HUMAN GAME

HUMAN GAME

The True Story of the "Great Escape" Murders
and the Hunt for the Gestapo Gunmen

SIMON READ

BERKLEY CALIBER, NEW YORK

BERKLEY BOOKS
Published by the Penguin Group
Penguin Group (USA) Inc.
375 Hudson Street, New York, New York 10014, USA
Penguin Group (Canada), 90 Eglinton Avenue East, Suite 700, Toronto, Ontario M4P 2Y3, Canada
(a division of Pearson Penguin Canada Inc.) • Penguin Books Ltd., 80 Strand, London WC2R 0RL,
England • Penguin Group Ireland, 25 St. Stephen's Green, Dublin 2, Ireland (a division of Penguin
Books Ltd.) • Penguin Group (Australia), 250 Camberwell Road, Camberwell, Victoria 3124, Australia
(a division of Pearson Australia Group Pty. Ltd.) • Penguin Books India Pvt. Ltd., 11 Community
Centre, Panchsheel Park, New Delhi—110 017, India • Penguin Group (NZ), 67 Apollo Drive,
Rosedale, Auckland 0632, New Zealand (a division of Pearson New Zealand Ltd.) • Penguin Books
(South Africa) (Pty.) Ltd., 24 Sturdee Avenue, Rosebank, Johannesburg 2196, South Africa

Penguin Books Ltd., Registered Offices: 80 Strand, London WC2R 0RL, England

This book is an original publication of The Berkley Publishing Group.

The publisher does not have any control over and does not assume
any responsibility for author or third-party websites or their content.

Copyright © 2012 by Simon Read
Jacket design by Daniel Rembert
Photos of the murdered POWs on pages viii and ix are
courtesy of the Imperial War Museum: HU1591 and HU1592

First edition: October 2012

Library of Congress Cataloging-in-Publication Data

Read, Simon, date.
Human game : the true story of the 'great escape' murders and
the hunt for the Gestapo gunmen / Simon Read.
p. cm.
Includes bibliographical references.
ISBN 978-0-425-25273-4
1. World War, 1939–1945—Prisoners and prisons, German.   2. Great Britain. Royal Air Force—
Officers—Crimes against.   3. Stalag Luft III.   4. Criminal investigation—Germany.
5. War criminals—Germany—History—20th century.   6. War crime trials—Germany.
7. Great Britain. Royal Air Force Police. Special Investigations Branch.
8. McKenna, Francis P., 1906–1994.   I. Title.
D804.G4R356 2012
940.54'7243812—dc23   2012005330

PRINTED IN THE UNITED STATES OF AMERICA

10   9   8   7   6   5   4   3   2   1

To my son, Spencer,
with love.

Then out spake brave Horatius,
The Captain of the Gate:
"To every man upon this earth
Death cometh soon or late.
And how can man die better
Than facing fearful odds,
For the ashes of his fathers,
And the temples of his gods?"

THOMAS BABINGTON MACAULAY,
LAYS OF ANCIENT ROME

"Who is in the right? The murderers who expect humane treatment after their cowardly attacks or the victims of those foul and cowardly attacks who in their rage seek their revenge? . . . We owe it to our people, which is defending itself with so much honesty and courage, that it not be allowed to become human game to be hunted down by the enemy."

NAZI PROPAGANDA
MINISTER JOSEF GOEBBELS URGING GERMANS
ON MAY 27, 1944, TO ATTACK DOWNED ALLIED AIRMEN

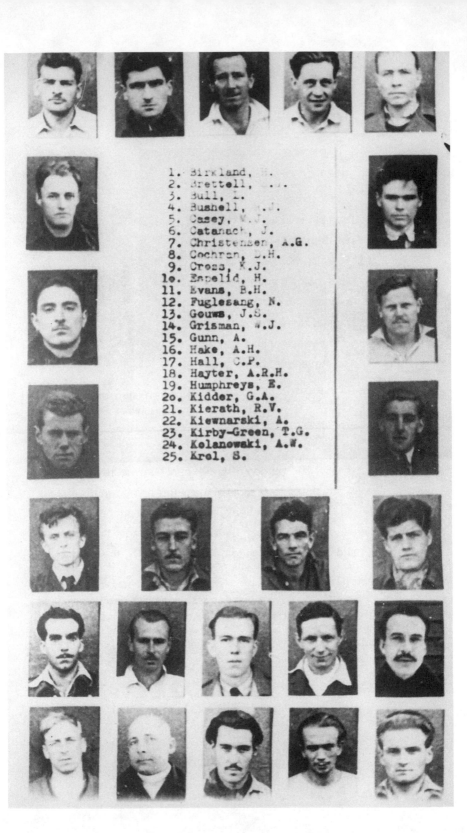

1. Birkland, H.
2. Brettell, E.G.
3. Bull, L.
4. Bushell, R.J.
5. Casey, M.J.
6. Catanach, J.
7. Christensen, A.G.
8. Cochran, D.H.
9. Cross, K.J.
10. Espelid, H.
11. Evans, B.H.
12. Fuglesang, N.
13. Gouws, J.S.
14. Grisman, W.J.
15. Gunn, A.
16. Hake, A.H.
17. Hall, C.P.
18. Hayter, A.R.H.
19. Humphreys, E.
20. Kidder, G.A.
21. Kierath, R.V.
22. Kiewnarski, A.
23. Kirby-Green, T.G.
24. Kolanowski, A.W.
25. Krol, S.

26. Langford, P.W.
27. Leigh, T.B.
28. Long, J.L.
29. Mc Garr, C.A.
30. Mc Gill, G.E.
31. Marcinkus, R.
32. Milford, H.J.
33. Mondschein, J.T.
34. Pawluk, K.
35. Picard, H.A.
36. Pohe, P.P.
37. Scheidhauer, B.W.
38. Skentzikes, S.
39. Swain, C.D.
40. Stevens, R.
41. Stewart, R.C.
42. Stower, J.G.
43. Street, D.O.
44. Tobolski, P.
45. Valenta, E.
46. Walenn, G.A.
47. Wernham, J.C.
48. Wiley, J.E.C.
49. Williams, J.E.
50. Williams, J.F.

CONTENTS

LIST OF CHARACTERS

ROYAL AIR FORCE INVESTIGATION TEAM

Squadron Leader Francis P. McKenna
Wing Commander Wilfred "Freddie" Bowes
Flight Lieutenant Stephen Courtney
Flight Sergeant H. J. Williams
Sergeant Wilhelm Smit
Flight Lieutenant Harold Harrison
Flight Lieutenant A. R. Lyon
Flight Sergeant R. M. Daniel
Squadron Leader W. P. Thomas
Sergeant J. Van Giessen
Flying Officer D. J. Walker

UPPER NAZI HIERARCHY

Adolf Hitler
Reichsmarschall Hermann Göring
Feldmarschall Wilhelm Keitel
Reichsführer-SS Heinrich Himmler

AT THE CENTRAL SECURITY OFFICE (RSHA) UNDER HIMMLER

SS *Obergruppenführer* and General of Police Dr. Ernst Kaltenbrunner
Gestapo SS *Gruppenführer* Heinrich Müller
Kriminalpolizei (Kripo) SS *Gruppenführer* Arthur Nebe

REGIONAL *KRIPO* AND GESTAPO PERSONNEL

BRESLAU

Dr. Wilhelm Scharpwinkel: Head of the local Gestapo
Max Wielen: Head of the local *Kripo*
Dr. Gunther Absalon: SS captain charged with prisoner-of-war security
   in Sagan region
Dr. Ernst Kah: Head of local SD, intelligence agency of the SS
Heinrich Seetzen: Inspector of local Security Police
Hans Schumacher: Senior officer with local *Kripo*
Max Richard Hansel: *Kriminal Inspektor* with the Görlitz Gestapo
Lux: Breslau Gestapo agent and chief executioner
Knappe: Breslau Gestapo agent and member of Scharpwinkel's murder
   squad
Kiske: Breslau Gestapo agent and member of Scharpwinkel's murder
   squad
Robert Schröder: Scharpwinkel's driver
Erwin Wieczorek: SS officer present at the shooting of four captured
   airmen
Laeufer: Breslau Gestapo agent and member of Scharpwinkel's murder
   squad

BRNO/ZLÍN

Hans Ziegler: Head of the Zlín Frontier Police, which served as an
   auxiliary to the Brno Gestapo
Wilhelm Nöelle: Head of the Brno Gestapo
Franz Schauschütz: Inspector with the Brno Gestapo
Hugo Roemer: Section chief in the Brno Gestapo

Adolf Knuppelberg: Senior Brno Gestapo official, who shot Thomas Kirby-Green

Friedrich Kiowsky: Driver for the Zlín Frontier Police (Gestapo)

Fritz Schwarzer: Hugo Roemer's personal driver

Erich Zacharias: Officer with the Zlín Frontier Police (Gestapo), who shot Gordon Kidder

Otto Kozlowsky: Brno Gestapo lawyer

DANZIG

Dr. Günther Venediger: Head of the local Gestapo

Erich Graes: Deputy director of the local *Kripo*

Kurt Achterberg: A deputy in the local Gestapo

Reinhold Bruchardt: Venediger's right-hand man

KARLSRUHE

Josef Gmeiner: Head of the local Gestapo

Walter Herberg: Local Gestapo agent assigned to the murder squad

Otto Preiss: Local Gestapo agent assigned to the murder squad

Heinrich Boschert: Local Gestapo agent assigned to the murder squad

Otto Ganninger: Deputy commandant of Natzweiler concentration camp

Magnus Wochner: Camp registrar at Natzweiler

KIEL

Friedrich (Fritz) Schmidt: Head of the local Gestapo

Johannes Post: Deputy in local Gestapo and chief executioner

Oskar Schmidt: Agent with the local Gestapo assigned to the murder squad

Hans Kaehler: Inspector with the local Gestapo

Franz Schmidt: Agent with the local Gestapo assigned to the murder squad

Walter Jacobs: Agent with the local Gestapo assigned to the murder squad

Artur Denkmann: Driver with the local Gestapo

Wilhelm Struve: Driver with the local Gestapo

LIBEREC

Bernhard Baatz: Head of the local Gestapo

Robert Weyland: Local Gestapo agent and suspected gunman

Robert Weissmann: Local Gestapo agent and suspected gunman

MUNICH

Dr. Oswald Schäfer: Head of the local Gestapo

Anton Gassner: Agent with the local *Kripo* in charge of Munich search operations

Greiner: Head of the local Kripo

Johann Schneider: Local Gestapo agent assigned to the murder squad

Emil Weil: Local Gestapo agent assigned to the murder squad

Martin Schermer: Local Gestapo agent assigned to the murder squad

Eduard Geith: Local Gestapo agent assigned to the murder squad

STRASBOURG

Alfred Schimmel: Head of the local Gestapo

Heinrich Hilker: Local Gestapo agent and gunman

Max Dissner: Section head of local Gestapo and suspected gunman

THE GREAT ESCAPE

Stalag Luft III sat in a clearing of dense pine forest just south of Sagan, some five hundred miles north of the Swiss border and two hundred miles south of the Baltic coast. Two fences measuring ten feet high, crowned in barbed wire, encircled the compound. The seven-foot space between the fences was a no-man's-land of additional barbed wire. Thirty feet inside the interior fence, strung no more than eighteen inches high, was a single strand of barbed wire that prisoners were forbidden to cross. Breaching the wire was likely to result in a deadly burst of machine-gun fire from one of the guard towers, which were strategically placed every 330 feet along the outer perimeter fence. At nightfall, guards in the towers swept the camp grounds with wide-beam spotlights.

Built on Hermann Göring's orders, the camp—its full name being Stammlager Luft III, or Permanent Camp for Airmen 3—was designed to be escape-proof. The compound's location was chosen, in part, because of the ground: yellow sand beneath a thin layer of gray, gravelly dirt. The soil's lack of solidity would make tunneling virtually impossible. If an intrepid group of men considered digging their way out, the tunnel's necessary length would most likely dissuade them from pursuing their scheme. The barrack blocks were set at least one hundred feet back from the fence; to reach the cover of the forest, a tunnel would have to stretch at least two hundred feet. The barracks, 160 feet long by 40 feet wide, with tarred roofs and timber-panel sides, were built with trapdoors in the floors and ceilings, allowing guards to make spot inspections to ensure prisoners weren't secretly stashing away contraband to assist in escape. In past breakouts from various camps, prisoners had tunneled their way out by removing the flooring of their barracks and digging into the ground directly underneath. Because the barracks at Stalag Luft III were set on stilts, this was not possible. Concrete pilings that served as foundations for the washroom and kitchen in each block, however, were dug into the earth. Through these, prisoners would have to dig before they even hit soil.

If such a task were possible, the next dilemma faced by a tunnel crew would be hiding the excavated dirt. The gray topsoil in the compound, the Germans believed, would thwart any attempt to discard and hide the yellow sand that was dug up from underneath. Little, however, was left to chance. The Germans sunk microphones ten feet underground to pick up the sounds of any subterranean activity. In addition to the guards in the towers, "ferrets"—as the prisoners called them—routinely patrolled the camp grounds and stalked the edge of the woods. Canine units covered the perimeter along the outer fence. During the summer months, the sun baked the camp and rendered the ground dry as bone. Winter brought temperatures below zero, heavy snow and torrential rains, turning the soil into a thick, sticky sludge. It was here to Stalag Luft III, the largest of six "main camps" built in Germany, that prisoners began arriving in March 1942. Squadron Leader Roger Joyce Bushell was thirty-two years old when he arrived in the autumn of that year. He had already been a prisoner of the Reich for two years.

His Spitfire was knocked from the sky on May 23, 1940, in combat over Dunkirk, when a Messerschmitt 110 challenged him head-on. Machine guns blazed, and both pilots found their mark. The Messerschmitt spiraled to earth, while Bushell—his cockpit filling with smoke—was forced to make an emergency landing. He brought the plane down in a field and escaped the fiery wreck with only a fractured nose. Not long thereafter, he was taken into custody and shipped off to Dulag Luft, the German reception center for captured Allied airmen, outside Frankfurt. The Germans quickly found out that Bushell was not a man content to sit out the war in relative safety.

He was born in South Africa, the son of an English mining engineer, but educated in England. He read law at Cambridge, where he excelled at academics and more physical pursuits, landing a place on the university's skiing team. His passion for speed earned him a reputation for fearlessness on the slope and the ranking of fastest British downhill skier on record in the early 1930s. During a competition in Canada, he suffered a nasty spill, the tip of one ski tearing at the corner of his right eye. The stitches required and the resulting scarring left him with a permanently drooped eye, giving him a somewhat sinister look. Scarred or not, Bushell could be an intimidating presence, an amalgamation of high intelligence, powerful build, and forceful personality. Such attributes served him well as a defense lawyer in the courtroom before the war and would prove an even greater asset in captivity. He joined the Royal Auxiliary Air Force in 1932 and was posted to 601 Squadron, where—just as on the slopes—he built his name on risk-taking, going so far on one occasion as to land his plane at a country pub for a pint. In October 1939, one month after the war's outbreak, he was promoted to squadron leader and charged with creating a night-fighter squadron on England's south coast. By the time Hitler unleashed his Blitzkrieg on France and the Low Countries in May 1940, Bushell's squadron was taking to the skies in Spitfires. It was shortly thereafter that he found himself in enemy hands.

By the time he arrived at Stalag Luft III, Bushell was a seasoned escape artist. His most recent adventure entailed jumping from a train while being transferred from one camp to another. Accompanied by a fellow escapee—a Czech officer with the RAF—he had made his way to Prague, where he and his compatriot were caught hiding in the apartment of a local resistance member. The two men, ratted out by a porter in the apartment building, were turned over to the Gestapo, who subjected both men to brutal interrogations. The Czech family that dared house the escapees was butchered. After failing to elicit confessions of sabotage, the Gestapo shipped both men off to separate camps: the Czech officer to Colditz,

Bushell to Sagan. Although Bushell never revealed what happened to him while in Gestapo custody, those who knew him beforehand noticed a harder edge to his personality upon his arrival at Stalag Luft III. In the camp already were numerous prisoners Bushell had conspired with in various compounds during his years of captivity. What the Germans believed to be sound policy, putting their most troublesome wards all in one camp, would prove a great asset to the determined Bushell. Assuming command of the camp's escape committee, dubbed "X-Organization," Bushell—codenamed "Big X"—hatched a plot to break out 250 inmates.

The audacious plan called for the simultaneous digging in the north compound of three tunnels named Tom, Dick, and Harry; speaking the word "tunnel" would be strictly forbidden. To avoid the camp's underground microphones, vertical shafts to each tunnel would be dug thirty feet down before horizontal digging commenced. Tom would cut west from Hut 123, which, of the three barracks selected, was closest to the wire but the farthest away from any guard tower. Dick would head in the same direction from the next hut over, number 122, slightly farther away from the camp's perimeter fence. Harry would start under Hut 104, directly opposite the camp's main gate, and cut a northern line into the woods. Elaborate trapdoors were devised to hide the entrance to each tunnel.

Tom was concealed in a dark corner of a hallway near the kitchen, above the stove's concrete foundation. The trapdoor was a mere eighteen inches square, just wide enough for a man to climb in and out. The entrance to Dick was in the washroom, beneath a grille-covered drain, which usually had several inches of wastewater sitting at the bottom, offering the perfect camouflage. To create the tunnel entrance, the prisoners drained the water, chiseled away a slab of concrete from one side of the drain and substituted their own manufactured replacement that could easily be lifted in and out. A sealant made of clay, soap, and cement was used to waterproof the slab's edges before the drain was filled again. A cast-iron stove in the corner of a room in Hut 104 was chosen to hide the vertical shaft that would grant access to Harry. The stove sat on a square bed of tiles, which had to be individually removed to access the hut's stone foundation beneath. The tiles were fitted into a special four-foot-square frame, which could be removed as one whole piece to gain entrance. The stove was always kept hot, so to remove it from the tile base, a set of lifting handles were made out of bed boards. A pipe extension, made of empty milk tins, was used to keep the stove attached to the hut's chimney when it was off the base.

The actual tunneling began in April 1943 and became "a standard pastime at Stalag Luft III." More than six hundred men took part in the escape's preparation and planning. An elaborate lookout system was established to monitor the guards. "Stooges," the name for prisoners serving as lookouts, were positioned throughout the camp and used a series of signals—the tamping of a pipe, the doffing of a cap, turning a page in a book—to notify the men in the huts of approaching "ferrets." One "stooge" would always be assigned to monitor the camp's main gate. Dubbed the "duty pilot," he would sit in a chair, perhaps appearing to catch some sun or idly flip through a book, all the while keeping track of the guards who came and went, relaying the information to other "stooges" through their various signals. The Germans were not entirely ignorant of the "duty pilot's" presence, though they were hard-pressed to ascertain the plot in which he played a role. Underground, the diggers sweat and toiled in miserable conditions. One digger would lie on his stomach and hack away at a wall of earth, piling the dirt and debris near his head. Eventually, he would push the pile down toward his waist, where the digger behind him would load it into a wheeled trolley. Another man, at the far end of the shaft, would pull on a rope to wheel the trolley in and load the dirt into sacks for later disposal. When done, the diggers would pull the trolley back to their end of the shaft, and the slow, painful process would repeat itself.

Men of large physique found the tunnel work particularly uncomfortable. Even for the smallest, lightweight man, conditions were too cramped to turn around. If one digger wanted to trade places with another, the two of them would often have to crawl over each other. The men worked in long, woolen underwear, which became increasingly uncomfortable as they perspired. Some men chose simply to work naked—but there was little relief from the stifling conditions. "Digging was the worst. You had a fat lamp by your head, you sniffed fumes all day, and when you came back up again you did nothing but spit black."

The digging generated tons of dirt, all of which had to be discarded somehow. Because the soil underground differed in color from the compound's topsoil, this presented a considerable problem—one that fell to Lieutenant Commander Peter Fanshawe, head of dispersal, to solve. He soon devised a contraption made from the cutoff legs of long, woolen underwear. The bottom of each leg was fastened shut by a pin attached to a length of string. The idea was to fill such trouser bags with dirt from the tunnels. More than one hundred prisoners, codenamed "penguins," would wear the contraption inside their trousers, the length of string from the bag easily accessible in their pockets. Pulling the strings would release the pins holding the sacks closed and discard the dirt down the penguin's leg. All they had to do was tread the small amount of dirt into the ground. Prisoners were more than happy to surrender their woolen underwear supplied by the Red Cross. Itchy and coarse, it was a despised piece of clothing.

As part of his ambitious plan, Bushell ordered that all escapees be issued with pertinent travel documents and identity papers. The task fell to a forgery department—named Dean and Dawson after the London-based travel agency—headed by Flight Lieutenant Gilbert Walenn, the twenty-six-year-old son of a London graphic artist, who shared his father's talent. Health-conscious and sporting a large, red handlebar mustache in the RAF style, Walenn neither smoked nor drank, believing both vices would inhibit his physical prowess should he make it out beyond the wire. His department relied very much on the camp's established blackmailers and scroungers to acquire the necessary German documents for replication. For bars of chocolate, cigarettes, a tin of real coffee, and assorted other goods that arrived for the benefit of prisoners via Red Cross packages, certain guards could be swayed to lend a hand. Once that line had been crossed, there was no going back. Walenn and his team of fifty artists would eventually produce four hundred documents, including forged travel passes, permits for foreign workers, identity cards, passports, and more. German gothic font and various emblems found on the source materials were painstak-ingly recreated by hand, as was any typewritten script. Official stamps were replicated by carving patterns out of boot heels; black boot polish was used for ink.

Australian Flying Officer Al Hake oversaw the production of two hundred compasses. The pointers were made from magnetized sewing needles, the compass bodies from shards of gramophone records soft-ened by heat and molded into shape. Pieces of broken glass were cut into circles for the compass covers and soldered into place using a makeshift blowtorch devised from a fat lamp and empty food tins. "Made in Stalag Luft III" read the inscription on the underside of each compass. Elsewhere in the camp, a tailoring department busied itself turning blankets and RAF uniforms into civilian suits, workmen's clothes, and German military apparel. A cartographic team was set up under Flight Lieutenant Des Plunkett to produce maps of Germany showing not only the locations of towns, villages, rivers, and other landmarks, but details of topographic features that might aid or hinder an escapee's progress. Information for the maps was passed on to Plun-kett and his men from turned guards and fellow prisoners familiar with Germany before the war. Knowledge, no matter how scant, of the cultures, customs, and languages of other European countries was also deemed beneficial to X-Organization's endeavor.

All the while, the digging continued, using makeshift tools and other materials scrounged from the camp or blackmailed from guards. Upon arrival in the camp, a prisoner was issued a "bed-stead and mat-tress, knife, spoon, fork, mess-tines, cup, 2 blankets, 3 sheets and 1 towel." Construction of the tunnels alone required the requisitioning of nearly 1,219 knives, 582 forks, 408 spoons, 246 water cans, 1,699 blankets, 192 bedcovers, 161 pillowcases, 1,212 pillows, 655 straw mattresses, 34 chairs, the frames of 90 bunk beds, 3,424 towels, 10 single tables, 52 twenty-man tables, more than 1,200 bed bolsters, nearly 1,400 beaded battens, 76 benches, 1,000 feet of electrical wiring, and 600 feet of rope. Four thousand bed boards were used to shore up the tunnels. Lights wired into the camp's electrical supply provided illumi-nation underground; air pumps made of discarded kit bags, empty powdered-milk tins, wood framing, wire mesh, and tar paper supplied fresh air to those doing the digging.

This mass scrounging by prisoners, when eventually discovered, would infuriate the enemy, as noted in a German report: "While bombed-out German civilians had to do their utmost and often failed to get at least something back of their belongings, the captured terror pilots treated their furniture and linen in a really devilish way and by doing so continued the war against the Reich successfully behind the barbed wire. No doubt, the P.O.W.s destroyed part of these articles on purpose to harm the Reich."

Digging underground was dangerous, as well as physically and mentally trying. The tunnels were no more than twenty-four inches square, leaving little room for maneuver; the constant threat of cave-ins only heightened the sense of claustrophobic dread. The fear that guards might discover one of the tunnels also played on the men's nerves. One detachment of guards constantly manned a listening station, keeping a check on any noises picked up by the subterranean microphones. Guards sat with headphones on and listened for anything that might suggest the digging of a tunnel. Starting in May 1943—some ten months before the escape—operators at headphone stations no. 53 and no. 54 started mentioning "heavy earth vibrations" in their monthly reports. They believed the noises were caused by laborers working in coal stores in the neighborhood of microphones.

By late summer 1943, Tom was 279 feet long—ten feet short of the woods, but long enough to deem it ready for use. Bushell ordered the entrance be sealed until a date for the escape was set. Eleven months of torturous work had brought the members of X-Organization to this moment, and it was now that disaster struck. Camp officials were beginning to suspect that laborers in the coal sheds were not responsible for the noises being picked up on the underground microphones. The sonic activity often continued throughout the night, when the coal stores were empty. On the morning of September 8, guards launched a series of inspections throughout the camp, methodically searching the barracks for any signs of escape activity. In the early afternoon hours, they turned their attention to Hut 123. A ferret inspecting a dark corner of the hut's main hallway near the kitchen tapped the ground with his metal probe. To his surprise, some of the sand-and-cement sealant used to hide the edges of the trapdoor chipped away, revealing Tom's entrance. The Germans, although dismayed such a massive excavation could have happened on their watch, were nevertheless impressed by the ingenuity displayed in the tunnel's construction. Newspaper photographers were summoned to the camp to snap pictures before a demolitions expert was brought in to pack the tunnel with explosives. The resulting detonation not only collapsed Tom but also blew apart Hut 123, much to the amusement of the prisoners who gathered to watch the spectacle.

It was decided after the New Year that work would move forward on Harry, while Dick would be used as a storage facility. Harry was almost one hundred feet in length; its vertical entrance shaft descended twenty-eight feet belowground. A railway with tracks made from the 1,400 beaded battens from the barracks above allowed diggers to move up and down the tunnel's length on flatbed trolleys. At Harry's midway point, the diggers constructed an interchange station for the two-trolley system and named it Piccadilly Circus. By the end of February, with the tunnel at nearly two hundred feet in length, a second station—this one dubbed Leicester Square—was built. Construction on Harry continued until March 14, when it was estimated the tunnel—at an impressive 336 feet—had reached the cover of the trees. The date for the escape was set for Friday, March 24, a moonless night.

In February, it was decided the first thirty spaces in the tunnel would be reserved for fluent German speakers—those most likely to escape successfully—and those traveling by train. The next forty spaces were held for those who made the greatest contributions to the digging and X-Organization's administrative work. Exit order was determined by writing names on scraps of paper and drawing them in a lottery. Although 600 men took part in the escape's preparations, plans called for only 200 men to break out. The remaining spaces in the tunnel were allocated by drawing from the 530 names still in the applicant pool. The ballot process complete, final preparations moved forward. Cover stories were rehearsed and aliases double-checked. Kit bags and disguises were inspected, and last-minute letters home were penned in the event of a grim conclusion. Forged documents and travel papers were stamped with the appropriate date. Maps and compasses were distributed, and several days' rations of a high-energy gelatin were handed out.

On the night of the escape, the first men were scheduled to clamber out of the tunnel at nine-thirty, but weather worked against them. Near freezing temperatures and a heavy snowfall had hardened the ground, making it near impossible to open the exit shaft. It took more than an hour to penetrate the final few inches of earth and clear a hole, revealing stars in a cloudless winter sky and a near-catastrophic problem. A miscalculation had resulted in Harry falling a good twenty feet short of the forest. A goon tower stood forty-five feet from where the tunnel broke ground near the main road that ran past the camp. After some frantic discussion, the decision was made to push ahead as planned: documents were date-sensitive, and postponement increased the likelihood of ferrets eventually finding the tunnel. Escapees would have to risk crawling across snow-covered open ground to the trees. A plan was devised to tie a length of rope to the top rung of the exit ladder. A man would hide beyond the tree line with other end of rope. In the tunnel, an escapee would wait to feel two tugs on the rope. Such a signal would mean the coast was clear. Progress through Harry proved to be cumbersome, the result of three tunnel collapses and—near midnight—an air raid. The target for Bomber Command that night was Berlin, some hundred miles away, but strong winds had blown much of the bomber stream off course. The sirens howled and the power went out, rendering the tunnel pitch-black. It took more than thirty minutes to light the grease lamps, which had been strung the length of the tunnel for such an event. By now, fewer than twenty men had made their escape, the rate of those passing through the tunnel being one every twelve minutes.

The outside nighttime temperature had sunk to thirty below zero. Underground, progress through the tunnel continued at its sluggish pace. The discomforting fear that 200 men were not going to make it out became a grim reality at two-thirty, when escapees 101 to 200 were ordered back to their bunks. Only fifty men had thus far got away, and time was quickly running out. Once dawn began breaking, the escape effort would have to cease. The first men out of the tunnel had been Flight Lieutenant Harry Marshall and his escape partner, Czech Flying Officer Ernst "Wally" Valenta; Roger Bushell and his partner, Bernard Scheidhauer, a member of the Free French forces, had followed close behind. Of these four, all but Marshall would be shot. By four in the morning, fewer than one hundred men had worked their way through the tunnel. With the first gray hints of daybreak showing in the east, it was decided the eighty-seventh man in the tunnel would be the last go. Aboveground, the sentry who patrolled the perimeter track around the camp deviated from his rounds and approached the edge of the woods to relieve himself. Nearing the trees, the guard noticed a wispy column of steam rising from the ground. He approached the anomaly with his rifle at the ready just as the eightieth escapee was about to emerge from the tunnel. Three escapees, waiting just beyond the trees, watched the scene unfold with growing dread and broke cover with their arms raised high. Startled, the guard fired a single shot into the air.

At 4:55 A.M. on Saturday, March 25, it all came to an end.

In Hut 104, pandemonium ensued. Men frantically stripped off their civilian clothes and tried to burn their forged papers and German currency. Some dashed from the hut for the safety of their own rooms but stopped when guards in the tower opened fire. Armed guards poured from the security hut near the main gate. They swarmed the compound and surrounded Harry's exit beyond the wire. Men still in the tunnel scrambled back the way they had come, fearful angry guards might claw their way down the shaft at any moment. In all the chaos, it took more than an hour for the Germans to discover the hut from which the tunnel originated. Not until a guard, armed with a torch and a pistol, lowered himself down Harry's exit shaft and followed the cramped passage back to Hut 104 was the point of origin determined. By six o'clock, a large contingent of guards, armed with machine guns, had surrounded the hut. The men inside were flushed out into a light snowfall and ordered to strip to their underwear.

It took nearly three hours to round up the rest of the camp and take roll call. When done, the numbers tallied were startling. Seventy-six men had escaped.

SUNDAY, MARCH 26

Hitler received the news with grave displeasure two days later at his mountain retreat, the Berghof at Obersalzberg. In the great anteroom off the villa's main hall, with its stunning views of the snowcapped Bavarian Alps, he read the report at his desk, his rage all-consuming. Hitler pushed the document away and summoned to his inner sanctum SS chief Heinrich Himmler, Air *Reichsmarschall* Hermann Göring, and the head of armed forces, *Feldmarschall* Wilhelm Keitel. The three men entered the room to a ranting, gesticulating Führer and immediately began assigning blame for the debacle. Responsibility for prisoners of war lay with a division of the *Oberkommando der Wehrmacht* (Army High Command), a point the proud and always pompous Göring was quick to make clear. Keitel bristled at the insinuation and thrust a finger in Göring's direction, reminding those present that Stalag Luft III fell under the *Luftwaffe*'s jurisdiction. Göring, at the war's outset, had requested all prison camps detaining airmen be placed under his control. A fighter ace in the previous world conflict, he felt a certain kinship with those who fought in the skies. Himmler watched, seething, as Göring and Keitel verbally assailed each other, before he, too, lashed out. The manpower required to track down seventy-six escapees, he said, would prove immense. The Breslau *Kriminalpolizei* (*Kripo*, or

Criminal Police)—responsible for the area in which the camp was located—had issued within hours of the escape a *Grossfahndung*, a national hue and cry ordering the military, the Gestapo, the SS, the Home Guard, and Hitler Youth to put every possible effort into hunting the escapees down. Nearly one hundred thousand men needed to defend the Reich were now being siphoned off elsewhere.

"It is incredible that this sort of thing should have occurred," Himmler said. "It should not have happened."

Mass escapes at prison camps across Germany had plagued the Reich in recent months. Forty-seven Polish officers had tunneled their way out of Oflag VI-B, a compound in Dössel, on the night of September 20, 1943. Twenty men were recaptured within four days, dispatched to Buchenwald concentration camp, and exterminated. Another seventeen were apprehended shortly thereafter and shot by the Gestapo. The remaining ten managed to get away. The night before the Polish breakout, 131 French soldiers escaped from Oflag XVII-A in Döllersheim; only two avoided recapture. Drastic measures had already been taken to prevent a repeat of such occurrences. In February, the German High

A stone slab now marks the spot to tunnel Harry's entrance. The wooden posts at the top of the picture show where the wall to Hut 104 once stood.

Command had issued *Stufe Römisch III*, an order dictating that recaptured prisoners of war, "irrespective of whether it is an escape during transit, a mass escape or a single escape, [are] to be handed over after recapture to the Head of Security Police and Security Service" and not the military. "The persons recaptured," the order stated, "are to be reported to the Information Bureau of the Armed Forces as 'Escaped and not recaptured.'" Inquiries from the International Red Cross and other aid organizations were to receive the same response. Recaptured British and American officers were to be detained by the police and handled on a case-by-case basis.

The Gestapo took things further on March 4—twenty days before the mass breakout from Stalag Luft III—and issued *Aktion Kugel* (Operation Bullet), which decreed that recaptured POWs be taken to Mauthausen concentration camp and executed. Prisoners were to be kept in chains for the duration of the journey, and no official record was to be made of their arrival at the camp. Upon reaching their destination, they would be stripped and sent to the "washrooms" in the cellar of the prison building near the crematorium, where they would die by gas or bullet. As with *Stufe Römisch III*, British and American prisoners were to be handled on an individual basis but held by the Gestapo until a decision could be made. The men at Sagan had been unaware of these ominous developments.

Hitler, presently ranting, ordered that all the Stalag Luft III fugitives be executed upon recapture. The proclamation brought the bickering between his deputies to an end. An example, he said, must be made, an action both punitive and deterrent in its effect. The idea offended no one, but the thought of covering up seventy-six murders posed a considerable challenge. Word of such an atrocity, Göring explained, might leak to the foreign press and result in fierce Allied reprisals. Himmler agreed, prompting Hitler to order that "more than half the escapees" be shot. Random numbers were suggested until Himmler proposed that fifty be executed—a suggestion that met with unanimous approval. Hitler ordered his SS chief to put the plan in motion and assigned to it the highest level of secrecy. The following day—Monday, March 27—Himmler addressed the matter with his second-in-command at the

German Central Security Office,* Dr. Ernst Kaltenbrunner. He dictated the content of a secret Teletype, which was transmitted to Gestapo headquarters throughout the country later that same day:

> The frequent mass escapes of officer prisoners constitute a real danger to the security of the State. I am disappointed by the inefficient security measures in various prisoner of war camps. The Führer has ordered that as a deterrent, more than half of the escaped officers will be shot. The recaptured officers will be handed over to Department 4 [the Gestapo] for interrogation. After interrogation, the officers will be transferred to their original camps and will be shot on the way. The reason for the shooting will be given as "shot whilst trying to escape" or "shot whilst resisting" so that nothing can be proved at a future date. Prominent persons will be exempted. Their names will be reported to me and my decision will be awaited whether the same course of action will be taken.

The order charged the *Kripo* with apprehending the Sagan fugitives and selecting who, upon recapture, would be handed over to the Gestapo. Kaltenbrunner delegated the logistics to his two immediate subordinates, Gestapo Chief Heinrich Müller and General Arthur Nebe, national head of the *Kripo*.

The same day the Sagan order went out, Nebe summoned SS *Obersturmbannführer* Max Wielen, head of the Kripo in Breslau and the man who sounded the national alarm after the escape, to his Berlin office. Wielen arrived by car at eight-thirty that evening and was ushered in to see his superior. Nebe occupied a ground-floor office at Central Security headquarters. Damage to the building from Allied bombs had forced Nebe to move offices several times in the past year. While the artwork he hung on the walls changed from one office to another, the furnishings—chairs in red leather and a slightly battered settee—remained the same.

---

* Otherwise known as the *Reichssicherheitshauptamt* (RSHA).

"You look tired," Nebe said, as Wielen entered and observed the familiar furniture. "I'll order some sandwiches and coffee to buck you up."

Wielen, surprised to find his chief in a generous mood, took a seat. Nebe picked up a phone and requested the refreshments be brought to his office. When finished, he tapped a typewritten communiqué on his desk. Hitler, he explained, "was very angry" and had ordered more than half the Sagan fugitives be shot. He slid the official order across the desk and allowed Wielen a moment to review it. Nebe made it clear to his subordinate that nothing could be done against a Führer Order. Wielen understood the implication and listened without protest to his assignment. Because most of the escapees had already been captured in the Breslau area, the majority of shootings would take place in Wielen's jurisdiction. Naturally concerned for his own skin, Wielen said he wanted no official responsibility in the killings. Nebe—who, according to Wielen, "looked extremely tired and was obviously suffering from very severe emotional strain"—said the Gestapo would be assuming full liability. Wielen's task was to hand over any condemned prisoners in his custody to Dr. Wilhelm Scharpwinkel, Gestapo chief in Breslau, who would assemble the necessary execution squads.

Wielen returned to Breslau on the night train and scheduled a meeting with Scharpwinkel early the next morning. The local Gestapo headquarters sat directly opposite the regional *Kripo* building. Wielen cared little for Scharpwinkel and the Gestapo in general—not out of any moral indignation, but for the Gestapo's penchant to view the Criminal Police as an inferior organization. He kept the meeting brief and relayed the order from Berlin. Scharpwinkel seemed pleased with his new responsibility.

"Yes," he said. "I shall do this personally."

By Wednesday, March 29, five days after the breakout, thirty-five escapees languished behind bars, four to a cramped cell, in the town jail at Görlitz. Those who remained on the run hoped to make destinations in Czechoslovakia, Spain, Denmark, and Sweden. Luck, however, worked against them. They were seized at checkpoints, betrayed by informants, or simply thwarted by freezing temperatures. Before long, all but three of the Sagan fugitives were back in captivity. That same week, a stack of index cards from the Central Registry of Prisoners of War began appearing on Nebe's desk. Each individual card contained the name, date of birth, rank, and other personal details of a Sagan escapee. He summoned his assistant, Hans Merten, a forty-two-year-old lawyer, to his office and pointed to the cards.

"You have heard about the Führer Order?" Nebe asked. "Then you know what to do. Müller, Kaltenbrunner, and I are lunching together. I will take them a list of men to be shot when I see them at lunchtime." Nebe shoveled some cards across the desk. "Have a look to see whether they have wives or children."

Merten did as instructed and returned the sorted cards to Nebe, who shuffled the deck and began flipping through them one by one, pausing momentarily to read the short biographical sketch of each man.

"He is so young," Nebe muttered, staring at one card. "No!"

He placed the card upside down on his desktop and picked up another.

"He is for it!" he said, slapping the card down.

This process continued for some time, until Nebe had two separate piles of cards on his desk, one larger than the other. He stared momentarily at both stacks, swapped one card for another, and at last seemed satisfied with his work. He handed the larger stack to Merten.

"Now, quickly," he ordered, "the list!"

Merten took the cards to Nebe's secretary and read her the list of names. He deliberately misstated the location where some prisoners were being held, in the vain hope that orders of execution would be misdirected. The "mistake," however, was noticed before the orders were sent down the wire. Nebe promptly dismissed Merten and sent him off to teach criminology at a school in Fürstenberg. It was, all things considered, a merciful decision—but Nebe's magnanimity did not extend beyond his office. He had a list of fifty names and an order to obey.

The killings began on Wednesday, March 29.

ONE

"THOSE ARE MY ORDERS"

"I have to acquaint you with a top secret matter."

Kiel Gestapo chief Friedrich (Fritz) Schmidt sat behind his desk with a single sheet of paper in front of him. It was Wednesday, March 29.

"It is an order from the Führer. Four prisoners, who are with the *Kripo* at Flensburg, will be shot at a place determined by me. They are enemy agents who were condemned to death and tried to escape to Denmark. You, Major Post, will go to Flensburg and interrogate the prisoners. It is not expected they will make any statement. You will leave Flensburg by car and shoot them at a pre-arranged spot. Oskar Schmidt will see that the cremation is carried out and all formalities complied with. For the firing, service pistols will be used. If, contrary to expectations, an escape should be made, service rifles will be used, as pistols will not be sufficient."

Thirty-eight-year-old Johannes Post was an ardent Nazi, fanatical in his loyalty to Hitler and intimidating to all who knew him. Although only five and a half feet tall, he boasted a solid physique—what some considered corpulent, and others thought imposing. His eyes—an arctic blue beneath a thick main of blond hair always brushed backward— rarely betrayed any emotion. Whatever moral convictions he possessed were solely defined by Nazi policy. He had, since the outbreak of the war and for the glory of the Reich, killed many he deemed inferior.

Married with three young children, he spent little time with his family, preferring instead the company of his mistress.

Next to Post stood forty-three-year-old Oskar Schmidt* and three other Gestapo officers. They received their instructions without protest, though some would later claim feeling ill at ease with their assignment. No such reservations burdened Post. He knew the condemned were British airmen, and he considered death by bullet too merciful. He listened attentively as Fritz Schmidt detailed what needed to be done. The shootings would take place in a meadow along a rural stretch of road about eight miles south of Kiel in the direction of Neumünster. The prisoners were to be escorted a good distance from the road so as to prevent any passing motorist from witnessing the murders. No official record of the slayings would be kept. Post was placed in charge of the overall operation.

"Anyone not complying with this order will have to reckon with immediate sentence of death and punitive measures against his family," Fritz Schmidt said. "The same applies to anyone talking about the matter with outsiders."

Schmidt walked around his desk and shook each man's hand, binding him to secrecy. The meeting, having lasted no more than ten minutes, was over.

At that moment, unaware of the dark machinations at work, Australian Squadron Leader James Catanach sat in a cell in the police prison in Flensburg. Freedom had seemed so close just three days prior. For two years he had sat in Stalag Luft III, having arrived there after being shot down over Norway. The twenty-two year old spoke fluent German and believed, the night of the escape, that he harbored a fair chance of ultimately making it to neutral Sweden. Before the breakout, he partnered with pilot officer Arnold Christensen of the Royal New Zealand Air Force. In the hours following the escape, the two men managed to

---

* No relation to Friedrich Schmidt.

make their way to the Sagan railway station and catch the 3:15 A.M. express to Berlin.

On the same train, also hoping to make Sweden, were fellow escapees Hallada Espelid and Nils Fuglesang, Norwegians with the Royal Air Force. They reached the capital shortly before 7:30 A.M., their journey having passed without incident. In the gray light of that cold winter morning, the men were perhaps satisfied to witness at ground level the devastation wrought by Allied bombers. The city was one of shattered architecture and gaunt, hollow expressions. They spent the night in Berlin, avoiding detection, and purchased train tickets the next day— March 26—to Flensburg on the Danish border. It was here, in this ancient city on the Baltic coast, that their bid for freedom came to an end. Catanach and Christensen were taken into police custody while walking along the Holm, a pedestrian thoroughfare in an area of the city that had thus far escaped bombardment. The two arresting officers were specifically on duty that night as a result of the Sagan breakout. In another part of town, Espelid and Fuglesang were apprehended at a police checkpoint on the Marienhölzungsweg. What aroused police suspicions and led to the arrests has been lost to history, the records having been destroyed by Allied bombs.

Once in custody, the men were taken to the local *Kripo* headquarters and briefly interrogated. Confessing to being officers of the Royal Air Force and fugitives from Stalag Luft III, they refused to surrender details regarding the escape's planning and execution. They gave only their names and ranks, military identification numbers, and the route they had traveled while on the run. Their information was noted and forwarded to the Central Security Office in Berlin, where it followed a bureaucratic paper trail to Kaltenbrunner's desk. From *Kripo* headquarters, the men were transferred to the city's police prison and put in a cell. Three days had now passed since their recapture; three days with no official word on what fate awaited them. They assumed the Germans would return them to a prison camp, as was normal protocol. The question was, were they destined once again for Sagan or a different compound altogether? On that Wednesday afternoon, an answer seemed close at hand.

The Gestapo men drove in two cars. Johannes Post and Inspector Hans Kaehler rode in a black four-seat Mercedes; Oskar Schmidt followed behind in a black six-seat Adler, with fellow officers Franz Schmidt (no relation) and Walter Jacobs. They arrived in Flensburg shortly after noon and stopped for lunch at the Harmonie restaurant. After their meal, they drove to the *Polizeidirektion*, where the four RAF officers were being detained. Prison officials, notified of the Gestapo's pending arrival, retrieved the airmen from their cell and seated them in the main corridor, ready for transfer.

Post and his comrades arrived at the prison and separated the airmen for questioning, but fifteen minutes of futile interrogation failed to yield anything beyond what was already known. At 3 P.M., the prisoners were handcuffed—their wrists shackled behind their backs—and marched to the waiting cars outside. Post and Kaehler took custody of Catanach; Christensen, Espelid, and Fuglesang were bundled into the Adler with the two Schmidts and Walter Jacobs. The vehicles pulled away in a convoy, with the Mercedes leading. In the backseat, Catanach stared out the window as the gothic architecture of Flensburg eventually gave way to open road. The cars traveled via Schleswig-Eckernförde in the direction of Kiel, the rolling country soon surrendering to a ravaged urban scene.

In the car's front passenger seat, Post eyed his captive in the rearview mirror. He played morbid tour guide, pointing out Kiel's once-great monuments and buildings recently devastated by Allied air raids. Catanach nodded and said he was most familiar with the city's architecture, having flown several combat operations against Kiel before his capture. Post shrugged and lit a cigarette.

"We must get on," he said. "I have to shoot you."

Catanach turned his gaze from the window, puzzled. "What did you say?"

"I am going to shoot you," Post repeated. "Those are my orders."

It was well known in local Gestapo ranks that Post took great pleasure in telling prisoners they were doomed to die. He enjoyed their

desperate pleas for mercy. Although Post knew Catanach spoke German, he addressed the airman in English.

"Do you mind?" the airman laughed, mistaking Post's statement
for a sick joke. "Another time. I have an appointment in the cooler of
Stalag Luft III. I've done nothing wrong except go under the wire. You
can't shoot me."

"Well," Post said, "those are my orders."

The car continued to navigate the city's shattered streets. As the
Mercedes turned a corner, Post barked an order to his driver, Artur
Denkmann. He had tickets for the theater that night, but with the business now at hand, he was doubtful he would make the performance on
time. Post directed Denkmann to an apartment building on the Hansastrasse. He pulled the tickets from the inside pocket of his gray leather
overcoat and ordered Kaehler to run them upstairs to his mistress. When
Kaehler returned several minutes later, the journey resumed without
another word. The Mercedes left Kiel and headed south in the direction
of Neumünster, along the Hamburger Chaussee. Roughly nine miles out
of Kiel, where the road curved sharply to the right, the car pulled onto
the right shoulder and came to a stop. Post ordered Kaehler, sitting next
to Catanach, to remove the airman's shackles, and got out of the vehicle.
During the car ride, when conversing with Catanach in English, Post
had seemed almost jovial. Now he barked his orders in angry German
and told Catanach to get out. The airman did as he was told but showed
no sign of concern, apparently still believing Post's earlier threat to be
a morbid joke.

Post ordered Catanach to cross the road, where, directly opposite
the Mercedes, a gate opened into a meadow bordered by hedgerow.
Kaehler got out of the vehicle and followed them across the carriageway.
Post stayed three steps behind Catanach and slid his right hand into his
coat pocket as they approached the gate. Entering the meadow, Post
marched Catanach to the left, concealing them behind the hedgerow.
Catanach kept walking, not bothering to look back. Without uttering
a word, Post pulled a Luger 7.65mm pistol from his pocket and fired.
Catanach screamed, the slug striking him between the shoulder blades,
and fell dead to the ground. As Post pocketed his weapon, he heard the

second car arrive. Engine trouble in Kiel accounted for the Adler's late arrival. Oskar Schmidt ordered his driver, Wilhelm Struve, to pull in behind the Mercedes and turned to the prisoners on the car's folding backseat. The journey back to Sagan, he said, would take several more hours. The men would be wise to relieve themselves. He got out and opened the car's rear left door for the airmen. Post stood watching impatiently at the gate, eager for what was coming.

Christensen, Espelid, and Fuglesang clambered out of the car—their wrists still shackled—with Walter Jacobs and Franz Schmidt behind them. Oskar Schmidt and his two partners marched the airmen across the roadway, toward the gate. It was five o'clock when they entered the meadow, and the men trod carefully in the fading light. Corralled by Post and the other agents behind them, they moved to the left of the gate. They were no more than seven steps from the gate when one of the airmen saw a dark object lying in the grass. The realization that it was James Catanach drew a panicked scream from one of the men. All three airmen jumped backward and tried to scramble as Jacobs and the two Schmidts drew their weapons.

"Shoot them!" Post roared. "Shoot them! Why don't you shoot them?"

Three gun reports echoed across the meadow in the evening gloom. Two of the airmen fell lifeless alongside Catanach; the third hit the ground in apparent agony and made a feeble attempt to get back up. He struggled, his wrists still chained behind his back, and opened his mouth as though wanting to speak.

"He is still alive!" Post screamed. "I shall shoot him."

He rushed at Kaehler and snatched the rifle from his hands. He approached the airman and put a bullet in his head. Satisfied the job was done, he ordered Kaehler to accompany him back to Kiel and told the others to guard the scene. Oskar Schmidt watched Post and Kaehler leave before turning his gaze to the bodies in the grass.

"He was not mine," he said. "Mine died instantly."

"And so did mine," said Franz Schmidt.

Post still hoped to make the theater on time. The Mercedes sped north, back up the Hamburger Chaussee toward Kiel. Coffins were needed to transport the corpses to the local crematorium. Post directed his driver to Tischendorf's, an undertaker at Karlstrasse 26. It was six o'clock when Post and Kaehler entered the establishment and spoke with Wilhelm Tischendorf, the proprietor. From the leather coats and long boots the men had on, Tischendorf presumed his customers were Gestapo.

"I need you to collect some prisoners who have been shot in the vicinity of the Rotenhahn," Post said by way of greeting, flashing his identification.

"What prisoners are they?" Tischendorf asked.

"French. Shot whilst trying to escape."

Post said no more and returned to his waiting car. He left Kaehler to handle the details. Suspicious of Post, Tischendorf asked Kaehler who the prisoners were.

"They're British airmen," Kaehler said.

"Are they some of the seventy-six airmen I have read about in the papers?"

Kaehler answered in the affirmative.

"I shall have a car ready to leave in half an hour," Tischendorf said.

Kaehler went outside and told Post, who nodded his approval. He ordered Kaehler to see the job through to its conclusion before demanding the driver return him to the apartment on the Hansastrasse, where his mistress waited with theater tickets.

The hearse—and two lidless, tin coffins—was ready sooner than expected. Tischendorf directed Kaehler to a parking lot behind the building, where he found two mortician laborers waiting in a burial van. Kaehler got in the front passenger seat and ordered the driver to get moving. The three men drove mostly in silence; Kaehler, giving directions, was the only one who spoke. As the van approached the right-hand bend on the Hamburger Chaussee, near the Rotenhahn, an inn and pub, Kaehler told the driver to slow down. The Adler was still parked on the right-hand side of the road, opposite the meadow's entrance. Kaehler pointed to the gate, which was open, and ordered the driver to turn left into the field. He did not want passersby on the carriageway to witness the bodies being loaded. The driver, Wilhelm Boll, although worried the van's wheels might get stuck in the damp earth, did as instructed. In the meadow, as he cut the van's engine, Boll saw three men—one armed with a rifle—standing several feet off to his left.

Kaehler climbed out of the van. He ordered Boll and the other laborer, Artur Salau, to retrieve the two coffins from the back of the vehicle. The men did as they were told without comment and placed the caskets alongside the four bodies. Oskar Schmidt, charged with ensuring the victims were properly disposed of, ordered the bodies be stacked two to a coffin. The Gestapo men simply stood and watched as Boll and Salau commenced the morbid task. The bodies, both laborers noticed, were dressed in what appeared to be new civilian suits. Two of the dead men had bullet wounds to the head.

"If the Russians get here, they'll do the same to us," muttered one of the Gestapo agents.

Boll and Salau, wanting only to be done with the job, heard the comment but did not respond. They placed the bodies in the coffins and loaded the caskets into the back of the van. Oskar Schmidt ordered the bodies be taken immediately to the crematorium in Kiel. The journey back to the city was made in two cars. Boll and Salau drove the burial van, while the Gestapo agents followed close behind in the Adler. At the crematorium, on-duty engineer Arthur Schafer knew better than to question official Gestapo business. It was six-thirty when the four agents arrived, accompanied by two undertakers hauling four bodies in a pair of cheap coffins. It was Oskar Schmidt who did the talking.

"Here are four corpses to be cremated."

"Do you have the necessary documents?" asked Schafer.

"Berlin has ordered it."

Schafer opened the crematorium's leather-bound register and reached for a pen.

"You will not make any entries."

Although notified in advance that such a visit was likely, Schafer found the circumstances peculiar. Regulations, he said, dictated that names of the deceased be recorded. Schmidt told Schafer to enter each body in the register only as a Roman numeral I through IV. The bodies were not to be assigned cremation numbers, nor were any notes to be made of the date.

"The corpses are those of prisoners who were shot whilst on the run," Schmidt said.

Schafer did as instructed and asked the undertakers to carry the coffins to the furnace. Before consigning the bodies to flame, Schafer gave each one a cursory glance. All four victims were dressed in civilian clothing, wearing woolen underwear, woolen stockings, and woolen pullovers. He didn't see any visible wounds. The four Gestapo men stayed until the bodies had been destroyed and the ashes relegated to four urns, each labeled with a Roman numeral I through IV. Walter Jacobs took possession of the urns, which were to be sent to Stalag Luft III for burial. By nine o'clock the agents were back at local Gestapo headquarters, their work done. Boll and Salau returned the burial van and checked in with their boss.

"Everything in order?" Tischendorf asked.

"Yes," Boll replied.

"What kind of bodies were they?"

"They were all shot from the back."

In another part of town, sitting with his mistress in a darkened theater, Johannes Post enjoyed that evening's operatic performance. He had made the show on time.

As senior British officer at Stalag Luft III, Group Captain Herbert Massey had approved plans for the mass breakout. It was, after all, the sworn duty of every captured officer to "harass, confuse, and confound the enemy." Had he not been crippled with a bad leg, perhaps he, too, would have crept under the wire—but merely strolling the compound was enough to cause the old wound to flare. He had permanently damaged his leg in a crash during the First World War but continued to fly. He suffered another grievous injury to the same limb in 1942 when enemy fire downed his Stirling over the Ruhr. He now walked with a cane, but it did little to improve his mobility.

It was Thursday, April 6, two weeks since the escape. Six men had thus far been returned to the camp and marched directly into "the cooler," the solitary confinement block. The fate and whereabouts of those still on the run remained a mystery to the men inside the camp. It was hoped, of course, that some would make it back to England, though most of the prisoners knew such optimism had no foundation in reality. German authorities once estimated that only 1 percent of all escape attempts actually proved successful—so why bother? Duty was too simplistic an answer. Perhaps youth had something to do with it. Most of the escapees were not yet in their mid-thirties; a vast number were still in their twenties. Young men, all of them, deprived of women, liquor, and their freedom; beyond the wire, life and the war were passing them by. A first-line defense against boredom, the planning and plotting of escape distracted one's mind from the banalities and deprivations of imprisonment. For men trained and eager to fight, but frustrated by captivity, escaping was their one means of striking at the enemy from behind the lines.

Now, on this Thursday morning, Hans Pieber, one of the camp's administrative officers, knocked on Massey's door with a summons from the *kommandant* for an eleven o'clock meeting. Pieber, generally a man of happy disposition, appeared solemn. In the days following the breakout, prisoners had been denied their Red Cross care packages and use of the camp's theater. Such reprisals, the prisoners had agreed, were minor by German standards. Presently, Massey wondered aloud if the *kommandant* had decided upon a more severe form of retribution. Pieber, his brow creased, said he only knew the *kommandant* had some "terrible" news.

At the prescribed hour, Massey left his barracks accompanied by his personal interpreter, Squadron Leader Philip Murray. Fellow prisoners watched the two men walk slowly across the compound. The camp's rumor mill had wasted little time generating numerous dark theories as to what hardships would soon befall the inmates. At the main gate, armed guards escorted the two men to the *kommandant*'s hut. Inside, they were led to a small office and took seats opposite the *kommandant*'s desk. *Oberst* (Colonel) Braune greeted the men with a silent nod, but remained standing. Pieber stood in one corner of the room, averting his gaze. Braune held a single sheet of paper in his hand and stared almost helplessly at the words typed across it.

"I have been instructed by my higher authority to communicate to you this report," Braune said, his voice quiet. "As a result of a tunnel from which seventy-six officers escaped from Stalag Luft III, north compound, forty-one of these officers have been shot while resisting arrest or attempting further escape after arrest."

Murray, translating for Massey, stopped mid-sentence.

"How many were shot?" he asked, disbelieving.

"Forty-one," Braune said, failing to meet Murray's gaze.

Murray struggled to keep his emotional response in check. He turned to Massey, who, upon hearing the translation, took in a sharp breath and repeated the same question asked by Murray.

"How many were shot?"

"Forty-one," Murray said, his voice thick in his throat.

Massey sat momentarily stunned, lost in the tumult of his thoughts. He fixed his eyes on Braune but addressed Murray when he finally spoke.

"Ask him how many were wounded."

Braune, now wringing his hands, said the "higher authority" allowed him only to disclose the shooting of forty-one officers. Massey, unmoved, asked Murray to repeat the question.

"I think no one was wounded," Braune said.

Massey leaned forward in his chair, anger laying waste to his calm reserve.

"Do you mean to tell me that forty-one men can be shot at in those circumstances and that all were killed and no one was wounded?"

Braune had no answer.

"Do you have a list of names?" Massey asked.

Again, Braune struggled, saying he knew nothing more beyond the details already relayed.

"I would like to have the names as soon as it is possible to get them," Massey said and rose from his chair.

Braune agreed without protest before pleading his case.

"I am acting under orders," he said. "I may only indulge what I'm instructed to by my higher authority."

"What is this higher authority?"

"Just a higher authority," said Braune, his voice dropping to a near whisper.

Before turning to leave, Massey asked that the bodies be returned to the camp for proper burial arrangements and the disposal of personal effects.

"I demand that the Protecting Power also be informed," he said in reference to the International Red Cross, which routinely visited the camp to ensure standards adhered to the Geneva Convention.

Braune agreed to Massey's demands but warned he could only arrange whatever the "higher authority" permitted.

Massey and Murray left the office and stepped outside, with Pieber following close behind.

"Please do not think the *Luftwaffe* had anything to do with this dreadful thing," he said, clearly distraught. "It is terrible."

Massey called the camp's three hundred senior officers—one for every room in each barrack—to a meeting in the compound's theater. The men received the news in quiet disbelief, and word of the atrocity quickly spread throughout the camp. That same day, eight more escapees returned under armed *Luftwaffe* guard and were put in the cooler. Massey, in his room, his game leg elevated on a chair, tallied the numbers at day's end. Out of seventy-six men, forty-one were dead; another fourteen were back behind the wire, and the fate of twenty-one men remained unknown. Massey's fate, however, was clear. In the weeks prior, the Germans had made arrangements to repatriate him back to Britain on medical grounds. He left the camp on April 11, bound for Switzerland on the first part of his return journey to England. In his place, Group Captain D. E. L. Wilson of the Royal Australian Air Force became senior British officer at Stalag Luft III.

In the early evening hours of April 15, a list identifying the victims appeared on the camp's notice board. A crowd quickly gathered and listened as the names were read aloud in a somber roll call. Quiet expressions of grief gave way to cries of outrage when it became apparent the list contained not forty-one names, but forty-seven. Two days later, Gabrielle Naville, a representative of the Swiss Protecting Power, visited the camp on a routine welfare inspection. Wilson pulled Naville aside, detailed recent events, and provided a copy of the list. Among the dead were twenty-five Britons, six Canadians, three Australians, two New Zealanders, three South Africans, four Poles, two Norwegians, one Frenchman, and a Greek. The Swiss government in May reported the killings to the British government. On May 19, Foreign Secretary Anthony Eden addressed the House of Commons. After relaying the basic facts of the case and voicing the outrage of His Majesty's government, he demanded Germany provide through Switzerland "a full and immediate report on the circumstances in which these men met their death."

In the weeks that followed, the Swiss learned of three additional victims, bringing the total number of those murdered to fifty. If some prisoners at Stalag Luft III remained skeptical of the news, the ashes brushed aside any lingering disbelief. Throughout May and July, the cremated remains of the deceased were delivered to the camp in forty-six urns and four boxes. On each container was engraved the city in which the prisoner had been shot. Braune allowed a group of prisoners to construct in a nearby cemetery a stone memorial in which the ashes were placed.

Eden made a second statement to Parliament on June 23, disclosing the new casualty figure. Germany, he said, had communicated through Switzerland its reasoning for the killings, asserting the victims were involved in sabotage operations that endangered the German public. Eden dismissed the accusation. "No orders," he said, "have at any time been given to British prisoners of war to take part, in the event of their escape, in any subversive action as is alleged in the German note." Regardless of the circumstances, he continued, there was no viable excuse for executing fifty men.

"His Majesty's Government must, therefore, record their solemn protest against these cold-blooded acts of butchery," he said in conclusion. "They will never cease in their efforts to collect the evidence to identify all those responsible. They are firmly resolved that these foul criminals shall be tracked down to the last man, wherever they may take refuge," swore Eden. "When the war is over, they will be brought to exemplary justice."

TWO

COLD CASE

Frank McKenna eyed the pile of documents on his bureau and pondered, not for the first time, the immensity of the task. More than a year had passed since the commission of the crimes detailed in the mountainous stack of folders and overflowing envelopes. He knew full well of Anthony Eden's promise to bring the killers to justice, but a politician's pledge was something one often accepted with a healthy amount of skepticism. On this evening in late August 1945, sitting in the cramped bedroom he rented from a police officer widowed during the Blitz, McKenna harbored his fair share of doubt.

He held the rank of flight sergeant, having joined the Royal Air Force and volunteered for bomber crew. At thirty-seven, he was an old man by aircrew standards but was nevertheless compelled by a fervent sense of duty. He was tall and lean, with sharp features. A well-defined chin and angular jaw gave him a somewhat hardened appearance; his pale eyes and thin mouth were not prone to easy laughter. A devout Catholic, he had been driven all his life by rigid ideals of right and wrong and doing what needed to be done. He believed in hard justice and the need to atone for one's sins. Such views propelled him in his civilian career. Before the war, McKenna had worked his way up to detective-sergeant in the Blackpool Borough Police. His physicality and dedication to police work earned him, among his fellow detectives, the sobriquet "Sherlock Holmes." He could have spent a relatively safe war ensconced in his police work, but that would have gone against McKenna's dutiful nature.

He flew thirty operations as a flight engineer on Lancasters with No. 622 Squadron and completed his tour of duty by Christmas 1944. His operational commitments met, McKenna joined the RAF Police and secured a posting with the Special Investigating Branch (SIB), headquartered at Princes Court Gate, South Kensington, London. He spent the better part of 1945 investigating routine crimes within the service, crimes that hardly differed from those he tackled as a copper on "Civvy Street." Stolen property and cases of assault were typical fare that neither challenged McKenna nor necessarily bored him. It was simply police work and appealed to his sense of righteousness. When Britain's Judge Advocate General's Office assigned the Sagan case to the Royal Air Force, Group Captain W. V. Nicholas, the head of SIB, knew McKenna's puritanical work ethic would prove a defining quality. And so, when the file hit his desk, he had sent McKenna off to review it and render an opinion.

It took McKenna a week to slog his way through the documents. They included an account of the Stalag Luft III breakout, many details of which had not yet been made public. He marveled at the escape's complexity and the audacity of those who'd planned it. But of the seventy-six men who made it through the tunnel, only three had managed to get back to England: Peter Bergsland and Jens Muller, lieutenants in the Royal Norwegian Air Force, and Dutch Flight Lieutenant Bram Van der Stok. Bergsland and Muller had made their way to Stettin, where Swedish sailors smuggled them aboard a ship and hid them in the chain locker. On the morning of March 30, the ship arrived in Stockholm. The two men—sore, but alive—disembarked and sought refuge at the British Consul. Their odyssey had lasted six days; Van der Stok's journey to freedom took four months. He traveled by train from Sagan to the Netherlands, where he went underground for several weeks and stayed with an old college professor. He next cycled into Belgium and dropped off the grid with the help of an uncle. Through a family friend, he acquired an address in southwest France and traveled by rail to St. Gaudens, where he made contact with the French Resistance.

There followed an arduous trek across the Pyrenees into Spain. From there, it was on to Portugal and then England.

The men, back on British soil, told the War Office what they knew of the escape's planning and execution based on their individual involvement. Their information was coupled with an account from Group Captain Massey—the repatriated senior British officer from Stalag Luft III—who provided what information he could on the violent aftermath. The documents, viewed in their entirety, were a threadbare tapestry of information when one considered the scope and immensity of the killings. The fog of war had effectively concealed many details of the crime. The identity of the gunmen remained a mystery, though the names of several high-ranking officials were put forward as most likely being involved in the murders. Some men of interest, noted Military Intelligence, might already be in custody. Allied prison camps were teeming with captives, but the daunting task of identifying the hundreds of thousands of prisoners behind the wire was far from complete. One man known to be in custody was Breslau *Kripo* chief Max Wielen. The British Army had picked him up after they crossed the Rhine, two weeks before Germany surrendered. In his statement to interrogators, Wielen detailed how national *Kripo* chief Arthur Nebe had ordered him to hand captured escapees in his custody over to Dr. Wilhelm Scharpwinkel, head of the Breslau Gestapo. British Intelligence placed considerable emphasis on this piece of information.

It was ascertained, through interviews with surviving escapees, that the majority of the Sagan fugitives—thirty-five them—had been captured in the Breslau area and imprisoned in the town of Görlitz. The Gestapo murdered twenty-nine men and shipped the remaining six back to Stalag Luft III. Scharpwinkel was a killer—but his whereabouts, indeed even whether he was still alive, remained a mystery. He had taken part in the defense of Breslau, besieged by the Red Army during the last three months of war. Having declared the city a fortress, Hitler ordered Breslau's defenders to fight to the last man. Scharpwinkel was most likely dead, but McKenna required hard evidence before accepting something as fact. Uncovering such evidence would not be easy. Seventeen months had passed since the killings—plenty of time for the

Gestapo to destroy incriminating files and send the perpetrators underground with forged papers and new identities. Germany, wrecked from
one end to the other, had been carved up among the Allies. Sagan,
conquered by the Red Army in February 1945, now lay within the Russian Zone of Occupation and was closed to British and American forces.

An intelligence report concluded: "In view of these difficulties, it
would appear that the best way of increasing the speed and efficiency
of investigations might be to set up temporarily a small unit to make
investigations in Germany. There can be little doubt that the employment
of a small group of officers with police experience and a knowledge of
German would be well justified having regard to the facts that, first, it
is one of the worst of the war crimes committed against British nationals
in general and the R.A.F. in particular; secondly, that it involves major
war criminals; thirdly, that a large number of victims are involved; and
fourthly, that is has aroused considerable public interest."

McKenna closed the file and shook his head. A week after receiving
the documents, he returned to Nicholas's office to deliver his profes-
sional opinion. There was, he told the group captain, little hope of
realizing Anthony Eden's promise. Nicholas leaned back in his chair
and tamped tobacco in a pipe. He sucked in a mouthful of smoke and
hissed it out between clenched teeth, listening as McKenna rattled off
various reasons as to why the case was destined to fail. Nicholas politely
acknowledged McKenna's arguments then casually brushed them aside.

"Listen," he said. "There appears to be little more evidence to be
gained from Allied witnesses. Although the outline is clear, the full
story cannot be learnt until more of the Germans connected with the
case are traced and interrogated."

McKenna realized, with a certain degree of alarm, that a decision
had already been made. When he opened his mouth to protest, Nicholas
raised his arm to signify the matter had been settled. McKenna, accompanied by Flight Sergeant H. J. Williams, an ex–Portsmouth police
officer, would venture to Germany and set about bringing the murderers
to justice. McKenna resigned himself to the mission, knowing any argument against the assignment would most likely result in a forceful
rebuff.

McKenna and Flight Sergeant Williams left England on September 3, 1945, six years to the day after Britain's declaration of war. They took off from RAF Northolt in a Dakota, thundered across the coast, and set a bumpy course over the English Channel. The bomber's interior smelled of grease and metal polish. The Pratt & Whitney engines rattled every screw and joint in the plane—or so thought McKenna, who feared the water. He made a point of not looking out the window as they crossed the sea and instead focused on bringing Williams up to date. The two men had to shout to hear each other over the fuselage noise. McKenna passed files to Williams and familiarized him with their prey. There was, of course, Scharpwinkel, followed by Dr. Gunther Absalon, an SS captain charged with prisoner-of-war security in the Sagan region. McKenna provided the relevant background.

"The camp's commandant at the time of the escape was Colonel Friedrich-Wilhelm von Lindeiner-Wildau, sixty-four, a decorated cavalry officer from the First World War and pro-British," McKenna shouted. "He had no patience for Hitler or the fanatics who towed the Nazi line. He knew any recaptured escapee would have to answer to the Gestapo, leaving him powerless to intervene on the prisoner's behalf. The morning of the escape, he made forty-two telephone calls to regional Gestapo and *Kripo* headquarters, alerting them to the breach. Max Wielen—who we have in custody—was chief of the Breslau *Kripo*, which had jurisdiction over the Sagan region. He issued a *Grossfahndung*, a national hue and cry placing all military and security personnel on the highest alert. That same afternoon, he ordered Gunther Absalon to conduct an investigation at the camp. Absalon stripped Lindeiner of his rank and placed him under arrest."

McKenna handed Williams a copy of Lindeiner's statement, taken by a British interrogator after the war, and summarized the main points.

"Nineteen of the escaped officers were recaptured in the vicinity of Sagan immediately after the escape," he said. "They were put in the local jail, where they were searched and identified by local *Kripo* personnel. At mid-day on Sunday, 26 March, Absalon was asked by Lindeiner to have the officers who were being held at Sagan prison returned to camp. Absalon refused the request peremptorily, explaining that he could accept no instructions from Lindeiner as the latter had been relieved of his post on account of the escape. On the evening of Sunday, 26 March, all nineteen officers were taken to Görlitz, and a further sixteen were brought there on various days. It's not possible to establish with certainty on whose instructions this transfer was carried out. The normal procedure was to return escapers captured by ordinary police to their camp, which applied to at least the officers of British and Dominion nationality. On Sunday evening, no instructions could have possibly reached the local *Kripo* to treat this particular escape in any different way, and the assumption is therefore that the *Kripo* took these measures on their own initiative."

McKenna braved a glance out the window and felt a weight lift when he saw land passing beneath the clouds. He turned back to the case file. Because Absalon had received orders to investigate the escape, he said, he would naturally have been required to interrogate recaptured prisoners. The facility at Görlitz had been a prison in the traditional sense before the war. The Gestapo, however, took it over once hostilities commenced and ran it as an interrogation center. Prisoners housed at Görlitz were mostly civilian and foreign workers accused of sabotage and other treasonous acts against the Reich. The prison, overrun with lice and fleas, was filthy. Prisoners received barely enough food to survive, their daily rations consisting of "200 grams of black bread and one liter of watery soup." Having been questioned, inmates were hauled before a special court where a panel of judges would sentence them to hard labor or condemn them to a death camp.

"Presumably," McKenna theorized, "it was Absalon who ordered the transfer of the officers to Görlitz, where interrogation and segregation could be more easily carried out."

As for Lindeiner, the stress of it all resulted in a coronary. He survived, only to be court-martialed—but the German capitulation spared him the hardship of a year in prison. Now held in London, he was cooperating with the British. Questioned after the war, former inmates of Stalag Luft III described the one-time colonel as "a good sort of commandant with a very difficult task, but well liked by his prisoners and staff." He had encouraged the prisoners under his charge to pursue various hobbies, from sports and gardening to amateur theatrical productions. He routinely violated protocol by shaking hands with inmates, accepting their invitations to tea, and joining them for a smoke. On three occasions, he presented senior ranking prisoners with wine and champagne on their birthdays. McKenna couldn't help but feel some sympathy for the man.

Turbulence rattled the plane as McKenna and Williams next focused on the upper echelons of the Nazi hierarchy. Hitler and Himmler were dead. Göring and Keitel were awaiting trial at Nuremberg, as was Kaltenbrunner, Himmler's second in command at the Central Security Office. That left Nebe, national head of the *Kripo*, whose whereabouts were presently unknown. The fate of Gestapo Chief Heinrich Müller, last seen on April 29, 1945, in Hitler's bunker, also remained a mystery. Their names had been added to the Central Register of War Criminals and Security Suspects in Paris, along with those of 106 other men wanted in connection with the Sagan murders. Britain's Judge Advocate General's Office had compiled the list, drawing the names from interrogations and intelligence reports. McKenna would have to determine who, on the list, had actually played a complicit role in the killings. It was understood that the list was a fluid thing, prone to change based on McKenna's findings. For all anyone knew, most men listed were already dead or languishing in Allied prison camps under assumed names.

"Where do we start?" asked Williams.

"The first task will be to ascertain that none of the wanted men are in fact held in the British, American, and French occupation zones," McKenna said. "It cannot be assumed that just because a name is not recorded in the Central Registry of Detained Persons that the individual is not in Allied hands. The next task is to make enquiries for the wanted persons in the German towns in the British, American, and French occupation zones. Saarbrücken, Natzweiler, Munich, Stuttgart. In these places, searches should be made where possible in the records of the Kripo and Gestapo offices."

There were additional avenues to explore, McKenna continued, including making inquiries in Berlin to review, if such material still existed, the records of the Central Security Office.

"If it is found possible to make enquiries inside the Russian occupation zone," he said, "full enquiries should be made at Breslau, Görlitz, Hirschberg, Oels, Liegnitz, Dresden, and Danzig."

The Dakota banked in a steep turn. McKenna looked out the window and saw a scene of utter devastation, a tortured expanse of twisted metal and shattered masonry: the skeletal remains of a city. Through the clouds, he could see people moving about the wreckage. It seemed remarkable that anything could live down there. Bombing Germany at night, all one could see was the glow of searchlights and the black clouds of flak illuminated by the fires below. It was impossible, under such conditions, to ascertain the true extent of the carnage being done. Now, in the light of day, McKenna felt a sense of pity—not necessarily for the people below, but that events had made such actions necessary.

The plane touched down with a heavy thud on a freshly bulldozed runway outside Rinteln in northwestern Germany. McKenna and Williams disembarked, cleared military customs, and were met by a representative of the RAF, who drove them by jeep to RAF Rinteln. Located on the banks of the Weser River, the ancient town had somehow escaped the ravages of war. Its medieval architecture and timber-framed houses were reminiscent of a Grimm's fairy tale. In stark contrast to the devastation McKenna had viewed from the plane, Rinteln was an oddity—a small vestige of simpler times. The jeep turned onto Waldkaterallee, a quiet, tree-lined street, and stopped in front of a guard gate. An RAF policeman, having checked identification papers, raised a red-and-white barrier and allowed the jeep to pass. McKenna admired the grounds and commented on the number of trees. It was an astute observation, said the driver. The English translation for Waldkaterallee is "Forest Hang Over Alley." They pulled up in front of a three-story barrack building with a heavily sloped roof. The RAF man led McKenna and Williams inside and helped get them situated. They were shown their sleeping quarters and their office, a spacious room of desks and filing cabinets. A large map of Germany dominated one wall. Then, with an utterance of good luck, their escort left McKenna and Williams to the task at hand.

The two men pondered their new surroundings and staked out their desks. McKenna spread the case files out in front of him and approached the wall-mounted map, which, he saw upon closer inspection, showed the Allied partitioning of Germany. The British occupied the northwest region of the country, while the Americans controlled the south. The French held territory along Germany's southwestern border with France. The Russians occupied the east. Berlin, although located in the Soviet Zone, was jointly held by the Americans in the south, the British in the west, the French in the north, and the Russians in the east. McKenna returned to his desk and sorted through the files. The ashes of the dead had been shipped back to Stalag Luft III in urns, many of which bore inscriptions identifying the place of execution. McKenna found the list of cities and returned to the map. Breslau, the site of the majority of killings, lay deep within the Soviet sector. The Russians, who now oversaw nearly a quarter of Germany's population, would most likely deny McKenna and his team access to the area. Cities such as Kiel, Hanover, and Hamburg fell within the British Zone and would pose no foreseeable problem. The British governed 23,000,000 people in their zone of occupation, which included the farmlands of the Rhine. Also under British control was the decimated Ruhr Valley. Once the industrial center of the Nazi war machine, its cities were now all but destroyed. American and British bombers had laid nearly 70 percent of Cologne to waste. "A staggering 93 percent" of Düsseldorf lay in ruins. In the American Zone, cities such as Frankfurt, Bremen, and Munich had suffered their own ordeal by fire.

With a general lay of the land, McKenna contacted the relevant Allied authorities in the American, British, and French zones, informing them of his arrival, the nature of the investigation, and the particulars of those wanted by the RAF. German police departments were also forwarded the wanted list. Meetings consumed the next several days. The commander of the North Western Europe War Crimes Investigation Unit offered McKenna the use of a holding facility in Minden. Officials at the American Authorities' Headquarters in Wiesbaden and

Frankfurt granted McKenna permits to enter the American Zone of Occupation. Records of recently captured Nazi officials were reviewed at Rhine Army headquarters and the Judge Advocate General Branch. These first several days seemed to pass in a flurry of papers, files, and index cards.

Back at his desk one evening, McKenna lit a smoke and pondered his next move. With no crime scene to examine, no witnesses to interview, and no evidence to analyze, the investigation lacked a clear starting point. Alongside the wall map he pinned mug shots of the murdered men, their solemn, black-and-white stares offering grim encouragement. Two of the victims were Flying Officer Robert Stewart and Flight Lieutenant Edgar Humphreys. Both men had been among the thirty-five prisoners to end up in the jail at Görlitz. McKenna flipped through the statements of the survivors who'd passed through the jail. The Gestapo had threatened to behead and shoot some of the recaptured men. Several prisoners were told outright that they would never see their homes or loved ones again. On the morning of March 31, 1944, roughly a dozen Gestapo agents—dressed in leather overcoats and fedoras—showed up at the prison and took ten inmates, including Humphreys and Stewart, away. Their ashes arrived at Stalag Luft III several days later in urns bearing their names and the place of cremation: Liegnitz. Humphreys was twenty-nine, Stewart thirty-two. McKenna took a drag on his cigarette and blinked the smoke out of his eyes. As a civilian police officer in Blackpool, he had become friends with a number of aircrew serving at RAF Squires Gate, the local air base. He often downed pints in the mess hall with Humphreys, a good-humored sort who showed him around the airfield and sparked an enthusiasm for the air force. A Blenheim pilot with No. 107 Squadron, Humphreys took off on December 19, 1940, for a daylight operation against the Channel ports and never returned. Stewart had also become a friend before being shot down over Duisburg on the night of April 27, 1943.

McKenna stared at their photographs and felt the weight of responsibility on him. He hoped to provide the fifty men with an epitaph worthy of all they had suffered. He stubbed out his cigarette, switched off the desk lamp, and retired for the night. The next day he dispatched a report to London, summarizing his first ten days in Germany. The odds of conducting a successful investigation were daunting but not impossible. His immediate plan was to comb the files of regional war crimes record offices in the hopes of establishing a lead, whether it be a name or an address that might put him on track. He also intended to visit the "camps and concentration areas" where the Allies were holding German prisoners. The challenge lay in the sheer numbers. There were a multitude of such facilities, housing millions of Germans, whom the Allies had to clear through a process of elimination. While there was a register listing all those in captivity, it was most likely, McKenna wrote, that many prisoners had assumed false identities prior to their apprehension. Despite such obstacles, McKenna believed the investigation would last several months at most. It was an optimistic assessment.

———

Listening to the voice at the end of the line, McKenna reached for a pen. He scribbled down an address and read it back to ensure he had it correct. The chief of the Düsseldorf Criminal Police confirmed the house and street number. McKenna uttered his thanks and hung up the phone. He held a short council of war with Williams and the newest member of his team. Fluent in German and English, Wilhelm Smit—a sergeant in the Royal Netherlands Air Force—had recently been seconded to the RAF's Special Investigating Branch and assigned to McKenna as an interpreter.

"We have a possible line of information," McKenna said, holding up the scrap of paper with the address. Responding to the wanted list he had wired out to regional police departments, McKenna said, authorities in Düsseldorf had just called with the address of Dr. Gunther Absalon's parents, who lived in the old Düsseldorf district of Heerdt.

Early the next morning, McKenna and his team set off by jeep. They traveled south through open country and small towns in the direction of Dortmund. The fields and hills on either side of the road at first appeared untouched by war, but the scenery morphed as they drew closer to the city. The greenery faded away and the woodlands thinned, consumed by scorched earth and a cratered landscape. Dortmund itself was mostly ash and rubble. The buildings that still survived stood without roofs or windows. On many, the walls had been blasted away, allowing passersby to stare at the devastated rooms within, the furnishings smashed and splintered, a lifetime of mementos and memories blown to pieces. People wandered aimlessly through the streets, pulling what possessions they still had in carts or simply carrying them in a bundle on their back. The RAF men steered clear of wreckage and bomb-ripped chasms, before passing once more into the country. They traveled the remainder of the way through battered terrain and finally reached Düsseldorf by mid-afternoon. The carnage here mirrored that seen in Dortmund. McKenna looked out at queues of people waiting for their weekly rations. Many appeared indigent and their clothes threadbare. The investigators made their way through the ravaged city center—blasted numerous times during the RAF's five-month campaign against the Ruhr in 1943—before crossing the Rhine into Heerdt.

Paul and Martha Absalon lived in a small house at Kribbenstrasse 20. The elderly couple answered the door, surprised to find three men wearing the dress blues of the British Royal Air Force standing on their doorstep. Speaking through Smit, McKenna introduced himself and stated the purpose of his visit.

"We're trying to locate your son," he said. "We need his help resolving an important matter."

The couple led them into a small living room, its windows still taped as a precautionary measure against bomb damage. Martha Absalon, unnerved by the British presence, remained shielded behind her husband. McKenna took a seat, offered what he hoped was a reassuring smile, and asked the couple when they last saw their son.

"It's vital we find him," he said, mindful not to mention the true nature of his visit.

Paul Absalon spoke in a halting voice, as though worried each word might reveal some transgression on the part of his son.

"We have not heard from him in a long while," he said. "He was in Breslau and wrote to us regularly, but we haven't received a letter from him since February 7. We don't know what's become of him or his whereabouts."

McKenna nodded and, with the couple's permission, ordered Williams and Smit to search the house. They turned out every drawer and closet but found nothing to suggest the Absalons were lying. McKenna looked about the sitting room. On the wall was an old family portrait, a picture of the Absalons in happier times, posing with their young son.

"Was Gunther married?"

"Yes," replied the mother. "She lives in Düsseldorf."

With an address in hand, the three RAF officers drove a short distance to Brunnenstrasse 42. Frau Gerda Absalon, having been left to care for two small children and her mother, appeared a pretty, though tired, woman. At her side clung a young girl, whom she gently ushered down a hallway into a back room. When she returned, she sat in an armchair, brushed a strand of dark hair aside, and rested her hands in her lap. McKenna noticed she wore no wedding ring. She caught him looking and managed a weak smile.

"You are here about Gunther," she said.

Smit translated and McKenna nodded.

"What can you tell us?" he asked.

"Not much," she said, explaining that the last she'd heard from him had also been a letter in February posted from Am Anger 10, Breslau. The missive had been brief, simply letting her know he was still alive. Her casual tone suggested the news bore little emotional weight. At thirty, she was three years Absalon's junior and eager to be done with him for good.

"Relations between my husband and myself have always been somewhat strained," she said. "My family and I are not members of the Nazi Party, whereas my husband was always a devoted follower. I'm sure he was in Breslau at the end of the war, and was either killed or taken prisoner by the Russians."

She paused and stared briefly at her bare left hand.

"If I do hear from him again," she said, "I will be asking him for a divorce."

She got up from her chair, moved across the room to a small writing desk, and retrieved a photograph from the drawer. Without giving it another glance, she passed it to McKenna.

"You can have this," she said.

McKenna looked at the picture and saw a young man of Aryan stock, about thirty, looking back at him. His blond hair shorn close to the scalp, he wore at a slight angle on his head a military cap bearing the death's head insignia of the SS. The mouth was a thin, straight line, the eyes cold, and the stare distant. From a British Intelligence report, McKenna knew Absalon always appeared "well groomed and smartly dressed." He pocketed the photograph, thanked Gerda Absalon for her time, and left.

They traveled back to Rinteln, traversing the same battered landscape in the dark. While Smit and Williams were quick to dismiss Absalon as dead, a casualty of the Russian onslaught, McKenna refused to accept the notion. Absalon could have survived and gone underground, or simply slipped away in the chaos of battle. Russian forces had encircled Breslau—the largest city in eastern Germany—on February 15. The fifty thousand defenders, a motley crew of depleted army units and local militia, faced thirteen Soviet divisions. Russian artillery and fighter planes blasted and strafed the city, leveling entire blocks, littering streets with rubble and human wreckage. The fighting raged among the ruins and exacted an awful, bloody toll. Hitler, despite an urgent plea from the commander of German forces on April 6, refused to surrender the city. On April 30, Hitler killed himself. Two days later, on May 2, Berlin fell to the Russians, but the fighting in Breslau continued four more days. Roughly sixteen thousand German civilians and soldiers were dead by the battle's end, and two-thirds of the city lay in a smoldering heap. The siege cost the Russians eight thousand lives.

McKenna arrived back in Rinteln desperate for a lead. He spent the days that followed visiting internment camps and cross-referencing the names of German prisoners with those on his wanted list. His rounds took him to Belsen near Hanover, now a place of incarceration for onetime Gestapo members. The British, for sanitary reasons, had torched the camp with flamethrowers shortly after its liberation in April.

SS guards, fleeing the advancing Allied armies, had left thirteen thousand bodies unburied. The living lay among the dead. So emaciated and racked with typhus and typhoid were the survivors, they were hard to differentiate from the corpses. The bodies were bulldozed into large trenches and quickly covered up to stop the further spread of disease. Now, five months later, macabre monuments to the atrocities committed in the camp still remained. The smell of decomposition and human waste lingered. Human bones, not yet buried, were stacked in large piles. Walking to the camp's registration office, McKenna eyed one large mound of earth after another, his revulsion growing at the realization they were mass graves.

His review of camp files turned up nothing, but being eager to put Belsen behind him, he found that the futility of his efforts hardly upset him. McKenna walked slowly back to his jeep. As a detective, he had witnessed man's capacity for violence in its infinite forms—but the camp defied understanding. Slaughter on the battlefield had a rationale behind it one could grasp, if not accept. Even the indiscriminate bombing of British and German cities served strategic aims one could argue for or against. The atrocities in the camps, however, went beyond any human reasoning. McKenna took comfort in his faith and did not believe in a vicious God, but how did one explain such barbarism? Lacking answers, he gunned the engine and turned the jeep around. As Belsen fell away behind him, he pondered the men on his wanted list. Would they express remorse for what they had done or simply swear blind allegiance to their cause? He mulled the questions over as he drove back to Rinteln, the sides of the road littered with rusting armored vehicles. He occasionally passed a bedraggled procession of the bombed-out and homeless, wandering from one town to another in search of food and shelter.

The dislocation of millions added another layer of complexity to the investigation, though it favored the men being sought by the RAF. Establishing the identities of those blasted or forced from their homes was all but impossible, as the vast number of displaced people had no way of confirming who they were. Those wanted by the authorities for war crimes and other transgressions could pass themselves off as anyone they so desired and disappear among the ruins. As McKenna considered this, something in his mind suddenly clicked. Noncombatants would have been evacuated from Breslau before the Russian siege began, and combatants desperate to avoid capture most likely slipped out before the Red Army overran the city. If he could find out where evacuees from Breslau were now located, he might get a line on Absalon or Scharpwinkel.

Back in Rinteln, McKenna paid a visit to the town's *Bürgermeister*—equivalent to a mayor—who said survivors of Breslau had fled to Rinteln and the surrounding area. Of course, he warned, some might have moved on, but many were likely to still be in the vicinity. Would the flight lieutenant care for the names and addresses of the host families? McKenna could hardly believe his luck and returned to his barracks with a long list of doors to knock on. He showed the list that evening to Smit. The two of them, he said, would have to start canvassing neighborhoods the following day. It was old-fashioned detective work and certainly preferable to the drudgery of cross-referencing files. They would work separately to save time, each covering his own ground. Although having been in the country for only three weeks, McKenna had picked up enough rudimentary German to stumble through the questions he needed to ask.

The rain fell dark and slow the following morning, September 27, as McKenna—his collar turned up against the cold—made his way door to door. His inquiries went nowhere that first day, and he returned to his barrack soaked through and foul tempered. At most houses, no one had answered the door. Those who were home said apologetically they were no longer housing refugees. A stiff drink and a smoke in the mess hall that evening put his mood right but did nothing to make the prospect of hitting the streets again any more appealing. When Smit pulled up a chair and reached for the bottle, McKenna hoped to hear some good news, but he felt his optimism fade when he saw the other man's grim expression. Between them, they easily conquered the bottle's contents and a pack of cigarettes before calling it a night.

The image, initially a blur, slowly came into focus. A field spread out before him beneath a gunmetal sky. Two figures materialized in the distance, one walking in front of the other. Watching them approach, McKenna realized the man in front was a young RAF officer, his uniform tailored to look like a suit. Behind him, a pistol in hand, stomped a member of the Gestapo dressed in a gray SS uniform. The two men stopped in front of McKenna and seemed unaware of his presence. Unable to move or cry out, he watched in horror as the Gestapo man raised the gun to the back of the airman's head and pulled the trigger. The young man's body convulsed and fell forward, the pistol's report echoing across the field like thunder.

McKenna jerked upright in bed. He stared into a dark corner of the room and listened to the rain beat a steady cadence against the window. The dream, which had plagued him for several weeks, lingered in his mind's eye. He lay his head back on the pillow, relieved when the after-image at last began to fade.

The rain, much to McKenna's extreme annoyance, continued into the morning. He prepped for the pending ordeal with several mugs of strong coffee in the mess. The second day of canvassing, September 28, seemed to be a depressing repeat of the first. One by one, he crossed names and addresses off his list, success having thus far steered clear of his efforts. It was near day's end when he knocked on the door of a small terraced house at Berlinstrasse 18a, and heard someone inside work a lock. The door opened a crack, and a young woman peered out. In German, McKenna fumbled his way through an introduction and asked if she was housing anyone from Breslau. The woman nodded and, in German and rough English, said she had living with her a man named Klaus Lonsky. He was out, but McKenna was welcome to wait for him if he so wished. Desperate to be out of the rain, McKenna accepted the invitation.

A little while later, sitting in the woman's living room, McKenna heard the front door open and close. When Lonsky entered the room, McKenna rose to greet him. He was younger than McKenna had expected, probably in his late twenties, but his movements were slow and his expression battle-weary. McKenna, wondering if his tongue would ever prove adept at German, began explaining the purpose of his visit. Lonsky cut him off and said he understood English.

McKenna allowed himself a quick smile.

"I'm investigating the murder of fifty Allied airmen who escaped from Stalag Luft III in March of last year," McKenna said. "One person of considerable interest is this man. Do you know him?"

McKenna retrieved the picture of Absalon from an inside pocket. Lonsky glanced only briefly at the photograph and nodded. He took a seat, his movements stiff, and explained that before the war he had attended school at the University of Breslau. He joined the *Wehrmacht* in 1939 and served in an artillery unit and tank regiment before being wounded in April 1943. Shortly thereafter, he joined the Military Police and was assigned to a patrol unit. His policing duties, he said, often brought him into contact with the Criminal Police.

"In this way, I got to know Dr. Gunther Absalon," Lonsky said. "He was in charge of the thirteenth section of the Criminal Police. I talked with Dr. Absalon on a number of occasions and learned he came from the Rhine district."

McKenna asked Lonsky what, if anything, he knew of the mass breakout from Stalag Luft III.

"Whilst I was in the Military Police, my own troop headquarters were at Sagan," Lonsky volunteered. "I know there was a prisoner-of-war camp there, and on occasions we used to hear that a number of prisoners had escaped. I remember a big number escaping, I think about eighty-one, about March 1944. My unit was advised of the escape, and I believe the whole garrison in Sagan was ordered to take part in the search for the escaped prisoners of war. I heard that a number of them were recaptured, but what happened to them I do not know. I believe some were recaptured in the Görlitz and Breslau areas, but I have never heard what happened to them."

"What instructions did you receive regarding the arrest of prisoners of war?" McKenna asked.

"We were to take them to the nearest Oflag or Stalag and hand them over."

"Did you know anyone associated with the Breslau Gestapo?"

"There was a Dr. Scharpwinkel," Lonsky said, prompting McKenna to lean forward in his chair. "I never met him and do not know his rank. I have seen his signature on papers, but I do not know his Christian name. I do not know where he came from, but he was probably a Silesian."

"And you fought at Breslau?"

Lonsky nodded.

"I remained in the Military Police until September 1944, when I was dismissed for not being a member of the Nazi Party. I believe at that time the authorities decided control of the home country should be taken over by the SS, and that a check was made respecting persons who did or did not belong to the Nazis. After leaving the Military Police, I obtained a post on the staff, which had been set up to prepare for the defense of Breslau."

When the battle commenced on January 20, 1945, Lonsky was assistant to the garrison commander's senior staff officer. He served in that capacity until wounded by a shell one month into the fighting. Bombed out of several hospitals, he was captured by advancing U.S. forces on March 27.

"And what about Scharpwinkel?" asked McKenna. "He was at Breslau, too, yes?"

"I had a good knowledge of the various fighting units that were engaged there and clearly remember a unit called *Einheit* [Unit] Scharp-winkel, which was made up of the Gestapo and Criminal Police of the Breslau district," Lonsky said, adding the unit—at its maximum strength—numbered 150 men. "It was engaged in the North-East of the fortress. I remember one particular incident with regard to the unit. The Russians had forced a spearhead in the direction of Deutschlissa, and headquarters directed that the spearhead must be wiped out. The commander in that sector replied that his men were exhausted and advised that the newcomers, the Gestapo—members of Unit Scharpwinkel—be engaged for this operation as they were fresh and would prove to be fanatical fighters."

"What happened?"

"Approval was given for them to engage," Lonsky said, "but they failed to wipe out the Russian spearhead. It is probable that they suffered severe losses."

"But you don't know for sure?" asked McKenna.

Lonsky gave an apologetic shrug.

"Do you know what happened to Scharpwinkel?"

"Since the capitulation of Germany, I have only met one person who I knew in Breslau," Lonsky said. "His name is Zembrodt. He was a lieutenant in an infantry regiment. In discussing the defense of Breslau, he told me that he and his wife had been taken prisoners by the Russians. He also mentioned something about Dr. Scharpwinkel being in a hospital in Breslau and the Russians coming to take him away."

"Where can I find this Zembrodt?"

"I met him in Rinteln recently," Lonsky said, "and he told me he lives in Barntrup."

McKenna knew the place by name, it being roughly twenty miles from Rinteln.

"What about Absalon?"

"I saw Dr. Absalon on occasions after I left the Military Police, as he used to come to the building where we had our staff offices and which had a restaurant underneath," Lonsky said. "He came there for a drink, as his police office was nearby—but I do not remember seeing him after Christmas 1944."

McKenna thanked Lonsky for his time and stepped once more into the rain.

———

Since the German capitulation, a man named Mercier had been aimlessly wandering the country. He considered himself lucky, having survived the slaughter at Breslau. He had slipped out of the city on May 6, mere days before the Russians completely overran the German defenses. Not sure where to go, he made his way down to the Oder River, where an armed Russian patrol robbed him of the few meager items still in his possession. Threatening to ship him off to a labor camp in Siberia, they marched him at gunpoint to a Red Army command post in the nearby town of Tarnow and held him for several days. During questioning, he identified himself as a French laborer forced to take up arms for the Nazis. "Where are your papers?" his captors asked. Mercier shrugged. All he had, he said, were the ragged clothes that hung from his gaunt frame. A Russian commander, taking the Frenchman at his word, issued the man new travel papers in the name of Mercier and let him go. So, from the town of Tarnow, he set off with only one goal in mind: to find his wife, whom he had not seen in more than a year.

He often walked alone but occasionally joined one of the many straggling processions of refugees that shuffled alongside the roads. The country he knew was gone. Food was scarce and shelter hard to come by. The glorious Reich, once resplendent in victory, giddy with conquest, now lay prostrate in ruins. He ventured through one flattened town after another, laying his head where he could. From a black marketeer, he purchased a ration card to help acquire food. He traveled west toward Görlitz, the great west-east exchange point for Polish and German refugees. At the local Polish Consulate, he presented his Red Army travel papers and secured a permit allowing him to cross the River Neisse into the west. His subsequent wanderings took him by rail into Prague then back into Germany through Lübeck and Hanover. All the while, he hoped to be reunited with his wife of twenty years—but like so many others, she had simply disappeared amid the chaos of war. He gradually made his way to Hamburg, where he found room and board at the Swedish Mission Hostel. To make money, he thought he might have a go at establishing himself in the wine trade as a salesman. He had often enjoyed a nice vintage before the war and was not ignorant on the subject. Whether he found his wife or not, he had to somehow make a living.

Several days later, a telephone rang in the Hamburg office of the RAF Security Police. A Sergeant Taylor took the call. The man on the other end of the line spoke in a low voice. At the Swedish Mission Hostel, the caller said, police would find a onetime *Obersturmbannführer* (the equivalent to a lieutenant colonel) in the SS lodging under the name Ernest Mercier. Before Taylor could ask any questions, the line went dead. He made his way to the hostel, navigating the wreckage-strewn streets, and checked with the clerk behind the desk. A look at the guest ledger revealed that Mercier had vacated his room several days prior but had left a forwarding address for any stray correspondence: a boardinghouse at Gurlittstrasse 23. The proprietress at the boardinghouse told Taylor that Mercier was out but expected back later that evening. Taylor gave the landlady his phone number and told her to call him the moment Mercier returned.

Taylor spent the next several hours back at his office, staring at the phone. On his desk sat the wanted list McKenna had circulated to Allied police units several weeks earlier. The name "Mercier" was not on it—but that meant little. The landlady called at seven to report that Mercier had just returned. Less than thirty minutes later, Taylor was back at the address and knocking on the door of an upstairs bedroom. When Mercier opened the door, Taylor pushed his way in and placed the man under arrest. Mercier put up little resistance but gave violent voice to his protests, insisting Taylor had made a mistake. He was, he said, a French national and had the papers to prove it. Taylor ignored the man's ranting and hurried him down to the car. Back at the RAF Police office, the man refused to submit to interrogation. He was turned over to the German civil police and taken to the local jail, where he promptly tried to break free of his guards and make a run for it. He spent the night in a cramped cell under constant supervision. The next morning, he was shackled and led to a dank interrogation room.

This time, under forceful questioning, Mercier's front crumbled. He slumped back in his chair and uttered his real name. Taylor's eyes dropped to a sheet of paper in front of him. He ran his finger down McKenna's wanted list. Dr. Ernst Kah, head of the Breslau *Sicherheitsdienst*—or SD, the intelligence agency of the SS—occupied the number-twelve slot.

Kah, now desperate to prove his willingness to help, began rattling off the names and whereabouts of other Nazis on the run, including one man in particular. Colonel Heinrich Seetzen, inspector of Security Police in the Breslau area, sat at number nine on McKenna's list. What about him? Taylor asked. At Kohlerstrasse 6, in Hamburg, Kah said,

British authorities would find Seetzen hiding under the name Gollwicer. Taylor asked for a description. Kah, after a moment's consideration, placed Seetzen in his mid-to-late thirties. Powerfully built, though comprised more of fat than muscle, he stood roughly six feet tall. His eyes were a watery gray beneath a fringe of fair hair. A motor accident had left scars on his arms and face.

"You will take us to him," Taylor said.

Kah could only agree.

It was past midnight when two RAF police cars, their headlights extinguished, turned onto Kohlerstrasse and moved slowly down the street. Kah sat wedged in the backseat of the rear car, between two RAF police officers. The cars passed darkened lots, some bearing the distinct silhouettes of small, cramped houses; others piled high with the wreckage of homes rendered flat by Allied bombing. Outside the house at number six, the cars came to a stop. Two officers, their sidearms drawn, emerged from the lead vehicle and rushed up the garden path. From where he sat, Kah could see the shadowy figures approach the door. They forced their way into the house, yellow light spilling from the doorway onto the darkened stoop. Kah could hear shouting and the barking of commands. Curtains were drawn across the windows, making it impossible to see the chaos unfolding inside. Several tense minutes passed before the two RAF policemen appeared in the doorway with a struggling man between them. They fought their way down the garden to the front of the car in which Kah sat. The driver turned on the headlights, illuminating the man's face. Kah nodded.

The officers bundled Seetzen into the first car and sped off toward police headquarters. His wrists cuffed behind him, Seetzen sat quietly in the backseat and worked the back side of his teeth with his tongue. He dislodged the cyanide capsule from his bridgework, positioned it between his teeth, and bit down. In the front of the car, one of the arresting officers turned around and saw Seetzen, his body wracked with spasms, frothing at the mouth. The driver turned the wheel hard and changed course for the hospital. They arrived within minutes, but it was too late. Seetzen lay dead across the seat, white residue dribbling from his lips.

THREE

VENGEANCE

Three Russian soldiers, two men and a woman, stormed the emergency ward of Breslau Hospital No. 6 on the morning of May 10, 1945. Armed with Tokarev rifles, they moved from bed to bed, prodding the burned and mangled casualties of the recent siege, screaming the same question over and over.

"Where is Lieutenant Hagamann?"

The Russian woman stomped through the ward, kicked the sides of beds, and fired the question at dazed and bewildered patients. The male soldiers, their rifles at the ready, followed in her wake.

"Are you Lieutenant Hagamann?" the woman screamed at one man, his body wrapped in bandages. When the man shook his head, she moved on to the next bed. "Where is Lieutenant Hagamann?"

The volatile questioning dragged on as one patient after the other denied being Hagamann. There was no doubt among those in the ward as to what fate awaited the unfortunate lieutenant should he be found.

"Are you Lieutenant Hagamann?"

Another man, his skin scarred and blackened, uttered a weak-sounding "No."

In a corner bed at the far end of the ward, a man raised his head and said, "I am Hagamann."

The Russians approached and ripped the sheets from his bed to reveal a lightly bandaged leg.

"You are Scharpwinkel," the Russian woman yelled.

"Yes," the man said. "I am Scharpwinkel, head of the Gestapo in Breslau."

The soldiers pulled Scharpwinkel out of bed and dragged him from the ward. Several minutes later, a car engine roared to life in the hospital courtyard below. The sound of squealing tires signaled the Russians' hasty departure.

The man telling McKenna the story paused and looked out the window of his small cottage, the rural serenity of his present surroundings far removed from the blood and antiseptic of the hospital. McKenna had tracked down Hubertus Zembrodt, twenty-seven, without a problem. Checking with the town *Bürgermeister* in Bartrup a day after questioning Lonsky, McKenna was provided an address on Alverdiessennerstrasse. Zembrodt—poor but pleasant—invited McKenna in and spoke freely. He told McKenna he'd joined the *Wehrmacht* before the war. He served in France and on the Eastern Front, where he was wounded in late 1944. He convalesced for two months before being sent to Breslau in January 1945. Three months later, enemy fire put him in the same hospital as Scharpwinkel, who had also been wounded in the Breslau fighting. The Russians imprisoned Zembrodt and the other patients after the city's fall but released him in July. Unable to find accommodations elsewhere, he settled in Bartrup—unemployed, but thankful to be alive.

"The Russians also arrested Dr. Mehling, who was the doctor in charge of all the hospitals in Breslau," Zembrodt said, returning to his story. "I have never heard of either man since that day and don't know what has happened to them."

"Is there anything about Scharpwinkel you can tell me?" McKenna asked. "Anything at all."

"The arrest at the hospital caused a certain amount of discussion among the patients and staff at the time," Zembrodt said. "As far as I can remember, Dr. Scharpwinkel was in the hospital about four weeks before he was taken away by the Russians."

"What about during the actual fighting?" McKenna asked. "Did you hear of a unit under his command codenamed Scharpwinkel?"

Zembrodt shook his head and said he knew little else about the man. McKenna concluded the interview and returned with Smit to their barracks at Rinteln. Brooding at the wheel, McKenna pondered Zembrodt's story. It failed to prove the Russians had liquidated Scharpwinkel. He drove and kept his thoughts to himself, the steady patter of rain and the rhythmic slapping of the windshield wipers the only sounds. When Smit, attempting to break the heavy silence, suggested they cross Scharpwinkel off their list, McKenna dismissed the idea. Scharpwinkel would remain a wanted man, McKenna said, until physical evidence dictated otherwise.

McKenna restored his spirits back at the barracks with a cigarette and glass of whiskey in the canteen. He returned to his office and studied the fifty mug shots on the wall. Under their watchful gaze, he took a seat and began sorting through the growing stack of paperwork on his desk. Since the investigation began, McKenna's team had received numerous tips from both anonymous and official sources. One in particular came from a Dr. Rudolf Diels and concerned General Arthur Nebe, the top man on the RAF's list. Presently, Diels was in British custody and preparing to testify for the prosecution at Nuremberg. The doctor served as the Gestapo's first chief from 1933 to 1934. When political intrigue forced him out of the job, he assumed command of security for the government of Cologne. Because of the various positions he'd held before and during the war, Diels was well versed on the inner workings of the Gestapo and *Kripo*.

Recently interrogated by British military officials, Diels said he had been arrested and sentenced to death for his alleged involvement in the July 1944 plot to kill Hitler. He claimed to have seen Nebe placed in the cell adjacent to his while imprisoned at Gestapo headquarters in Berlin. According to information passed on to McKenna's team by the Judge Advocate General's Office:

Nebe was regarded as a most interesting prisoner by the Gestapo because the case against him for treason was allegedly clear cut.

Nebe had disappeared from his office sometime after the Hitler plot, and his arrest was ordered. He was eventually captured. Dr. Diels had thought that Nebe might still be alive, but he has since seen a friend in the Bad Oeynhausen district and had been told that a man named Huebner, who was in the next cell to Nebe, had been shot. It was the practice to shoot prisoners in batches of eight and he presumed that Nebe must, therefore, have been executed.

McKenna pulled a copy of the wanted list from his desk drawer. To the right of Nebe's name he wrote, "Believed dead but not yet confirmed." In the number-ten slot, alongside Absalon's name, he scrawled in pencil: "Believed killed or taken by the Russians." The pages of his notebook were filled with rumors and speculation but nothing concrete. Definitive leads remained elusive despite twenty-six days of investigative footwork. As he sat pondering the list, the phone on his desk rang. Sergeant Taylor, at the end of the line, informed McKenna of Kah's apprehension and the subsequent arrest and suicide of Heinrich Seetzen. Neither man, he said, answering McKenna's question, had mentioned Scharpwinkel or Absalon. Kah was now being transferred to No. 1 Civilian Internment Camp (CIC) at Neumünster. The British Army planned to hold him in isolation for fourteen days' interrogation. Once they were done, Taylor said, McKenna would be free to question Kah himself.

McKenna hung up the phone and picked up his pencil. Satisfied, he drew a line through Seetzen's name at number twelve and checked off Kah at number seven. Two down.

McKenna and Smit left Rinteln several days later for Berlin, where they hoped to uncover information on Scharpwinkel. They traveled by jeep to Helmstedt and cleared an army checkpoint before leaving the British Zone of Occupation behind. McKenna doubted they would make Berlin by nightfall. Showing their papers at another checkpoint beneath a red sickle-and-hammer flag, they passed into the Russian Zone. They traveled on for another forty-five minutes, racing against the fading light and mindful of the storm clouds overhead, before the jeep's engine died without warning. McKenna cursed and guided the jeep onto the road's center divide.

"This is a hell of a mess," he said, looking up at the darkening sky. "No one will come through now."

The two men remained in the jeep and considered their next move. They were still roughly ninety miles from Berlin. The minutes ticked by until, in the evening gloom, the distant sound of an engine signaled an approaching vehicle. Two American officers in a jeep screeched to a halt alongside McKenna's stricken ride and asked if he needed help. On him, McKenna had his French and American travel passes, a copy of the wanted list, and his notebook.

"I have papers here that I don't want to get into anybody else's hands," McKenna said. "Would you be kind enough to take them with my sergeant to Berlin, and I'll sit and wait for the Aid Department to come out. Please tell them exactly where I am."

The Americans agreed to help and drove off toward Berlin with McKenna's papers and Smit. McKenna watched the taillights vanish into the night and suddenly felt very alone. The surrounding landscape was completely still and cloaked in a heavy silence. He climbed back into the jeep and wrapped himself in an overcoat and blankets. It would be at least four hours, he guessed, before help arrived. Snow began to fall and quickly piled high against the jeep's windshield. He settled in for the long wait and gradually drifted off.

Low voices and footsteps in the snow dragged him from a shallow sleep. Through the fogged passenger window, he saw several men approaching the jeep, their features faintly lit by the pale glow of oil lamps. Their vehicle—a large, canvas-topped truck with chains around the tires—sat alongside his. A gloved hand knocked on the driver's-side window and motioned for McKenna to get out. He could now hear the men more clearly and realized they were speaking Russian. Wearily, he got out and tried to identify himself using the few Russian words he knew. The soldiers, heavily bundled in long coats, rifles slung over their shoulders, shook their heads. One nudged McKenna out of the way and peered inside the jeep.

"*Papirosi*," the soldier said when done with his cursory examination.

It was McKenna's turn to shake his head.

"*Papirosi*," the soldier said again, bringing an imaginary cigarette to his lips.

"No," McKenna said. "No cigarettes—no *papirosi*."

The Russians decided to check for themselves and rummaged through the vehicle. McKenna eyed their firearms and kept silent. He stood shivering in the snow as the soldiers foraged through the glove box and checked under all the seats. Satisfied McKenna was not holding out, the Russians turned and walked back to their truck. One soldier flashed a broad grin and shook McKenna's hand before joining his comrades. His teeth chattering and his shoulders hunched against the cold, McKenna watched the Russian transport pull away and disappear into the dark. He retreated quickly to the relative warmth of the jeep's interior and continued to wait. At about midnight, a car came speeding down the autobahn from the direction of the capital and pulled in behind McKenna. From it emerged a visibly annoyed squadron leader from RAF headquarters in Berlin.

"You should have abandoned the car," the squadron leader bellowed. "What does it matter?" He examined the jeep and shook his head. "We can't tow this thing anyway with a broken axle. We'll have to get out a heavy aid detachment in the morning."

McKenna shrugged off the superior officer's displeasure.

"Have you seen my sergeant interpreter?" he asked.

"Yes," the squadron leader said, still examining the jeep, "we've got all the papers in Berlin."

"Well," McKenna said, "that's all that matters."

The squadron leader drove McKenna to Berlin and left the stricken jeep by the roadside. McKenna borrowed a car the next morning and returned to check on the vehicle and wait for a towing crew. He arrived at the spot mid-morning and found the jeep gone; four tire marks in the snow were all that remained. Desperate locals must have raided the jeep for scrap, McKenna theorized, picking it apart piece by piece.

McKenna drove to the nearest military checkpoint and called the local RAF authorities to report the jeep stolen.

"Are you sure there were no papers in it?" asked the group captain who took the call.

"Yes, sir."

"Right, then forget it," the group captain said. "We'll write it off."

McKenna returned to Rinteln without his jeep or any worthwhile information on Scharpwinkel.

Naked bulbs hanging from exposed wires in the ceiling bathed the interrogation room in a harsh white light. Dr. Ernst Kah sat at a long table and raised his shackled wrists to his mouth. He took a long drag on his cigarette and smiled at his inquisitors. Two weeks had passed since Kah's initial arrest. The army, having obtained from him whatever information it sought, had now made him available to the RAF. McKenna, along with Squadron Leader W. P. Thomas, recently dispatched from England to assist in the investigation, arrived at No. 1 CIC at Neumünster on the afternoon of October 17. Expecting the onetime chief of the Breslau Security Police to be an ardent Nazi, they were surprised when he voiced, by way of greeting, his admiration for the British.

"I think you are prepared to help us with information," said Thomas.

"Yes," Kah said. "Germany has lost the war. Germany will not recover again. It is too late. England is the only country which can lead Europe and to establish Europe again. I do not say this as a joke."

"If you do not tell us the truth," Thomas said, "it will be your responsibility and not ours."

Kah nodded, taking in another lungful of smoke. "I want to help you voluntarily," he said, "because Germany cannot now do anything."

The RAF men asked Kah if he knew of Scharpwinkel. Kah answered in the affirmative and explained that the man had served as chief of the local Gestapo in Breslau. The last he heard, Scharpwinkel had been shot in the left leg during the Russian assault and most likely remained in the city. But such information, he warned, was based solely on secondhand intelligence he'd picked up in the days following the battle.

"Do you know what happened to him?"

"No," Kah replied. "The capitulation was so much in a hurry. The report came in on a Sunday that the capitulation would be during the night of Sunday or Monday. During Sunday—and during the night—many fled to other parts, away from the Russians. That is what I did. We were surrounded, but many people succeeded in getting out. It was a matter of life and death. I left Breslau alone in the night of Sunday."

Kah suggested a number of individuals on the RAF's wanted list had been killed in the fighting at Breslau or were now in Russian custody. It would, of course, take time to corroborate such information. The Russians had thus far ignored McKenna's various requests for assistance. Arrangements were promptly made to ship Kah back to England for further interrogation at the London Cage, a prisoner-of-war facility run by British Intelligence out of a grand house in Kensington Palace Gardens.

Still lacking strong leads, McKenna once more channeled his energy into canvassing the internment camps and focused on the British Zone of Occupation. New to the team was Flight Lieutenant Stephen Courtney who, accompanied by a large German shepherd of questionable demeanor named Fritz, had arrived in Rinteln in early October. McKenna tasked Courtney with searching the holding facilities in the American Zone. The camps, miserable in ideal conditions, were utterly wretched in the cold damp of winter. Drenched in rain, the grounds were rendered muddy swamps; the wooden huts reeked of rot. Over the course of several weeks, Courtney and Smit, serving as interpreter, made their way from one compound to another. It was monotonous and tiring work rife with bureaucracy. Authorization was required to travel from one town to another, and permission was needed to access the camps. On November 29, Courtney arrived at Dachau, the Nazis' first concentration camp, located roughly ten miles outside Munich, on the grounds of an old munitions factory. A GI standing sentry ushered Courtney's car through the main gate, the wrought iron bearing the phrase *Arbeit macht frei*—"Work makes one free." Entering the grounds, Courtney thought of a jingle he had heard shortly after his arrival in Germany:

Lieber Herr Gott, mach mich stumm
Das ich nicht nach Dachau komm.

[Dear God, make me dumb
That I may not to Dachau come.]

Men—some in tattered civilian clothing, others in faded uniforms— milled about the compound as though waiting for something to happen. In a cold interrogation room, Courtney questioned prisoners known to have served in the Gestapo. He asked them about Scharpwinkel, Absalon, and others on the RAF's wanted list. Some prisoners spat invective; others refused to talk. Some minor gains, however, were made. Information Courtney obtained from several inmates led to the arrest in early December of Colonel Ernst Richard Walde at a private residence outside Hannover. Walde, who had served as a *Luftwaffe* administrator at Stalag Luft III, was number twenty-four on McKenna's list. Another informant steered the team to General Inspector Walther Grosch— Walde's superior and number twenty-three on the list—who was hiding outside Kiel. Also apprehended in the same region was General Rudolf Hoffman, number twenty-six, overall commander of *Luftwaffe* installations, including Stalag Luft III, in Lower Silesia. The men were transferred to the London Cage, where, although cleared of direct involvement in the Sagan murders, they—as witnesses—confirmed the roles of other men being sought by the RAF.

The investigation continued to advance on the hearsay of others. For a detective with nearly two decades' policing experience, McKenna found it discomfiting. He craved personal interaction with the suspects, longed to confront them with the facts, back them into a corner, and elicit a confession. In mid-December, the Judge Advocate General's

Branch of the British Army of the Rhine forwarded McKenna a dossier on Fritz Panzinger, number seventy-five on the wanted list and onetime adjutant to Gestapo Chief Heinrich Müller. Panzinger's last known address was in Berlin, where he and his wife had lived in a second-floor flat at Yorckstrasse 72. On April 28, with the Red Army closing in, Panzinger joined other Gestapo officials on a flight out of Berlin, bound for Thuringia in central Germany. The aircraft reportedly crashed on takeoff, the fiery impact killing all on board. The story, however, was impossible to verify as the Gestapo had destroyed all pertinent records prior to the capitulation. What Allied investigators had managed to ascertain was that Panzinger's wife, two days after the plane supposedly went down, bit into a cyanide capsule and killed herself. Panzinger's mother and brother had been located in Munich and would be questioned in due time.

"The Americans," the dossier concluded, "are interested in locating Panzinger and will pass on any information they may obtain."

McKenna was happy to let the Americans worry about it; he had enough to deal with.* He remained desperate for one solid lead, a cornerstone upon which he could slowly build his case.

––––––––

On the afternoon of December 2, 1945, Dr. F. V. van der Bijil—a Czech lawyer who'd flown with the RAF during the war—returned to his room at the Hotel Esplanade in Prague, took pen to paper, and began a long letter to the British ambassador. A steady rain pummeled the window and distorted the view of the city's ancient steeples and spires.

Restored after Germany's defeat, the Czechoslovakian government was conducting its own investigation into wartime atrocities. On May 27, 1942, Prague Gestapo chief Reinhard Heydrich—"head of the Reich Security Service, Deputy Reich Protector of Bohemia and Moravia, administrator of the concentration camps, and a specialist in Nazi

––––––––

* The man was never found.

terror techniques"—had had an appointment with Hitler in Berlin. He left for the German capital that morning in an open-air car driven by his chauffeur. The black Mercedes pulled away from Heydrich's villa in the suburb of Paneské Břežany and traveled along the Dresden-Prague Road. At an intersection, where the car slowed to maneuver a hairpin turn, two Czech patriots trained by British Intelligence lay in wait. Shortly after 10:30 A.M., as Heydrich's car navigated the bend, one of the assassins stepped into the street and tossed a grenade at the vehicle. The resulting explosion wrecked the car and wounded Heydrich, who died several days later in a local hospital. His killers fled and took refuge in Ss. Cyril and Methodius Cathedral. Rather than surrender to the German troops who soon besieged the church, they took their own lives and became martyrs to the cause.

Response to the assassination was immediate and brutal. The Germans rolled into the small town of Lidice on the morning of June 9 and rounded up every male sixteen years of age and older. The 173 men were taken to a local farm and shot. "Seventeen rows of corpses in bloody clothes, with shattered skulls, brains and guts spilling out, lay on the ground in batches of ten" by the time the killing was done. German soldiers destroyed the town's graveyard and desecrated four hundred graves. Women and children were shipped off to concentration camps, their homes looted and set ablaze.

The Czechs cast a wide net in their search for the perpetrators and hauled in more than their intended catch. Czech officials had been receptive to the British plea for help in the Sagan investigation. The government had a vested interest in the case. Flying Officer Ernst Valenta, a Sagan escapee, was a Czech national and one of the murdered fifty. After the war, Czech officials ensnared in their dragnet a onetime driver for the Gestapo. Under interrogation, the man confessed to participating in the murder of two escapees from Stalag Luft III: British Squadron Leader Thomas Kirby-Green and Canadian Flying Officer Gordon Kidder. Van der Bijil, having informed the Czech government of his personal interest in the Sagan murders, was granted access to the Narochi Vybor prison in Zlín and allowed to question the man.

Now, in his hotel room, writing to the British ambassador, van der Bijil put what he knew down on paper:

Sir,

Detailed information has just come into my possession regarding the alleged murder of two Royal Air Force officers on March 29th, 1944. I have personally questioned a former Gestapo man who was an eye-witness of the murder. I have every reason to believe the complete accuracy of the report, which I submit to Your Excellency, although more than this I cannot certify.

Thomas Kirby-Green. British. Born in Nyassaland on 28th February, 1918. Gave his rank as "Major" of the Royal Air Force; i.e. Squadron Leader. I think there is little doubt this was Squadron Leader Kirby-Green who was formerly officer i/c of training of 311 Czechoslovak Squadron R.A.F. whilst stationed at R.A.F. East Wretham, Norfolk.

He was prisoner of war at Sagan in Lower Silesia. He escaped and was arrested at Zlín, Moravia, at 11.00 hours on the 28th March, 1944 by the German Criminal Police. Charge: "Escape from Prison Camp."

With Squadron Leader Kirby-Green was a Canadian flight lieutenant, and the story applies equally to him.

Following their arrest and interrogation, wrote van der Bijil, the prisoners left Zlín in two Gestapo cars:

The driver of one was Kiowsky, at present in custody in Zlín. I was invited to personally question Kiowsky at the Narochi Vyber, Zlín, on November 30, 1945. The driver of the other car— Schwarzer—has not been caught.

Also along for the ride was a Gestapo man named Erich Zacharias. According to information obtained by van der Bijil, Zacharias was married and now living in Gartenstadt in the British Zone. Military authorities in the region, oblivious to the man's past, had classified Zacharias "a harmless person." According to Kiowsky, Zacharias had already murdered three people in Zlín, one being an eighteen-year-old girl. The letter went on to detail the murders of Kirby-Green and his Canadian companion:

> *Arriving at a spot somewhere between Frydek and Moravska Ostrava about 10 kms from Moravska Ostrava, the cars were stopped to permit the prisoners to relieve themselves. Kiowsky was some few meters away when, hearing a shot, he turned and saw Erich with a revolver in his hand having shot Kirby-Green in the back by the shoulders. As Kirby-Green swung round from the shot, he then shot him in the head and Kirby-Green collapsed, dead. The Canadian officer was murdered in a similar manner.*
>
> *It is asserted that these murders were ordered by the Chief of the Gestapo in Zlín, Hans Ziegler. . . . Ziegler forbade any discussion of this incident for fear of Red Cross investigation.*

Van der Bijil concluded his letter with a plea for immediate action:

> *I, therefore, request [Your] Excellency to arrange for an immediate enquiry into these alleged murders and, in particular, for the immediate interrogation of the alleged murderer, Erich Zacharias.*
>
> *I would add that I am deeply interested in the fate of S/Ldr. Kirby-Green, who was a gallant and distinguished officer with whom I had the honour to serve in the Royal Air Force.*

Van der Bijil signed his name to the page and dropped the letter in the hotel's outgoing mail.

FOUR

ZLÍN

Squadron Leader Tom Kirby-Green, with his mop of thick black hair, Clark Gable mustache, and chiseled features possessed a bohemian streak that both entertained his fellow prisoners and gave him an exotic air. One contemporary remembered him looking like "an overgrown Spaniard." He wore bright-colored kaftans and played the maracas. He enjoyed Cuban music and was enthralled by Latin American culture. While others sat around and played cards, he reclined on his bunk and read French literature.

The son of a colonial governor, Kirby-Green was born in what is now present-day Malawi. His parents soon shipped him off to school in England, where he earned something of a reputation at Dover College. Accustomed as he was to a more adventurous upbringing on the subcontinent, he irked the headmaster early in his school days by shooting the ducks on the college pond. It did not take long, however, for him to earn the respect of his teachers and fellow students with his intellectual acumen and prowess on the rugby field. When done with school, he joined the ranks of RAF Bomber Command in 1936 intent on becoming a pilot. Coupled with his lust for adventure was a concern over Europe's growing fascist threat. He served with several squadrons—including a Czech training unit—before joining No. 40 Squadron, flying Wellingtons out of RAF Alconbury in Cambridgeshire. On the evening of October 16, 1941, he took off on his thirty-seventh operation, the target being Duisburg. Enemy fire knocked his bomber from the sky on the return flight and brought it down near Reichswald Forest in north Germany. He was captured near the wreckage. The Germans considered the incident a propaganda coup to the extent that Lord Haw-Haw, the traitorous Briton turned Nazi broadcaster, announced it over the airwaves. Not long thereafter, Kirby-Green ended up in Stalag Luft III.

In a letter to his wife, Maria, dated September 30, 1943, he described the horrifying ordeal of bailing out:

> We were on our way home when we were extremely hard hit, all controls were completely "dead" and the aircraft was spinning and losing height extremely fast. I gave the order to jump. My parachute opened almost at the same time as I hit the ground with the result that I injured my spine and could not walk.
>
> The aircraft crashed about three seconds after I landed and about 30 yards from me. Martin was found in the tail of the aircraft dead. The others were found some short distance away but on very much higher ground with their chutes open, killed instantaneously.

During the escape's planning phase, Kirby-Green helped handle security matters and took part in digging the tunnels. All the while, his thoughts centered on Maria and their young son, Colin. Wandering the camp one afternoon, he paused and gazed through the wire at the surrounding pine forest. The trees, he wrote home later that day in his neat, cursive writing, "don't do well. Few are growing, but anyway I feel we'll be together before they grow much bigger."

And so the days, marked only by the slow lengthening of tunnels and the sluggish growth of the trees, bled one into the other until, at last, all was ready. Prior to the breakout, Kirby-Green partnered with Canadian Flying Officer Gordon Kidder, a twenty-nine-year-old navigator who had done his part helping planned escapees learn German. Prior to the war, he had briefly attended Johns Hopkins University in the States, intent on gaining a master's in German before deciding to

try his luck in the real world. When war broke out, he joined the Royal
Canadian Air Force and was posted as a navigator to No. 156 Squadron,
a Pathfinder unit that flew in ahead of the main attack force to light
the target area with colored flares. On the night of October 13, 1942,
Kidder's Wellington suffered heavy flak damage over Kiel and lost an
engine. The pilot fought to maintain altitude as he turned the bomber
for home. Over the North Sea, the second engine gave out. The plane
came down hard in the water and killed all on board except Kidder—
who suffered a broken ankle—and the radio operator. The two men
managed to scramble aboard the aircraft's emergency dinghy and spent
the night bobbing about on the waves. They were picked up early the
next morning by a German minesweeper. Kidder had subsequently
languished in Stalag Luft III since Christmas 1942.

On the night of the escape, as nervous men again checked their
forged travel documents, repeated whatever German phrases they had
learned, and hoped their civilian disguises passed muster, Kirby-Green
took a break from the frantic last-minute preparations and penned
another letter home:

March 24, 1944

My beloved adored darling,

*I hope you are well and Colin too. My sweetheart, I am thinking
so much of you now and I long so hard for you with every part
of my soul and body. I am so lonely in my heart and a burning
fire consumes my body longing to cool in the heat of yours, my
darling lovely girl. I live only for the moment when I shall take
you in my arms which have been so sadly bereft of the softness
of your waist and hips and thighs, as hungry have my lips been
for yours and your lovely body. No love in the world can compare
with ours, Maria. Darling love, how feeble are my words, how
hard to express the wild tumult of my heart when I think of you.
I feel so grateful for your love and tenderness and so humble, my
girl, my darling love, and I shall be able to make the world a*

paradise for you with God's help, if love and adoring passion can
bring joy for you and for Colin. God bless you and keep you
Maria. I love you, darling, what more can I say?

Kisses to you,
Your Thomas

Kirby-Green and Kidder were among the first two dozen men to
make it through the tunnel. Posing as Spanish laborers, the pair hoped
to make it to Hungary and establish contact with friends of Kirby-
Green's. Once Kidder had been pulled through the tunnel, Kirby-Green
crawled onto the shaft's flatbed trolley. He lay on his stomach and held
his suitcase out in front of him. Calamity struck when, more than
halfway through the shaft, the trolley slipped off the rails. When Kirby-
Green tried to fix the problem, he inadvertently knocked a shoring plank
out of place and brought three feet of tunnel crashing down on him. It
took an hour to pull him free, excavate the dirt, repair the damage, and
situate the trolley back on the rails.

Despite the setback, the two men eventually emerged from underground and made their way through the pine forest to the Sagan train
station. It was after midnight. Both men saw a number of fellow escapees hanging about the platform, trying to look anonymous. Unfortu-
nately, they also noticed some off-duty guards from the camp waiting
for a train. Among them was a female officer who took a sudden interest
in Kirby-Green and Kidder. She approached them and demanded, in a
barking tone, to see their papers. The other escapees milling about tried
to ignore the scene. The two men presented their travel passes and
explained to her in Spanish they were foreign workers. The guard told
them to stay where they were and ran off to show their papers to a
military police officer on duty at the station. The policeman gave the
passes a quick looking over and nodded his approval.

The pair, much relieved, boarded the 1 A.M. train to Breslau. They
took their seats and felt a flicker of hope as the train pulled away into
the night. The journey passed without incident, and they arrived at the
Breslau station an hour and a half later. In the booking hall, the men

purchased two tickets to Czechoslovakia. They got as far as Hodonin
in southern Moravia, where they were arrested on March 28 and taken
to a prison in Zlín.

––––––––––––

Wing Commander Wilfred "Freddie" Bowes was broad of beam, powerfully built, and possessed a jovial disposition and forceful nature. At
forty-two, he had served in the RAF since 1918, the year it was established as the world's first independent air force. His weathered face
conveyed the dual nature of his personality, quick to smile at an off-
color joke but just as prone to flash anger at the stupidity of others and
what he perceived to be bureaucratic meddling. He never hesitated to
speak his mind, caring little for what others thought of his opinions
and making good use of profanities when he deemed a situation worthy
of blunt language. In his subordinates, he instilled fear, respect, and a
fierce loyalty. He did not suffer fools gladly and could harshly dress
down those who failed to meet his expectations, but he bristled at the
thought of anyone else reprimanding those who served under him.

By early December, Bowes had been promoted to chief of the Special
Investigating Branch, British forces, Occupied Germany. He arrived in
Germany that month to assume overall command of the investigation.
McKenna, also in line for a promotion, was made squadron leader,
which gave him greater pull when requesting help from senior officers.
The two men admired each other but approached their work differently,
one's personality and methods serving as a good counterbalance to the
other's.

On January 24, 1946, the letter written by van der Bijil—delayed
by diplomatic protocol and intelligence assessments—reached Bowes
in Germany, along with a directive from SIB headquarters in London:

> We can now accept as an established fact that the department
> charged with the responsibility for carrying out these murders was
> the Gestapo. The apprehension . . . of Ziegler and the heads of
> the Gestapo-stellen at the various places where officers are known
> to have met their deaths becomes a Category A priority.

Bowes—opting to pursue the lead himself—left Germany for Czechoslovakia on February 12, 1946, accompanied by the newest member of the team. Twenty-eight-year-old Flight Lieutenant A. R. Lyon was quiet by nature and prone to losing himself in thought. He was tall and thin, and enjoyed smoking a pipe, which gave him a professorial air. In civilian life, he distinguished himself as a top student at the Hendon Police Staff College before working his way up the ranks of the Metropolitan Police Service to detective-inspector. He eventually joined the RAF and put the expertise he had acquired questioning criminal suspects to good use with the Air Directorate of Intelligence. His job was to question captured *Luftwaffe* scientists and learn what he could about Germany's highly evolved aeronautical technology. Returning to England from one such interrogation, Lyon found himself delayed by weather in Brussels. At the hotel bar he struck up a conversation with one Major Pancheff, deputy commander of the London Cage. During their talk, Lyon mentioned the fact he spoke fluent German. Pancheff suggested Lyon transfer to the RAF's SIB, which he did shortly thereafter.

Bowes and Lyon arrived in Prague on February 16 and established themselves at the British Embassy. There followed a series of meetings with officials from the Ministry of Defense and Third Army Intelligence in which various permissions were obtained to interrogate members of the Gestapo now in Czech custody.

The men traveled by train to Brno on February 18 and reached the local prison that afternoon. They were given a tour of the facilities and set up an interrogation room in an empty office. Throughout the day, prisoners—malnourished, their skin a sickly pallor—were led into the room at gunpoint. They had all served in varying capacities with the Gestapo. Some were guilty of nothing more than filing paperwork; others had carried out more ominous duties as field agents. Lyon translated Bowes's questions into German, but their queries only met with defiant stares. Even in the dank confines of Brno Central Prison and most likely facing death at the end of a rope, the onetime Gestapo men refused to cooperate. If anyone had information on Ziegler, the Gestapo chief who oversaw the Kirby-Green and Kidder murders, they were keeping it to themselves. The hours ticked slowly by with nothing to show in the way of progress. Finally, the guards brought in Franz Schauschütz. Bowes quickly glanced over the man's file. In November 1942, the thirty-three-year-old Schauschütz—having previously served with the criminal police in Berlin—joined the Brno Gestapo as an inspector. His superior was a major named Hugo Roemer. Bowes made note of the name and asked Schauschütz if he knew anything about the Sagan murders or the whereabouts of Hans Ziegler.

Schauschütz pushed a pair of horn-rimmed spectacles up his nose and considered the question. Eyeing the two armed guards who stood on either side of the door, he seemed resigned to his fate and, unlike those before him, started talking. In the middle of March 1944, he said, Roemer dispatched him to Zlín as temporary head of the local police station. The station's regular commanding officer, Hans Ziegler, was due for leave. Schauschütz, who claimed he knew nothing of the killings, said he arrived in Zlín the morning of March 29 and relieved Ziegler. He spent the following two weeks tending to routine police business and overseeing a manhunt for two enemy agents allegedly dropped into the area during a nighttime air raid. On the evening of April 13, Roemer visited the station for an update on the search. That same night, a senior Gestapo official from Brno, Adolf Knuppelberg, also made an appearance. Because the station was equipped with a run-of-the-mill teleprinter, it could not receive secret messages from Berlin; classified communiqués had to be hand-delivered. And so it was that Knuppelberg arrived with a secret message in hand for Roemer. Sitting in Schauschütz's office, Roemer opened the sealed envelope, read the document, and shared its contents.

"As he handed me the documents in question, he said briefly that two English fliers, who were to have been transferred to Moravska Ostrava, had been shot on the way in compliance with orders from high quarters," Schauschütz said. "The facts had to be reported in an incident report to Berlin in such a way as to show that both the English fliers had attempted to escape while relieving themselves on the journey and had therefore been killed."

It was, Schauschütz said, the first he knew of the murders. Now in the know, he was ordered to write a formal report stating the airmen had been shot while attempting to escape. Knuppelberg, who gunned down one of the fliers, told Schauschütz the airmen had been let out of the car during the journey to relieve themselves but took off running into the woods. Knuppelberg and another Gestapo officer—the name of whom Schauschütz could not remember—were forced to draw their sidearms and open fire.

Schauschütz prepared a report for Berlin, which Roemer and Knuppelberg approved without alteration.

"I had nothing further to do with the affair," Schauschütz said, angling for merciful treatment. "Right up to the end of the war, I never heard of a case when local Staatspolizei or Sichereitspolizei chiefs ever received authority to decide questions of life and death in respect to prisoners of war."

"Do you know who else may have been involved in this incident?" Lyon asked.

Schauschütz listed the usual suspects: Kaltenbrunner, Himmler's deputy at the Central Security Office, and Gestapo Chief Müller. At the regional level, he named Wilhelm Nöelle, head of the Gestapo in Brno and last seen in Prague in November 1944. Depending on the rumor one chose to believe, said Schauschütz, Nöelle was imprisoned somewhere in the French Zone or was dead—executed for defeatism in the dying days of the war.

"Nöelle would have had to transmit the orders received from Berlin to the departmental head in question," Schauschütz explained. "In this case, it was Kriminalrat Roemer. On receiving the orders from Nöelle, Roemer would seek a suitable man to carry out the job. He chose Knuppelberg. I know definitely that another official was involved, but I cannot recall his name."

"Did Erich Zacharias play a role?" Bowes asked through Lyon.

Schauschütz shrugged. "I can only say that is quite possible," he said. "I know Zacharias too little to pass an opinion as to whether he was a suitable person for carrying out such an affair."

At the time of the shootings, Schauschütz said, several Gestapo drivers were employed in Zlín. He provided their names, listing among them Friedrich Kiowsky.

"I have been told that driver Fritz Schwarzer was also involved," he said. "I can say that I consider this extremely possible. Fritz Schwarzer was Roemer's personal driver. He's an extremely safe driver and has a reputation for keeping his mouth shut."

The interrogation done, Bowes motioned the guards to remove Schauschütz from the room. Bowes considered the man intelligent and believed he would make an eloquent witness when the case went to trial. More importantly, he was able to detail the general channels through which the orders sanctioning the murder were transmitted. Over the course of two days, Bowes and Lyon questioned another one hundred prisoners. One inmate shed light on the possible whereabouts of Fritz Schwarzer, saying rumor placed him in the northern Czech town of Teusing, where he worked as a mechanic. Bowes made a note to follow up on the lead.

As Bowes and Lyon continued their line of inquiry, they were partnered with one Captain Vaca of Czech Army Intelligence, an expert on local Gestapo activity. The captain, eager to assist the British investigation any way he could, felt compelled to shed light on the Nazi atrocities perpetrated in his homeland and took the two investigators to the prison at Pankratz. He led them down a dank, stone-constructed hallway lined on either side by fifteen cramped cells. Here, Vaca explained, the Gestapo imprisoned enemies of the Reich before placing them on trial. Through an arched doorway at the end of the hall, the three men entered the courtroom. Behind the judge's bench, a black curtain stretched the length of the room. The verdict of those brought before the judge, Vaca explained, was never in doubt. The trials were merely for show. The guilty verdict rendered, the condemned was shoved behind the curtain. Vaca pulled the black cloth aside and revealed a number of nooses dangling from a moveable rail. The Gestapo could efficiently hang one prisoner after the other and move the bodies along the rail, disposing of them accordingly. Through another door, Vaca led Bowes and Lyon into a small room, its only furnishing a guillotine in the far corner. The blade still bore evidence of its bloody work. The RAF men stared at the contraption. Bowes, a man whose vocabulary could rise to any occasion, said nothing.

That evening, Vaca took Bowes and Lyon to a watering hole frequented by members of the local Gestapo during the war. The three men ordered beer at the bar. Bowes took a long pull of his drink and eyed the place over the rim of his glass, noticing for the first time a large mural on one of the walls. In a scene both whimsical and, to Bowes, strangely sinister, determined satyrs pursued naked nymphs through a forest of flowers and tall grass. The satyrs appeared serious about the task at hand, their pointy faces devoid of any joviality or humor. One, its expression particularly intense, with narrowed eyes and furrowed brow, chased a well-proportioned nymph riding atop an angel-winged pig. Bowes put down his glass and approached the wall, struck by an odd sense of familiarity. Closer inspection revealed the satyrs to be more than simply the figment of an artist's imagination. In the mural, members of the local Gestapo had been rendered by the painter's brush into randy cherubs. There was Schauschütz and Ziegler, and other men Bowes recognized from various mug shots he had seen. He gave voice to his astonishment and ordered another pint of lager.

"This is Knuppelberg," said the bartender, jabbing his finger at one cherub in particular. "They never paid a bill in five years."

Bowes took a picture of the mural, believing it might come in handy at some point. On the morning of February 22, he and Lyon proceeded to Uherske Hradiste and met with Judge Molovsky, a magistrate with the local People's Court, who granted the RAF men access to Friedrich Kiowsky. The interrogation took place in Molovsky's office, wood-paneled and elegant; not the sort of place one associated with such proceedings. Kiowsky was forty years old and appeared thin and frail when guards led him into the room. Seeing the RAF uniforms worn by Bowes and Lyons, he swallowed hard and cast a fearful glance at the judge. The guards placed him in a chair, his wrists shackled, and retreated to a corner of the room. A German typist sat off to one side, her fingers poised and ready.

Lyons, speaking German, introduced himself and Bowes and stated the nature of their business. "You are obliged to say nothing," Lyons said, "unless you wish to do so. Anything you do say could be used in evidence."

Asked if he understood his rights, Kiowsky answered yes and began talking. Instead of an official Gestapo branch, Zlín had the Frontier Police, with whom Kiowsky had been employed as a driver since June 1939. The police took their orders from the Gestapo office in Brno. On the evening of March 28, 1944, while working the night shift, Kiowsky's superior, *Kriminalrat* Hans Ziegler, summoned him to a meeting.

"I entered his office and saw Ziegler, Zacharias, and a Gestapo official from Brno," Kiowsky said. "I recognized the Gestapo official but don't know his name." Bowes silenced Kiowsky with a raised hand. He reached for a folder and placed a number of photographs on the table.

"Do you recognize any of these men?" Bowes asked through Lyons.

Kiowsky sifted through the images.

"This is the man," he said, tapping a picture of Knuppelberg.

Resuming his statement, Kiowsky said Ziegler ordered him to retrieve two English airmen from the local prison, bring them to the police station for interrogation, and then transport them to Breslau. Sworn to secrecy, Kiowsky left the office and readied his car. He drove to the prison with an interpreter and took charge of the two airmen. He remembered both men wore sports jackets. They sat in the backseat and said nothing on the return journey to the station.

"Both officers were handcuffed," Kiowsky said. "We drove into the garage, and then Erich Zacharias and I accompanied them to the cells. The larger of the two was then brought out and led into interrogation room number three."

From the physical description, Bowes and Lyon knew Kiowsky meant Kirby-Green.

"As I was curious, I looked into the room and saw that the handcuffs were being taken off the flier," Kiowsky said. "It was at this moment Ziegler entered the room."

Ziegler watched as a guard struggled to remove one of the cuffs from Kirby-Green's wrist. When it appeared the cuff wouldn't unlock,

Ziegler stepped forward and tore the cuff away, pulling it hard over skin and bone. He turned to the interpreter and said, "Tell him in English that when vagabonds are encountered on the streets, they will be treated like vagabonds."

Kiowsky left the room and returned to the driver's quarters to await further instructions.

"I received the order to depart about midnight," he said. "This order was given by Ziegler personally. I asked Ziegler before our departure what we would do about petrol, as I did not have [enough] to get to Breslau. Ziegler replied, 'You will not have to drive to Breslau.' Although I said nothing to Ziegler, I got the impression the two fliers would not reach Breslau alive."

The prisoners, once again manacled at the wrists, were brought down to the garage and put in two separate cars. Kirby Green rode with Knuppelberg, the Gestapo official from Brno; Kidder traveled with Zacharias and Kiowsky. Guiding his car on the darkened street heading out of town, Kiowsky asked his companion what was to become of the airmen. Zacharias said nothing and simply gave a thumbs-down sign.

"I knew for the first time," Kiowsky said, "the two were going to be shot."

Outside of Zlín, he turned the Mercedes onto a country road that ran between the towns of Friedeck and Moravska Ostrava. Knuppelberg's car followed close behind. Zacharias stared out the window in search of an ideal spot and found one at a point where the side of the road fell away into a drainage ditch. He ordered Kiowsky to pull over onto the grassy shoulder. In his side-view mirror, all Kiowsky could see of the other vehicle was the sharp glare of its headlights. Next to him, Zacharias, one hand buried in a coat pocket, opened the door and got out of the car.

"I knew that he was carrying a gun," Kiowsky told his interrogators. "I had seen him load it in Zlín and put it in his pocket. He told the officer to get out and relieve himself. The officer was still handcuffed."

The driver from the second vehicle— Schwarzer—now approached Kiowsky's car, leaned through the window, and asked for a smoke.

"I gave him a cigarette, and at the precise moment when we were lighting the cigarettes, two shots were fired almost simultaneously: one by my car and the other by the second car. I immediately turned to see what was happening. I saw the officer collapsing on the roadside, to the left and slightly to the front of Zacharias. At the same moment as I saw this officer collapsing, Zacharias fired a second shot," Kiowsky said. "At the time, this officer was handcuffed with his hands in front of him. The officer fell into the ditch. I immediately got out of the car and saw that the second officer was also lying in the ditch. The Brno official came to Zacharias and told him to take the handcuffs off the officers, so that no one would notice the two officers were manacled. I saw nothing that gave me the impression that the officers had wished to escape or made an attempt. I stood by the ditch and saw the two bodies lying there. There was a lot of blood on the snow, but I saw no wound on the bodies. Zacharias told me—without my asking him—that his first shot was in the back and the second in the head as he was collapsing."

Knuppelberg ordered Kiowsky and Zacharias to remain with the bodies while he drove to Moravska Ostrava to notify authorities. He returned about two hours later with a police van in tow. In the van, Kiowsky made out one man behind the wheel and another, wearing "the dark uniform of the Czech police," in the passenger seat. The two men got out of the van and loaded the bodies into the back. Knuppelberg assured Zacharias all would be taken care of and asked him to relay the news to Ziegler. Once back in Zlín, Zacharias did as instructed and reported, "Herr Kriminalrat, everything has passed off smoothly. The bodies have been taken to the crematorium in Moravska Ostrava and a doctor will be there to make an examination."

"What happened next?" asked Lyon.

"Ziegler then gave us the strictest instructions to discuss this occurrence with no one."

About one month later, Kiowsky and the others involved returned to the scene of the crime on Ziegler's orders to coordinate their stories, thus ensuring everyone had his "facts" straight. Otto Kozlowsky, a

Gestapo lawyer with the Brno office, accompanied them to the killing field and helped orchestrate their stories down to the smallest detail.

"He showed us a plan of the scene that was completely at variance with the actual facts of the case," Kiowsky said. "He explained that it was possible that someone might come from the International Red Cross to investigate the matter, and instructed us as to what we should say."

"And what were you supposed to say?" Bowes asked.

"If asked, that the two fliers had tried to escape whilst relieving themselves and were shot in the fields at a distance of twenty to thirty meters."

Done for now with Kiowsky, Bowes and Lyon questioned other Gestapo men held in the town. A man named Urbanek—captured in September 1945—said he and Erich Zacharias had both been issued papers by the American military stating they were "harmless persons and ex-customs officials." Together, they found work on a farm in the Mittenwald region of Bavaria. Zacharias soon moved on, Urbanek said, and was now with family in Wesermünde. Urbanek gave the RAF men what he believed to be the addresses of Zacharias's parents and brother. The wanted man's wife, who, by sheer luck, happened to live locally, could confirm the information. She invited Bowes and Lyon into her home and offered them a seat. An electric fire cast a pallid, flickering glow on the worn carpet but did little to heat the room. A young boy materialized from the hallway to check out the visitors and, just as quickly, scurried from the room. Through Lyon, Bowes stated the purpose of their visit. It soon became apparent that whatever feelings Frau Zacharias once had for her husband had died long ago. He was an ardent Nazi, but she had never taken up the cause. He had abandoned the family in April 1945 to escape the advancing Russians. Yes, she said, answering a question put by Bowes, he had family in Wesermünde at the addresses provided by Urbanek. With any luck, they could find him there.

On the morning of February 23, Bowes and Lyon traveled to Zlín and toured the building formerly used by the Gestapo as its regional headquarters. The place had been cleared of all relevant files near the

end of the war. In the cellar, they inspected the squalid cells in which
Kirby-Green and Kidder were imprisoned prior to their execution. They
were dark, cramped spaces of stagnant air and, like the cells they'd seen
in Pankratz, not adequately large enough to accommodate a full-grown
man. The Zlín authorities made available for questioning a onetime
clerk in the building, who recalled seeing the prisoners shortly after
their arrest. One of them, he said, spoke excellent German.

"I spoke to both the officers in English," the clerk said. "The captain
was a Canadian. He told me he studied languages at Quebec University
and was shot down in Flanders in 1941. He said he improved his knowledge of German during his captivity. He was dressed in grey civilian
clothes and told me he was not married. The major was about six feet
tall, well-built, and told me he lived in England. He told me he was
married and had one child. I was with them about half an hour and,
as I was leaving, I saw them being put into the small cells at the end of
the corridor."

Both Ziegler and Zacharias, said the clerk, were present when the

Members of the Royal Air Force Special Investigating Branch reconstruct the shooting
deaths of Squadron Leader Thomas Kirby-Green and Flying Officer Gordon Kidder.
BRITISH NATIONAL ARCHIVES: WO 309/1369

airmen were interrogated. At the local civil police station, Bowes examined the Prisoners' Record Book. An entry dated 28.3.44 showed Kirby-Green and Kidder had been taken into custody at eleven that morning and turned over to the Gestapo at eleven that night. Bowes turned away from the book, satisfied with the progress being made. Now he wanted to see the actual crime scene. Kiowsky was temporarily released into the RAF's custody and directed Bowes and Lyon to the killing field. The men traveled by jeep, passing through Moravska Ostrava and continuing several miles south on the road to Frydek before Kiowsky told them to stop. Bowes pulled the jeep over. The RAF men got out and surveyed the landscape.

"It's open country," Bowes said, "which gives no possible cover to anyone attempting to escape."

Kiowsky led Bowes and Lyon to a nearby ditch, the ground sodden and muddy underfoot. It was here, he said, the officers fell when shot. Lyon snapped pictures of everything. As the camera bulbs flashed, Kiowsky mimicked the positions of Kirby-Green and Kidder before and after the execution. In the car for the return journey, Bowes and Lyon silently pondered the fate of their fellow airmen. They stopped in Moravska Ostrava, where inquiries led them to a policeman who, on orders from the Gestapo, had transported the bodies to the local crematorium. The officer said he arrived at the scene in the early morning hours, sometime between five and six. When he got out of his car, he saw two Gestapo agents pulling the victims from a ditch alongside the road. "The body of the first man was stronger and bigger," the officer said. "When this body was being put in to the car, I noticed a wound on the right side of the face directly in front of the ear. The area around it was strongly burnt and proved beyond any doubt that the man was shot from close range. I noticed no wounds on the body of the second man. I saw only blood flowing from the nose, mouth, and one ear."

The bodies loaded in the backseat of his car, the officer followed the Gestapo agents to the crematorium in Moravaska Ostrava. "The two Gestapo men took the bodies into the crematorium, and I drove off to the police station," he said. "Before I left, I was ordered by one of the Gestapo officials not to talk about this case whatsoever."

Frantisek Krupa, the crematorium attendant, was still on the job.

Krupa said he arrived at the crematorium on the morning in question to find three Gestapo agents waiting outside. On the ground were two bodies, which they dragged into the mortuary. Krupa watched as the agents patted down the corpses and removed watches, rings, and other personal effects. When done, they sealed the door to the mortuary and told Krupa that no one was to enter. Not until nine-thirty the following morning, March 30, were the bodies destroyed. "The Gestapo men came with two other men," Krupa said, "and I was ordered to cremate the bodies in succession without coffins. They were cremated in their suits."

As the bodies were loaded into the incinerator, Krupa made a mental note of the physical injuries evident on each: a gunshot wound was visible in front of the ear of one man and behind the ear of the other. The ashes of the two dead men were placed in separate urns, numbered 6385 and 6386. The next day, a Gestapo agent turned up at the crematorium and took possession of the urns. "I don't know where the urns were taken," Krupa said. "I made a notice in the crematorium book of cremations, showing the urns had been sent to the family. This meant the urns had been taken away by the Gestapo."

On February 28, with multiple corroborating statements implicating Zacharias, Ziegler, and Knuppelberg in the Zlín murders, Bowes and Lyon returned to Prague. From a local war crimes investigator, they learned that a Czech state policeman had seen Ziegler and Kozlowsky at a hotel in Zell Am See, Austria, no more than two weeks ago. Although it was impossible to substantiate the sighting, Bowes deemed it worthy of immediate attention. His plan was to travel to Weisbaden, where McKenna was currently working his end of the investigation. There, he would personally hand over the information acquired on Zacharias and task McKenna with the man's apprehension. The weather, however, had turned foul in recent days and grounded flights out of Prague. Desperate, Bowes and Lyon hitched a cold and bumpy ride with a U.S. Army transport truck bound for Schweinfurt Airfield. They sat in the cab, alongside the driver, wrapped in coats and struggling to keep warm. The journey lasted well into the night; the later the hour, the greater their discomfort. At the airfield they caught a ride, equally rough, on another truck, heading for Weisbaden. They reached the city aching and exhausted. McKenna met them on arrival and was debriefed on Zacharias. There was little time to socialize. After a night spent in a local hotel, Bowes and Lyon traveled on to their final destination. In Zell Am See, Bowes made contact with the U.S. Military Government and coordinated the raid on the Landhaus Brichta hotel.

A sliver of moon cast watery silver light on the bare tree branches and thin covering of freshly fallen snow as the jeep followed the winding country lane that led to the Landhaus Brichta. With Lyon behind the wheel, Bowes sat in the passenger seat and watched the bleak scenery scroll past his window. A U.S. Army truck with a contingent of armed men followed in the jeep's wake. The two vehicles reached the crest of a hill and rounded a bend, dimming their headlights in the process. The hotel windows were dark. The jeep and the army truck came to a stop several yards down the road. Men, gripping sidearms and rifles, jumped out of the vehicles and moved quickly toward the hotel, skirting the sides of the road. The Landhaus Brichta was a typical Alpine structure, with a sharp-angled roof and colorful flower boxes, now barren, beneath the shuttered windows. The frigid night air stung Bowes's eyes and burned his lungs as he closed in on the building. He and Lyon, along with two armed officers, made their way to the hotel's back entrance. The American soldiers, rifles at the ready, covered the hotel's front and sides.

Bowes and his team took up position behind a row of foliage and studied the building's façade. All appeared silent and still. Bowes squinted at his watch: the top of the hour was minutes away. Since Czechoslovakia, he had thought many times of Thomas Kirby-Green and Gordon Kidder, falling in a sodden field and lying in muck. He glanced at his watch again, impatient to get the job done. At 0100 hours, the Americans took the hotel from the front. A violent banging on the door announced their arrival, startling the sleeping guests and dispelling the darkness. The place sprang to life with noise and light. Bowes and his men rushed across a patch of frozen lawn and entered through the back door. Guests who tried to flee their rooms were ordered back inside. It took several minutes to restore some level of peace and order. A bewildered Frau Brichta, in her nightgown, pleaded to know what was happening. Bowes showed his identification and stated his business. The woman seemed incredulous. "No Gestapo from Brno, or anywhere else," she said, "has stayed here since the capitulation!"

A room-to-room search of the premises turned up nothing. Guests were questioned and the hotel registry examined, without results. That afternoon, Bowes interrogated Herr Brichta at the CIC in Salzburg. He admitted local Gestapo officials had once stayed at a hotel he owned in Brno. "They bled me white," he said. "They had food and drink for which they offered nothing in return. They said that if events ever went wrong, they would come and stay at my hotel in Zell Am See, but they never did." Bowes left the camp disappointed. Although he had found the Brichtas to be "undesirable types," he could see no reason for them to lie. "With regard to the question of harbouring Gestapo officials, they were telling the truth," he cabled London. "I consider it extremely probable that should Brichta get an opportunity of cutting of their throats, he would do so."

Two days later, on March 11, McKenna—accompanied by Dutch translator Lieutenant Colonel Vreugdenhil—arrived in the American-held port of Bremen. He met that morning with officials from the U.S. Counter Intelligence Corps and presented what information he had on Erich Zacharias. Records showed that a German national by that name currently worked as a clerk at the No. 256 U.S. Army Refrigeration Plant on the city's main dock. McKenna moved quickly. Through the U.S. Army's regional public safety officer, Lieutenant Freshour, he arranged a military police escort and descended on the docks that afternoon. The men, armed with automatics and mug shots of the wanted man, dispersed and went in search of their prey. It was 2:14 P.M. when McKenna, standing outside the refrigeration plant, saw Zacharias heading in his direction. McKenna approached the man; Vreugdenhil and Freshour drew their Colt .45s and covered Zacharias from behind.

"My name is Frank McKenna," he said, as he drew closer. "I'm an officer with the Royal Air Force investigating the murders of fifty British airmen from Stalag Luft III. Show me your papers."

The man fumbled inside his jacket and produced an American-issued identity card in the name of Erich Zacharias. Because the Americans had classified him as "harmless," he'd had no reason to assume a false identity. McKenna pocketed the card and took the man by the arm. McKenna drove Zacharias to the CIC at Wesermünde. The prisoner was stripped and searched for poisons before being moved under armed guard to the American-run prison in Karlsburg. Later that day, McKenna sought permission from U.S. authorities to transfer Zacharias to the War Criminals Holding Centre in British-controlled Minden. Approval, he was told, would have to come from U.S. forces headquarters in Frankfurt Am Main and would take several days. Determined not to lose the RAF's first major catch to the Americans, McKenna settled into a cheap hotel and waited.

He did not have to wait long: the necessary clearances came through the following day. He reported that afternoon to Freshour, who met him with a grim expression and news that Zacharias had escaped. As guards walked him to an army truck parked in the prison courtyard, Zacharias broke free and ran through the open prison gates. He put the truck between himself and the guards, who raised their rifles to fire, and disappeared into the nearby wreckage of a bombed-out building. McKenna phoned Bowes in Rinteln, who voiced his displeasure in the bluntest terms. There was nothing McKenna could do but lend whatever assistance the Americans might need. McKenna returned to Rinteln to let the manhunt run its course, but he held out little hope of success. A break came some weeks later when investigators, monitoring the mail services, intercepted a letter addressed to a friend of Zacharias. "Erich has been ill," it read, "and will soon be on his way." The return address was a house in Fallersleben, in the province of Brunswick, mere miles from the Russian Zone of Occupation. American soldiers stormed the house at one o'clock on the morning of March 31 and found Zacharias packing for a long trip. McKenna traveled to Wesermünde on April 2, took Zacharias into custody, and conveyed him to the British holding facility in Minden. A strip search revealed in his possession a silver wristwatch of the kind worn by British aircrews.

"Where did you get this?" asked McKenna, holding up the watch for closer inspection.

"I bought it in Zlín," said Zacharias, unable to provide additional details.

"Why did you escape from the American prison at Wesermünde?"

"I was afraid."

"Of what?"

"I know why you arrested me," Zacharias said. "Wasn't it on account of two English Luftwaffe officers? I only did my duty; I will tell you all about it. I have had many sleepless nights of worry since the happening."

McKenna informed Zacharias of his rights and allowed him to proceed. Zacharias made no attempt to assert his innocence. From 1938 to 1945, he had served with the Gestapo in Zlín under *Kriminalrat* Hans Ziegler.

"I last saw him in Zlín just before I left," Zacharias said. "I don't know where he is now. I don't know where any of the other Gestapo are. I would tell you if I knew."

Zacharias now played a familiar card.

"I carried out the task first because it was an order," he said, "then because I was assured that nothing could happen to me later, and also because I justified myself in that there was a war on and that the airmen might have killed already many hundreds of civilians by bombing."

He said that when he and Kiowsky retrieved the two airmen from the prison in Zlín, Kirby-Green voiced his anger at being shackled.

"I reported this to Ziegler at the office," Zacharias said. "He replied that the two prisoners did not look like officers, but like tramps and therefore could not be treated in any other way until it had been established that they really were captured officers."

After the prisoners were interrogated and their identities established, they were bundled into separate cars for their alleged transfer back to camp. It was about two o'clock in the morning when the journey commenced.

"I had the Canadian officer in my car," Zacharias said. "I believe his name was Gordon."

At four-thirty that morning, roughly six miles outside Moravska Ostrava, the two vehicles pulled over.

"I made the prisoner get out of the car and go to the kerb to pass water there," he said. "I took up position about one meter obliquely to the left and behind him and observed what was happening at Knuppelberg's car. I noticed that there, too, everything had gone according to plan and his prisoner was also standing at the kerb. Then Knuppelberg raised his right hand holding the pistol and pointed the barrel at the back of his prisoner's head. This was for me the time for action. I drew my service pistol, which was all ready for firing, from the side pocket of my coat and fired obliquely in the left side of my prisoner to hit his heart."

Zacharias said he and Knuppelberg fired their weapons simultaneously.

"I fired a second shot at the prisoner as he was collapsing," Zacharias said, "hitting him above the right ear."

Zacharias knelt beside the body, checked for a pulse, and felt none. Shining a torch in Kidder's eyes, he saw no change in the pupils.

"I ran to Knuppelberg and saw his prisoner lying with a bleeding wound at the back of the head," Zacharias said. "I then tried to make him hurry up and get to Moravska Ostrava to fetch an ambulance. I wanted the corpses to disappear as quickly as possible from the road so as not to give an exhibition to the many workers going to work."

Once the bodies had been removed and taken away for cremation, Zacharias returned to the police station with Kiowsky and detailed the killings for Ziegler.

"He replied, 'Good, that's all right. You go home and sleep because you look terrible.'"

FIVE

THE LONDON CAGE

On April 5, 1946, McKenna escorted Erich Zacharias to the London Cage. The men took off from an airfield outside Minden and flew by Dakota to RAF Croydon. By jeep, they traveled into London proper, a wounded city. Zacharias stared out the window and took in the damage. What he saw fell far short of claims made by Nazi propaganda, declaring that German bombs had rendered the British capital a desolate wasteland. Surface air-raid shelters still lined cratered streets, and rubble-strewn holes marked where buildings once stood, but the city still thrived. Londoners appeared to be going about their business: heading to work, shopping, attempting to live as normal an existence as circumstances allowed.

The London Cage occupied three large white mansions in Kensington Palace Gardens, an exclusive enclave of grandiose architecture and old money. The eloquent exteriors of numbers 6, 7, and 8 belied the brutality that occurred within. Only a single barbed-wire fence separating the houses from the main street gave any indication of something amiss. Operated by MI9, the branch of the War Office charged with the interrogation of captured enemy personnel, the Cage had opened for business in July 1940. The interior of the houses had been modified to serve their unique purpose, with five interrogation rooms and cells to house up to sixty prisoners at any given time. A dozen noncommissioned officers served as interrogators and interpreters. Soldiers, selected "for their height, rather than their brains," guarded the prisoners around the clock. Lieutenant Colonel A. P. Scotland oversaw the facility's day-to-day operation. Now in his mid-sixties, the blunt Scotland was the ideal man for the job. British-born, he had traveled in 1904, at the age of twenty-two, to South Africa and taken a job managing a branch of South African Territories, Ltd., a "grocery and provisions trade." His work brought him into contact with German officials who invited him to join the German Army in southwest Africa to oversee the distribution of its food supplies. He served in the German Army from 1903 to 1907 and acquired unique insight into its military philosophies and tactics. The knowledge proved useful when, during the First World War, he worked as an interrogator for British Intelligence. He toured Germany twice between the wars, fascinated as he was by its people, and again went to work for British Intelligence as an interrogator during the Second World War.

The London Cage, despite its elegant setting, was a brutal place. Visiting the Cage, an RAF airman was surprised upon entering the premises one evening to find a German naval officer in full regalia on his hands and knees, scrubbing the floor to the entrance hall. Over him stood a broad-shouldered guard, a cigarette clamped in one corner of his mouth, with a heavy boot placed squarely on the prisoner's back. Scotland possessed no qualms about the methods employed under his watch. "Abandon all hope ye who enter here," he thought each morning as he settled behind his desk. Prisoners who refused to share what vital information they had were eventually broken. From the threat of violence to psychological browbeating, Scotland's men excelled at their specialized trade. At night they roamed the halls and knocked on cell doors every fifteen minutes to deprive inmates of their sleep. Those who did not initially crack were threatened during interrogations with torture, needless surgical procedures, and execution. Others were told they would simply vanish and never be heard from again. Beatings were not uncommon, while making a prisoner stand at attention for more than twenty-four hours straight proved an effective method of wearing down a man's resolve.

Vicious though such treatment may have been, Scotland felt justified in the steps taken to extract information. He was, after all, dealing with members of the Gestapo and the SS. Hadn't they perpetrated far greater evils on countless others? If anything, they deserved the harsh measures being meted out. Besides, his work served an important purpose. The statements he extracted from prisoners sent a number of Nazis to the gallows.

The Red Cross, which monitored prisoner-of-war facilities, initially knew nothing of the Cage. Only when the name and location of the Cage was inadvertently added to a list of camps submitted by British authorities did it come to the aid organization's attention. In early 1946, they sent an inspector to Kensington Palace Gardens to ensure the treatment of those imprisoned behind its ornate white walls adhered to the Geneva Convention. Scotland would have none of it, and the inspector was promptly turned away at the door. Scotland explained his actions in a letter to his superiors at the War Office. Those imprisoned in the London Cage, he wrote, were either civilians or war criminals within the German military, neither of whom were protected under the Geneva Convention. Allowing the Red Cross to inspect the Cage, he argued, would severely limit his ability to do his job—especially when it came to questioning those suspected in the Stalag Luft III murders. Should the Red Cross persist in gaining access to the Cage, the interrogation of Sagan suspects, he wrote, "must proceed in Germany under conditions more closely related to police methods than to Geneva Convention principles."

SS Captain Fritz Knoechlein, arrested for his part in the slaying of ninety-nine British soldiers near Paradis, Pas-de-Calais, France, in May 1940, made note of his experiences in the Cage prior to his 1949 execution. When he refused to surrender information sought by his interrogators, Knoechlein claimed he was stripped, starved, and deprived of sleep for nearly a week. The guards routinely beat him, he said, and forced him to exercise until he passed out. Among the physical exertions forced upon him were walking in a tight circle for four hours and running through the Cage's landscaped back garden while carrying a heavy log. Complaining to Scotland about his treatment only made matters worse. He was tossed down a flight of stairs and beaten with a club. On one occasion, he wrote, he was forced to strip and stand near a hot gas stove. When he could no longer tolerate the heat, guards dragged him into a shower stall and blasted him with freezing water. Other prisoners, he claimed, were treated in a similar manner and begged their captors to kill them. Scotland dismissed Knoechlein's story of brutality as "a lame allegation." He later recounted the SS man's last few nights in the Cage before being shipped to Hamburg to face trial. "[He] gave us an example of what might have been regarded in another man as pitiful behavior, but from him it seemed merely contemptible," Scotland wrote. "He began shrieking in a half-crazed fashion, so that the guards at the London Cage were at a loss to know how to control him. At one stage, the local police called in to enquire why such a din was emanating from sedate Kensington Palace Gardens."

When Scotland received Zacharias at the London Cage, the Gestapo man struck him as being "a wild young brute." The prisoner's "abnormally large, powerful hands [and] remarkably thick neck" impressed him. McKenna warned the colonel that his new inmate had a penchant for escaping. Scotland dismissed McKenna's concerns with a wave of the hand. Escape, he said, was a near impossibility with the Scots Guards watching the premises. Satisfied, McKenna left London and returned to Germany.

Zacharias proved forthcoming during interrogation. He recalled once torturing a captured airman at Gestapo headquarters in Zlín. Outside the airman's cell, a young secretary sat waiting in the stone corridor with a business matter that required Zacharias's attention. Emerging from the cell and fearful the girl might have heard the airman's screams, Zacharias asked her out to lunch. They got in his car and drove out of town into the surrounding countryside. He occupied the young Czech girl with friendly conversation. She seemed not to notice the winding route he took through the woods, taking them farther away from civilization. Only when he ceased the friendly banter and pulled the car off the road did she ask what was happening. He got out of the car and dragged the girl from the vehicle. He pulled her away from the roadside and raped her among the bushes. As the girl lay prostrate, he drew his Walther pistol and put a bullet in her head. He walked back to his car and retrieved a shovel from the trunk. Beyond the tree line, he dug a shallow hole and disposed of the body. He brushed the dirt from his uniform and did his best to hand-iron out the creases before returning to his car. He drove back to Zlín, enjoyed a lunch out, and returned to work.

"He showed neither remorse for the act," noted Scotland, "nor compunction about describing it." He made Zacharias strip and kneel for hours on a concrete floor—an interrogation tactic he knew the Gestapo had frequently employed. Having already confessed his involvement in the Kirby-Green and Kidder murders to McKenna in Germany, Zacharias again repeated his story for Scotland's men. "Take him away," said Scotland, turning to a guard, "and feed him on kindness and cups of tea."

Zacharias was soon transferred to a holding facility at Kempton Park Racecourse in Middlesex. On the night of May 13, he took the tin plate on which he'd been served dinner and began scratching away at the wood surrounding the lock on his cell door. It was tedious work, but he eventually scraped away enough wood to release the door's lock mechanism. He snuck his way into the prison yard and scrambled up the side of a twelve-foot-high outhouse, its roof layered with barbed wire. He crossed the roof, crushing the wire underfoot, and leapt into a tree. He shimmied along a branch and lowered himself onto a guard walk, fenced on both sides by ten-foot-high wire palisades. Spotlights swept the walkway, but four trees—their branches thick with leaves—provided ample cover. A sentry on duty a hundred yards away saw nothing. Near the end of the walkway, Zacharias found an iron bar, which he used to separate the wire in one of the palisades. He wormed his way through the hole, losing a shoe in the process, and scurried off into the night. In his pocket were rations he'd saved from his meals, which he hoped would last him at least a day or two. He moved quickly, half-expecting to hear at any moment the blare of an alarm—but all remained silent behind him. Not until eight hours later, when making their morning rounds at five, did guards discover Zacharias missing.

Officials sounded a national alarm. The BBC, at the urging of the War Office, broadcast news of the escape and warned listeners to be vigilant. Erich Zacharias, "a Nazi police officer," was extremely dangerous. "His escape," proclaimed the *Sunday Times*, "is one of the boldest and most desperate from any prisoner of war camp in Britain during and since the war." Reports described the fugitive as wearing "a dark blue reefer jacket with zip fastener down the front and blue trousers, and one brown shoe." A break developed late that morning when a guest at the nearby Weir Hotel reported seeing a man who answered the fugitive's description, hiding in the shrubbery of a local park along the River Thames. An army of police officers and three hundred soldiers armed with tommy guns descended on the scene and fanned out through the park. Armored cars and radio vans from the Metropolitan Police Service blockaded nearby streets. RAF reconnaissance planes thundered over the park at tree level. Although area residents were urged to stay in their homes, curious onlookers began to congregate near the park and outside the prison camp. Noted one reporter: "Italian prisoners of war, who were also at the camp, were paraded outside the guardroom preparatory to repatriation, and smilingly enjoyed the temporary notoriety when scores of sightseers, who had heard of the escape, stopped to peer at them."

Police found Zacharias later that day, hiding beneath a bush and nursing a sprained ankle. He was returned to Kempton Park and kept under continual watch until his eventual transfer to Hamburg to stand trial.

A newspaper clipping detailing the escape of Erich Zacharias from the prison camp at Kempton Park Racecourse. Zacharias was hanged for his participation in the murders of Squadron Leader Thomas Kirby-Green and Flying Officer Gordon Kidder.
BRITISH NATIONAL ARCHIVES: ADM 40/2492

SIX

PRIME SUSPECTS

The urns of four Sagan escapees returned to Stalag Luft III bore inscriptions identifying the place of cremation as Danzig, but details surrounding the deaths of Flying Officer Henri Picard and Flight Lieutenants Edward Brettell, Romas Marcinkus, and Gilbert Walenn had been slow to materialize. The Russians had thus far denied British investigators access to the city. Not until Flight Lieutenant Courtney—accompanied by three translators and his German shepherd—located a man named Erich Graes at an American camp in Neumünster did the case begin to unravel. Graes had been deputy director of the *Kripo* in Danzig and charged with coordinating the local search for Sagan fugitives shortly after the escape. He dictated for Courtney the order that went out to all police and military installations following the breakout:

> *Most Immediate: To all stations of the Criminal Police, State Police, Commanders of the Security Police, and Frontier Posts.*

> *Subject: Mass Escape English-American Officers from PW Camp Sagan.*

> *Degree of Search: Nationwide Hue and Cry*

In the night of 24 March 1944, 84 (?) British-American Air Force Officers escaped from PW Officers' Camp Sagan. Direction of flight unknown. They will attempt to escape by sea or to neutral countries.

For the territory of the Greater German Reich nationwide hue and cry is ordered. All available forces are to be employed. Exact nominal roll follows. Success messages by most immediate teleprint direct to Central Office for War Searches.

The document was signed by Kaltenbrunner. Graes told Courtney four British officers were subsequently arrested on a passenger train at Schneidemühl on the night of March 26 and taken to a prison camp in Marienburg. They were transferred by truck the following day to *Kripo* headquarters in Danzig for interrogation. The men arrived in the evening, after Graes had gone home for the night, but he left instructions with his prison commandant to place them "in the best room in the police station." Graes said he and his men were not accustomed to handling British fugitives and dealt primarily with Russian prisoners of war who escaped from the nearby labor camps.

"The next morning, when I went to the office, I immediately phoned the police prison and enquired after the officers," Graes said. "I learned to my immense surprise that they had been taken away by officials of the Gestapo in Danzig and had not been brought back."

Calls were placed to the Danzig Gestapo chief, a man named Dr. Günther Venediger, who said the matter was classified "Top Secret" and could not be discussed. Graes said his superior officer, visibly upset, informed him several days later the Gestapo was transporting the cremated remains of the officers back to Breslau. He could only conclude that the Gestapo had shot the prisoners. In recounting the story, Graes nervously tapped his fingers while he spoke. He said he learned shortly thereafter the Gestapo had executed "forty-three or forty-seven" Sagan escapees. Several months after the killings, he picked up a Swiss newspaper and read an account of Anthony Eden's promise to Parliament. Graes drove that day to Gestapo headquarters and confronted Venediger in his office. He slapped the newspaper down on Venediger's desk and pointed to the article. "Is this true?" he asked. "Were these men murdered?"

"We do not do that sort of thing in Matzkau," Venediger said, brushing the newspaper aside.

"Matzkau?" asked Courtney.

"It's a rather distant suburb of Danzig," Graes explained. "There was a penal camp there for persons who had been sentenced by the SS and police courts. As far as I know, there was an average of 10,000 prisoners there."

Graes's tone and expression took on sudden anger.

"I am at any time ready to substantiate my statements on oath before the court," he said. "It is a question of an action that can never be justified."

Courtney nodded. "What can you tell me about Venediger?"

"He's big and elegant looking and holds himself well. Somewhat aristocratic," Graes said. "He's slim and about six feet tall, has very dark—almost black—hair with a parting on the left. No mustache, thirty-eight years old. His home was in Danzig, but he's rumored to have been seen in Hamburg after the capitulation. He might be found in Magdeburg, as his wife's parents live there. He'll certainly have false papers."

Dr. Venediger now joined the ranks of the hunted.

McKenna and his men continued the arduous task of canvassing Allied prison camps in the British and American sectors for leads. It was a painstaking process that offered no alternative. At one camp after another, they reviewed countless prisoner files and dossiers, the pages of many stained with details of atrocities so heinous one could not help but feel physically ill. At No. 4 CIC near Recklinghausen in the British Zone, two of McKenna's team reviewed the records of eight thousand internees. Named in the files was a onetime Gestapo agent who appeared on the RAF's wanted list for his alleged involvement in the murders of Squadron Leader Roger Bushell and Lieutenant Bernard Scheidhauer in

Saarbrücken. Possessing "the manners and appearance of a thug," the man confessed to knowing of the crime but denied direct involvement. He identified Saarbrücken Gestapo chief Dr. Leopold Spann, number forty-two on the RAF's list, as the mastermind and—possibly—the gunman.

While the investigation made slow but steady progress in the British and American zones, efforts were under way to uncover leads in the French sector. Records at the French War Crimes and Political Prisoners Bureau in Paris were poorly organized—a result of the French frequently moving prisoners from one camp to another. The French were busy dismantling their smaller camps and transferring prisoners to larger facilities. Not until the process was complete and the smaller camps had been abolished was there any hope of the files being properly organized. In their sector, the French had assumed the role of conqueror and did little to hide their disdain for the vanquished population. As far as they were concerned, being a German—regardless of whether or not one was a Nazi—was crime enough. They had a grudge to settle. In the latter stages of the war, French forces—following behind the Americans—marched into Stuttgart and raped an estimated three thousand women and eight men. Likewise, in the small town of Freudenstadt, they raped women as old as eighty, burned homes, and shot civilians. It was the sort of behavior one associated more with the Red Army, which, in the vast areas of Germany it overran, unleashed a frenzy of "looting, destruction and rape." Noted one Danish journalist, "It was not that a sex-starved Russian soldier forced himself upon a girl who took his fancy. It was a destructive, hateful and wholesale act of vengeance. Age or looks were irrelevant. The grandmother was no safer than the granddaughter, the ugly and filthy no more than the fresh and attractive."

Help from the Russians was nonexistent outside the Berlin area, but McKenna hoped to establish a personal contact through the British-Russian Liaison Authorities in the German capital. Both McKenna and Bowes believed the Russian Zone "held the key" to the Sagan investigation, seeing as the majority of murders took place in what was now

Soviet-controlled territory. Despite the Russian stonewalling and French disorganization, McKenna allowed himself a measure of satisfaction with the progress made thus far. "The enquiry," he wrote in a report to Bowes, highlighting recent developments, "appears to be opening up on lines which promise to track down the actual killers of the murdered officers."

Mystery still surrounded the whereabouts of Breslau Gestapo chief Dr. Wilhelm Scharpwinkel and the SS captain charged with prisoner-of-war security in the Sagan region, Dr. Gunther Absalon. Last seen in Hitler's bunker days before the Red Army claimed Berlin, *Gruppenführer* Heinrich Müller—national head of the Gestapo—remained a top priority for the Allies. Rumors surrounding his fate were plenty, and McKenna's men heard most of them while canvassing the internment camps. Some believed him to be dead, killed by the Russians or his own hand. Others claimed he had gone underground with false papers and fled Germany for South America.

Five of the executed men from Stalag Luft III—Squadron Leader John E.A. Williams, Flying Officers Reginald Kierath and John Stower, Flight Lieutenants Lester Bull and Jerzy Mondschein—were captured on the German-Czechoslovakian border. British Intelligence knew the men had been held in Liberec, a fourteenth-century city sixty miles north of Prague surrounded by the snowcapped peaks of the Izera Mountains. Bull, Mondschein, Williams, and Kierath were believed to have been executed together. Inscriptions on their urns indicated the men were shot in Liberec and cremated in Brüx. The location of Stower's death remained a mystery. He had escaped from Sagan in the company of Flight Lieutenant I. P. Tonder, who, although captured and imprisoned with the other men prior to their deaths, had not been marked for execution. It was Tonder's affidavit taken by the RAF in late 1945 that provided some insight into what happened at Liberec. Bowes, returning to Czechoslovakia with Lyon to work the case, read the document during the flight to Prague.

Tonder and Stower were numbers twenty-one and twenty-two, respectively, out of the tunnel. They planned to catch the 1 A.M. train from Sagan to Laubau but were late to the platform. Not wanting to hang around until six in the morning, they decided to take their chances and walk. They set off to Halbau, a town twelve miles away, and kept to the woods for cover. A thick layer of snow covered the ground and hampered their progress. Dressed only in civilian suits, they were ill-equipped to handle the near-freezing temperatures. They reached the town by daybreak but, fearful of capture, spent the day sleeping in the woods. They woke that evening cold and aching, their suits wet from lying in the snow, and struggled onward. They walked for two days before reaching the town of Kohlfurt.

They by now realized the futility of their situation. Traveling by foot would get them nowhere. They broke cover and made their way to the town's train station, where they purchased food and two tickets to Liberec. They changed trains at Görlitz and continued on their way. Some miles past the town of Sittau, as the train approached its final destination, two plainclothes policemen from the Liberec *Kripo* made their way through the carriage to check papers. Tonder and Stower showed the agents their forged travel documents, which passed inspection. Their clothes, however, proved their undoing. Although there was nothing out of the ordinary in their appearance, the suits they wore were strikingly similar in style and color to the tailored clothing worn by other recently captured escapees.

The agents took the two RAF men to *Kripo* headquarters in Liberec. They were photographed, stripped of all their personal possessions, and placed together in a cell. From a *Kripo* official who processed their arrival, the two men learned that Bull, Kierath, Mondschein, and Williams were also in custody in the same building. After Tonder and Stower had been questioned individually, they were moved to a cell upstairs and locked up with the other four escapees. The men told the new arrivals they had caught the 6 A.M. train out of Sagan. They had got as far as the Czech frontier and were seized by a military patrol while crossing the mountains on the Silesian Czechoslovak border.

The following day, a *Kripo* official informed the prisoners they were being handed over to the Gestapo. The men were ushered downstairs, where two Gestapo agents sat waiting. Bull, Kierath, Mondschein, and Williams were asked to sign some paperwork. "During this time," Tonder told RAF investigators, "Stower and I had the impression that S/L Williams had learnt something about his fate. He was not normally a nervous man, but he was clearly pale and scared. I have no reason to suppose that he had behaved in a provocative manner during his interrogation or that there was any cause for him to be more alarmed than the others. After this, we were taken back to our cells. Stower and I continued to share a cell, and the others were nearby. We were not badly treated, and we were able to talk through the walls."

The next morning, Wednesday, March 29, Tonder and Stower were allowed to use the washroom. They were joined by a Russian prisoner who told them he'd seen the Gestapo taking the other airmen away at four that morning. Tonder asked a guard what had happened to his comrades. They had been shipped back to Sagan, the guard said. The men were not seen alive again. As Tonder sat on a cot in his cell that evening, the heavy iron door swung open and the two Gestapo agents from the previous day walked in.

"You are a Czech and a traitor," one of the agents said, before he and his partner turned and promptly left.

Tonder told Stower through his cell wall that he expected the worst. Should Stower make it back to Stalag Luft III, he was to report Tonder's fate to the proper officials. At eight on the morning of Friday, March 31, a Gestapo agent appeared outside Stower's cell and said he was being escorted back to Sagan. Tonder remained in Gestapo custody for another six months before ending up in Colditz, where he sat out the rest of the war. Urns bearing the names of Bull, Kierath, Mondschein, and Williams arrived at Stalag Luft III on March 29. Stower's ashes arrived two days later in an urn stamped only with the date of execution: March 31.

Bowes closed the file. The RAF Dakota banked through heavy clouds and landed in Prague on a wet and gray afternoon. Bowes and

Lyon checked into their hotel, finished the day with a drink in a bleak watering hole, and commenced their inquiries the following morning.

Checking with local military officials, the RAF men were dismayed to learn there were no members of the Liberec Gestapo in Czech custody. The Czech Security Police, however, had raided Gestapo and *Kripo* headquarters in Liberec at the end of the war and seized a number of documents. The men traveled by rail to the town and were granted access to the paperwork. Sifting through folders and cartons, Bowes and Lyon found the cremation order for Williams, Kierath, Bull, and Mondschein. It was dated March 28, 1944, and signed by *Obersturmbannführer* Baatz, chief of the Liberec Gestapo. The Prisoners Record Book from *Kripo* headquarters revealed that the men did not leave the building until the early morning hours of March 29, meaning the cremation order had been signed a day *before* the executions. No records for Flying Officer Stower were found.

"This," said Bowes, turning to Lyon, "is conclusive proof of premeditation of the crime."

Bowes and Lyon visited the crematorium in Brüx. The attendant they found on duty, Anton Sawerthal, expressed little surprise when the two RAF investigators presented themselves. He had a story to tell and had always known he would have the opportunity to someday share it. On the morning of March 29, 1944, shortly after seven o'clock, Sawerthal's boss called him at home and told him to report to work. The Gestapo had four bodies it wanted cremated. Sawerthal arrived just minutes before five Gestapo officials showed up with the bodies in the back of a truck.

"As the bodies were being unloaded, I heard the Gestapo officials speaking German with a high German accent and therefore gained the impression they were born and bred in Germany," Sawerthal said. "One of the Gestapo officials told me that the dead men had been shot, but I did not see the wounds personally. They were cremated in their clothes without coffins."

"Do you have a record of the cremation?" Bowes asked.

Sawerthal nodded and pulled from his desk drawer a leather-bound ledger. He flipped through its yellowed pages and turned the book around on his desk so Bowes and Lyon could read it. When they examined the entry dated 29/3/1944, this is what they saw:

Kierath, Reginald	6923
Williams, John	6925
Bull, Leslie	6926
Mondschein, Jerzy	6927

The cremation number, Sawerthal explained, corresponded to the number on the urns. An entry at the bottom of the page read, "Shot while attempting to escape." It had been assumed that Stower was gunned down with his comrades, though records and Sawerthal's statement now seemed to disprove that theory. Nevertheless, Bowes and Lyon theorized the same parties were responsible for all five murders. Sawerthal could not recall if any of the Gestapo men referred to one another by name. "The two chief Gestapo officials wore four stars on their lapels," he said. "The other three had either one or two stars."

Four stars, Bowes told Lyon, denoted the rank of *Sturmbannführer*, the equivalent of a major. They traveled to Liberec, where the prisoners had been held prior to execution, and obtained from town officials a list of men who had once served in the local Gestapo. Only two men, Robert Weyland and Robert Weissmann, had achieved such a rank. Their names—along with Baatz—were promptly added to the RAF's wanted list.*

"It is possible," Bowes conceded to Lyon that evening over drinks, "that one of the *Sturmbannführers* present at the cremation of the officers came from Brüx, having been contacted by the Liberec Gestapo for assistance." Bowes pondered the bottom of his glass. For now, there was nothing more to go on. He returned to his hotel in a despondent

---

* Baatz was captured by the Russians but released early and never seen again. Weyland disappeared into the Russian Zone; the French captured and imprisoned Weissmann.

mood but was buoyed by a message from the British Embassy in Prague. Polish authorities—responding to an earlier request—had authorized Bowes and Lyon to pursue their investigation in and around Breslau, where twenty-seven of the fifty Sagan escapees had been shot. The Polish now controlled the region, but the Russians continued to exert a heavy influence in the area. The two RAF men picked up their visas the next day from the Polish Consul in Prague and arrived in Warsaw on April 13, 1946. Two days of meetings followed with various local officials, who let it be known they cared little for the British presence in Poland. It took another ten days and the intervention of the British Foreign Office to sort things out and move the inquiry forward.

A meeting with the Polish colonel in charge of the local security police secured a promise of cooperation. Bowes handed over a Polish translation of the RAF's wanted list. Sitting behind a cluttered desk, the colonel eyed the document and assured Bowes all Gestapo and *Kripo* personnel in Polish custody would be made available for inter- rogation. On April 23, Bowes and Lyon—accompanied by a security officer—left Warsaw by jeep and arrived in Breslau early the following day. The city was indistinguishable from the countless others they had seen in Germany: a wasteland of rubble and shattered architecture. Cramped and tired from their overnight journey, they forewent check- ing into their lodgings in favor of meeting with the attorney for the district. The encounter proved short and disappointing. The man met Bowes and Lyon in his office and spoke through an apologetic smile. The security officer translated, saying no members of the *Kripo* or Gestapo were—or ever had been—in local custody. Bowes, who, until now, had maintained his temper for the sake of diplomacy, shed his English reserve and unleashed a verbal broadside. He told the attorney that officials in Warsaw had promised to cooperate with the investiga- tion. The attorney simply shrugged. How could he produce prisoners who simply weren't in custody? Bowes, feeling his physical restraint slipping, stormed from the office.

Bowes and Lyon spent another ten days in Breslau, attempting to garner some sort of lead. At every turn, they met with resistance. When Bowes sought permission to travel to Görlitz, Hirschberg, Oels,

Liengitz, and other towns in the region, he was denied. When he requested a meeting with General Siedwidski, the area's military commander, he received a curt reply saying such a meeting would not be possible. While Bowes found the Polish in Breslau to be uncooperative, the local German populace found them unforgiving. Members of the local Polish police had no qualms beating Germans and "extort[ing] food and money." One Breslau resident later remembered standing "in a queue of expellees in front of the railway station. The Poles who were doing their jobs there took what they liked from our baggage and threw the things they took onto a large pile. They also took from us what we were carrying. My father had a satchel with our birth certificates. They took these from him and threw them with the papers on the pile."

A visit by Bowes and Lyon one afternoon to what remained of Stalag Luft III underscored the depressing nature of their recent inquiries. The *Luftwaffe* evacuated the camp on the night of January 27, 1945, with the Red Army rapidly approaching from the east. More than two thousand inmates were forced to march nearly fifty miles in temperatures well below zero. After spending the night in barns, sheds, makeshift tents, and anything else that might shelter them from the freezing elements, the exhausted, frostbitten men arrived in the town of Spremberg. There, the Germans loaded them into the backs of trucks and shipped them off to new camps. American prisoners were dispatched to a compound just outside Munich. The inmates from North Compound, from which the escape took place, were taken to a facility near Bremen. They remained there until April 9, when their captors again decided to evacuate and forced them to march nearly one hundred miles to a camp outside Lübeck. The barracks were so overrun with lice, rodents, and filth, the prisoners were held in two neighboring farms instead, until their liberation by British troops on May 2.

Bowes and Lyon walked about the camp grounds in silence, the barracks now falling into disrepair. The surrounding pine forest had yet to reclaim the site. A monument to the fifty built by inmates not long after the escape still stood a short distance from the compound. It was made of gray stone from a local quarry. Three large slabs atop the monument bore the names of the dead. The two RAF men read the names and bowed their heads.

There was nothing more for Bowes and Lyon to do in Breslau—nothing, in fact, they could do. An embittered Bowes arrived back in Rinteln toward the end of May. Although the Breslau inquiry had gone nowhere, he was pleased to learn of great strides made in the Munich investigation.

SEVEN

MUNICH

Lieutenants Johannes Gouws and Rupert Stevens, both South Africans, were among the first men to make it out of the tunnel. Gouws joined the air force on May 14, 1940—four days after Hitler unleashed his blitzkrieg on the west—and received his commission early the following year. He was posted to a fighter-bomber squadron in Abyssinia that mostly flew low-level reconnaissance operations. During one such mission in August 1941, engine problems forced Gouws to crash land his Hartbee. When it touched down, the plane flipped over and trapped Gouws under the fuselage, forcing his crewmate to dig him out. Bruised but upright, the two men walked away from the wreckage and spent the better part of a week trudging across the barren landscape, sheltering in the huts of locals at night, before rejoining their squadron. Eight months later, on April 9, 1942, two Me-109s shot down Gouws and his Tomahawk over Egypt. This time, he did not evade capture.

Rupert John Stevens received his wings shortly after Britain's declaration of war. Less than six months later, he was flying combat operations over the Western Desert. The target for Stevens and his crew on the morning of November 14, 1941, was a German airfield in Derna, Libya. Nine Martin Maryland light bombers took off on the raid and fell into formation over an endless expanse of desert. They made their objective and bombed and strafed the airfield before setting a course for home. On the ground, anti-aircraft guns opened fire and threw up heavy clouds of shrapnel. Flak hit the port wing of Stevens's aircraft and punctured the fuel tanks. Within seconds, the damaged wing was hemorrhaging fuel. It took only minutes to completely empty the tank. The bomber's controls grew sluggish and the aircraft began losing altitude. As had been the plan in case of emergency, Stevens turned the stricken bomber toward Tobruk, dropped the plane's undercarriage, and ordered the crew to fire the colors of the day from their flare guns. The men, however, mistook the German-held port of Bardia for Tobruk. Flak again battered the plane as it came in low. Shrapnel pierced the cockpit, wounding Stevens and knocking him unconscious. The navigator seized the controls but died on landing when the plane's nose caved in. Although suffering life-threatening injuries, Stevens and the two air gunners survived the ordeal. They were captured and sent to a German hospital, where they slowly recovered from their wounds. Once in better health, they were dispatched to various prison camps. It wasn't long before Stevens found himself, along with Gouws, in Stalag Luft III.

Their plan the night of the escape was to travel by train to Breslau and then Switzerland. They picked their way through the pine forest surrounding the camp and arrived at the Sagan station only to see their intended train pulling away from the platform. They hung about the station for more than an hour, wrestling with frantic nerves, before boarding the one o'clock express to Breslau. It was in the booking hall at Breslau station the two men were last seen, doing their best to blend in with the other travelers. Their ashes arrived at Stalag Luft III several weeks later. An inscription on the underside of each urn gave the date of death as March 29, 1944, and identified Munich as the place of cremation.

It was all the RAF had to go on.

———

The investigation commenced in November 1945. Because their canvassing of internment camps in the American sector would take them to Munich, McKenna tasked Flight Lieutenant Courtney's team with investigating the Gouws-Stevens murders. Early on, Courtney and his men traced a onetime member of the Munich *Kripo* to the southern

Bavarian town of Garmisch-Partenkirchen, a ski resort popular with the Nazi leadership before the war. It was here Hitler had opened the 1936 Winter Olympics and presented himself as the benevolent dictator. In preparation for the hordes of spectators, the Nazis removed the numerous "Jews Not Wanted" signs displayed prominently about town prior to the games. Only five months earlier—at the party's annual rally—the regime had enacted the anti-Semitic Nuremberg Laws designed to safeguard the "purity" of the German race. By the time Hitler took his seat in the Führer's Gallery to watch the games, his minions were busy shipping political opponents and those of inferior blood off to concentration camps. It was to this Alpine idyll that Hermann Göring had escaped in the wake of Hitler's failed coup in Munich in 1923. And it was here Hitler initially planned to build a mountain retreat, before he finally settled on Berchtesgaden.

The Americans now maintained an internment camp at Garmisch-Partenkirchen. Flight Sergeant Williams, a member of Courtney's team, arrived at the facility on January 21, 1946, to interview Anton Gassner. The onetime *Kripo* agent refused to answer questions put to him by a member of the Royal Air Force. Williams lit a cigarette and explained in a casual manner that a cell awaited Gassner in the London Cage. Cooperation now might go some way in helping his situation in the future. Gassner took a cigarette from the packet Williams placed on the table and signaled his acquiescence by asking for a light.

"Are you a party member?" asked Williams.

"Yes," Gassner said, "since the first of May 1937."

"When were you arrested?"

"On 30th June, 1945."

Gassner said he became a police officer in 1913, at the age of twenty-three, and joined a small gendarmerie in the town of Augsberg. He transferred in July 1919 to the Munich Town Police, which was taken over by the state in 1938 and absorbed into the *Kripo*. He spent the entire war in Munich and achieved the rank of *kriminalrat,* or detective. In the waning days of the conflict—with the U.S. Army closing in—he fled Munich and went into hiding at his sister's house in Reichenhall. It was there the Americans took him into custody.

"Do you remember," asked Williams, "that in March 1944 there was a mass escape from a stalag at Sagan?"

Gassner said a teleprint from the State Security Office in Berlin had come through to Criminal Police headquarters in Munich on the afternoon of Saturday, March 25, 1944. The message detailed the escape from Stalag Luft III and ordered all regional police agencies to join the search effort. The escapees were officers of the Royal Air Force and most likely carrying false papers and disguised in civilian clothing. Gassner said his superior, a man named Greiner, placed him in charge of search operations in and around Munich. Gassner focused his efforts on area train stations, which quickly led to the apprehension of three RAF officers. Taken first into custody was Lieutenant Neely, arrested on an express train outside Donauwoerth. Neely spoke "excellent German," Gassner said, and made "a good impression" on his captors.

"The flying officer asked me what would happen to him," Gassner said. "I gave him to understand that I supposed he would be returned to Sagan, but that instructions would have to come from the State Security Head Office. Until then, he would have to remain in the prison of the police headquarters in Munich. Before taking leave of him, I asked him whether he required anything or had enough to eat and smoke. He indicated to me that he did not require anything. I told him that if, during his stay, he required something after all, he should mention it to me or my deputy."

Gouws and Stevens were arrested shortly thereafter on separate trains. A Munich police inspector took one into custody on the Buchloe-Lindau express just outside Kaufbeuren, roughly fifty miles from Munich. The other man was riding in a second-class compartment on the slow train from Rosenheim. Both men were taken to Criminal Police headquarters in Munich and questioned. All three arrests, Gassner said, took place between March 25 and April 3. After the two South Africans were apprehended, Gassner had to leave Munich for a War Search Conference in Dresden. Upon his return on April 11, he learned that Neely had been sent back to Stalag Luft III.

"The two other officers," he said, "had been taken away by the State Police."

Less than a week later, Greiner's deputy—a man named Haselsberger—asked Gassner to transport two wrapped parcels to Criminal Police headquarters in Breslau.

"At first, Haselsberger did not want to say what they contained," Gassner said. "I replied that in that case, we would simply open the boxes—but this, Haselsberger would not permit. Then he intimated to me, pointing out that it was top secret, that the parcels contained urns of two English Air Force officers. He did not tell me from which department this top secret matter had originated, but I guessed immediately it must be a question of the English flyers who had been in custody. How these officers met their death and at whose hands I did not find out at that time."

Gassner said all evidence relating to the murders had since been destroyed.

"About a fortnight before the arrival of the American Army," he said, "all secret documents, and thus also the Sagan file at the Criminal Police headquarters in Munich, were destroyed by orders of Greiner."

"And what happened to Greiner?" Williams asked.

Gassner said the U.S. Army seized Greiner in June 1945. The Americans confirmed they had the former Munich *Kripo* chief in custody. Courtney handled Greiner's interrogation but gleaned little information. The man claimed to have been away on sick leave at the time of the Sagan escape, but Courtney pushed forward with his questioning. Greiner, an experienced interrogator himself, offered only vague answers.

"What happened to the two RAF officers?"

"They were handed over to the Gestapo," Greiner said. "That is all I know. I learned from Gassner that two urns were taken to Breslau by an official."

"Did you see the urns?"

"No."

"Do you know what happened before the urns were filled with ashes?"

"I don't know," said Greiner. "It was all very hush-hush."

"As head of the Munich Kripo," said Courtney, more than a little incredulous, "didn't you enquire?"

"No," replied Greiner, matter-of-factly. "The matter finished for me after the Gestapo took the case over."

Courtney, not wanting to waste any more time, left the room and made the necessary arrangements to transfer Greiner to the London Cage for a more thorough interrogation. In the meantime, the canvassing of American camps continued. For Courtney and his team, it was akin to fumbling about in the dark. They weren't always sure what they were looking for until they found it. At an internment camp in Ludwigsburg, they came across a man named Josef Achter. A onetime Bavarian police officer turned Gestapo agent, Achter detailed the night Gouws and Stevens were murdered. He was working the night shift at Gestapo headquarters in Munich with another agent named Emil Weil. He remembered the occasion well because one of the on-duty drivers, a man named Schneider, turned up to work with a Russian tommy gun.

"I had not seen a model like that before," Achter said. "Schneider told me it was his own property; that he had brought it back with him from active service in the East."

Shortly before eleven that evening, Munich Gestapo chief Dr. Oswald Schäfer summoned to his office Weil, Schneider, and two other men identified as *Kriminalkommissar* Martin Schermer and *Kriminalsekretär* Eduard Geith. Achter, whose desk faced Schäfer's office, said the men met behind closed doors for roughly ten minutes. When the meeting concluded, none of the participants seemed eager to share details.

"Weil resumed his seat opposite me," Achter said. "I asked Weil what was up. He evaded answering and gave it to be understood he was not allowed to talk about it. I never discovered anything about the nature and purpose of the job—either in the course of conversation, or by rumor—so that I forgot about the incident."

Not until after his arrest at war's end, Achter said, did he put the pieces together. In an American-run internment camp, Achter learned from a colleague that two escapees from Stalag Luft III had been murdered in the Munich area.

"Until then," he said, "I did not know this fact."

"What happened to Weil, Schermer, and Geith?" Courtney asked.

"I heard Weil worked for the Americans in Munich after the capitulation but had later been arrested," Achter said. He believed the Americans had also seized Schneider. "According to an eye-witness account, Schermer committed suicide by shooting himself. It's also been said that Geith is in some American internment camp."

"What about Schäfer?"

"There are various opinions about Schäfer's whereabouts," Achter said. "According to his deputy, he is said to have left on a bicycle with very little luggage the day before the troops marched into Munich. He was supposedly seen in the Tyrol a few days later. It is generally assumed that he first fled and then later committed suicide. As far as I know, his family was living in a village near Prien when the war ended."

Achter's information cleared away the fog of mystery long obscuring the murders. Courtney now added Weil, Schneider, Geith, and Schäfer to his wanted list. A search of Munich city records produced a death certificate for Schermer, who apparently hanged himself from a tree prior to the Americans entering the city.

At about this time, interrogators at the London Cage were busy questioning a recently captured staff member from the Central Security Office named Peter Mohr. Mohr had joined the Bavarian Police in 1926 before transferring to the Munich *Kripo* one year before the outbreak of war. A promotion in February 1944 to the rank of *Kriminalkommissar*—the equivalent of a detective superintendent—saw him transferred to security headquarters in Berlin. He was assigned to Section C, which helped coordinate nationwide manhunts for wanted individuals. One month later, word reached Berlin of the mass breakout from Stalag Luft III. Believing this episode would provide Mohr valuable insight as to how one organized a large-scale search, Mohr's superior placed him in charge of the Sagan case files. Consequently, Mohr was well versed in all aspects of the case and possessed knowledge relevant to the Munich investigation. Part of Mohr's job was to catalogue the possessions of those escapees murdered by the Gestapo.

While processing Gouws's and Stevens's personal effects, Mohr learned that the Munich Gestapo had deducted the cost of the coffins and cremations from the cash the prisoners had on them. If the Gestapo had been forced to pay cremation expenses, then the bodies had most likely been destroyed at the city's only public crematorium, located in Munich's East Cemetery. No cost would have been incurred had the Gestapo destroyed the bodies at the Dachau concentration camp, Mohr told his London interrogators. In Munich, Flight Sergeant Williams reviewed the cemetery's records and found copies of receipts for the two cremations. At an abandoned building previously used as the police prison, he discovered a document—left behind in the mad rush to vacate the building prior the arrival of American forces—stating that Gouws and Stevens had been held in cell number thirty-two upon their capture. Williams made his way to the holding area on the lower levels and found the cell in question. "It was two feet wide and about five feet long," he noted, "and you could see the marks on the walls where the poor devils who were kept there for any length of time had gone demented, and beaten and scratched the wall."

The search for Emil Weil took Courtney back to Dachau once the Americans confirmed they had the man in custody. On May 16, 1946, a visibly frightened Weil provided Courtney an eyewitness account of the killings. Originally a civil police officer in Bavaria, Weil had been posted to the Gestapo in Neustadt in 1938 to help oversee security during construction of the Siegfried Line, a stretch of fortifications along Germany's western frontier. The following year—at the age of twenty-nine—he was transferred to the Munich Gestapo and remained there for the war's entirety, assigned to the Counter Espionage Branch.

The Gestapo in Munich operated out of the Wittelsbach Palais, former royal palace of the Bavarian monarchs. One night, toward the end of March 1944, Weil was catching up on paperwork at his desk. At about ten o'clock, he heard a car pull up in the courtyard below his office window. He glanced out and saw Geith, Schneider, and Schermer exit the car and enter the palace. Roughly two hours later, Weil said, Schermer came into the duty office and told him he would be taking part in the transporting of two prisoners early the next morning. When Weil questioned the assignment, Schermer waved a dismissive hand and said, "Orders are orders." At four-thirty in the morning, Weil was summoned downstairs to the station's holding cells. He saw two men in civilian clothing being moved from one of the cells at gunpoint and placed in a six-seater car out back. He, along with Schermer, Schneider, and Geith, got in the car with the two prisoners. They got on the autobahn and drove in the direction of Ingolstadt. They rode in silence. Thirty miles into the journey, Weil said, Schermer ordered the car onto the shoulder. Everyone was told to relieve himself. The air was cold and a frost covered the ground. Weil walked past the front of the car and into a meadow that fell away from the roadside. Behind him, the two prisoners were ushered out of the car and marched to a position about six feet to Weil's right and less than two feet in front him.

"On the right of the prisoners was Geith, also slightly in front of me," Weil said. "I did not see whether or not the prisoners were manacled. While I urinated, two shots from an automatic weapon fired in quick succession. I saw the first prisoner on the left falling forward and, immediately afterwards, the one on the right. I turned at once towards the car and saw Schermer standing before the rear right door. At the same moment, I noticed Schneider at the back of the car. He had a submachine gun in his hand. Then I saw Schermer going to the two who were lying there. He looked at Schneider and told him to fire more shots at each. Schneider approached the two corpses and fired a few shots with his sub-machine gun, as he had been ordered. Schermer ordered that a covering be fetched from the car and the bodies covered. I did not go to the bodies nor did I cover them."

Weil drew a nervous breath before continuing.

"Schermer said he had to drive to the municipal legal official and medical officer, and told me and Geith to remain with the bodies in the meantime. After about twenty minutes, two policemen came along on their beat. Geith showed them his papers and said our commanding officer had gone to the authorities. As far as I remember, one of the policemen remained with us, and the other left us after a while."

Schermer and Schneider returned in a van roughly one hour later with a police officer and a civilian worker. The latter approached the bodies and pulled back a corner of the blanket.

"They're dead," he said.

Schermer summoned the officer and civilian to the back of the van, where they conferred in quiet tones. What they said could not be heard by the others, who remained by the bodies.

"Shortly afterwards," Weil said, "the civilian and the police officer drove off in the direction of Ingolstadt. At Schermer's instruction, Schneider, Geith, and I had to put the bodies in a hollow to prevent their being seen so easily from the autobahn. We also had to cover them with pine twigs so that we could take the covering with us. One of the policemen remained with the bodies. Schermer, Geith, Schneider, and I then returned to Munich. At Allerhausen (or some such name) we stopped at the police station where Schermer, I presume, telephoned the funeral office at Munich to collect the bodies. On our return to the office we had to swear an oath of secrecy before Schäfer."

Not until April 1945, with the Americans only days away from the city, did the matter come up again. A panicked Schäfer dispatched Weil to the local funeral home to remove the airmen's names from the undertaker's registry. Weil did as instructed, using a pocketknife and typewriter eraser to eliminate the names from the pages of the book. Reporting to Schäfer upon completing the job, Weil was ordered to do the same with the booking ledger at the police prison, where Gouws and Stevens had initially been held. The police, Weil said, did not object to his mission, as they planned on destroying all records prior to the arrival of the Americans.

Courtney had Weil transferred to the British military prison in Minden and crossed the man's name off his list. He now turned his attention to combing the American camps for Schneider and Geith. Although the U.S. Army had seized both men in a postwar roundup of Nazi collaborators, locating them among the hundreds of thousands of people now interned in Allied camps posed a significant challenge. Inaccurate record keeping and the in-and-out flow of transfers from one camp to another meant some individuals got lost in the shuffle. Oswald Schäfer's whereabouts, however, were a different matter. Depending on whom Courtney spoke with, Schäfer was either dead or on the run. Until the man's fate could be firmly substantiated, his name would remain on the wanted list.

The search for Schneider eventually took a turn in the right direction when Courtney located the man's wife. She said her husband was being held in Hammelburg, a small town in Bavaria and the site of a large internment camp. The lead was forwarded to the Americans, who confirmed several days later that Johann Schneider's name appeared on the camp's list of identified prisoners. The journey from Munich by jeep took Courtney through the snowcapped Bavarian Alps, a stunning reprieve from the depressing drudgery of shattered cities and mud-swollen camps. His arrival in Hammelburg, however, brought him back to reality. The camp sat in a forested area roughly two miles south of the city. Initially a training facility for the German Army, the camp was used to hold enemy combatants during both world wars. It was here the Germans imprisoned Americans captured during the Battle of the Bulge. Conditions at the camp, designated Oflag XIII-B, were grim during the best of times and had grown increasingly dire as the war turned against the Reich.

Each of the seven five-roomed barracks in the camp's American compound housed nearly two hundred GIs during the war. Lighting in each room, provided by two single fifteen-watt bulbs, was extremely poor—as was insulation against the elements. Temperatures in the barracks during the winter averaged no higher than twenty degrees and forced the incarcerated men to gather whatever clothes and blankets they could spare and burn them in the single stove that furnished each room. Because the camp received no clothes from the Red Cross, staying warm during the cold months became a matter of basic survival for the inmates. There were no washrooms. The men had to retrieve any water they needed from a faucet in the camp's kitchen to fill the few sinks in their barracks. Because of fuel rationing, the camp was not equipped with hot water. Comfort could hardly be found in the daily rations, which consisted of "one-tenth of a loaf of bread, one cup of ersatz coffee, one bowl of barley soup, and one serving of vegetables." Occasionally, the diet was supplemented by a teaspoon of sugar and a small slice of margarine. Toward the end of the war, many men in the camp were bedridden by malnutrition.

As the war swung in the Allies' favor—and air raids over Germany wrought ever-increasing carnage—tensions between the Americans and their German captors ran increasingly high. The camp's commandant had strict rules in place dictating the proper protocol during an air raid. When air raid sirens in the vicinity of the camp signaled an impending attack, the prisoners had three minutes to get back to their barracks. One evening, the sirens began to wail, and four American officers, standing at the barbed-wire fence and chatting with several Serbian POWs in the neighboring compound, did not immediately seek shelter. They eventually returned to their barracks with a slim margin to spare and were spotted by a guard standing post seventy-five yards away. The guard fired at the four men and struck one in the back. The bullet tore through the prisoner's lung and blew out his chest. Another POW was shot, on a separate occasion, in the back of the head by a guard after failing to understand an order barked at him in German. One order in particular irked American officers imprisoned at Oflag XIII-B. The camp's commandant deemed it necessary for all Americans, regardless of rank, to salute German officers first. The regulation, naturally, led to a fair number of ugly confrontations between guards and prisoners.

In late March 1945, Lieutenant General George S. Patton—commanding the U.S. Third Army—ordered the creation of a special task force to penetrate fifty miles behind enemy lines and liberate Americans imprisoned in the camp. Patton issued the order under the official guise of a rescue operation, but his true intent may have simply been to free his son-in-law, who was captured in Tunisia in 1943. The task force, codenamed "Baum" after its commander, Captain Abraham J. Baum, was drawn from Third Army's 4th Armored Division. Numbering 314 men, 16 tanks, 28 half-tracks, and 13 other assorted vehicles, the task force set off at 21:00 hours on March 26 from the American bridgehead south of Aschaffenburg. They ran into heavy resistance almost immediately outside the nearby town of Schweinheim. Intense German fire destroyed two Sherman tanks and bogged the task force down for hours. Not until the early morning did it punch a hole through the German defenses and continue on its way, thundering along Reichsstrasse 26. Reaching the town of Gemünden at 0800 hours on March 27, the force again encountered blistering enemy fire and lost three more tanks. Unable to break through, the Americans were forced to retreat and find another way to the camp. They followed the Sinn River north and turned in the direction of Hammelburg before making visual contact that afternoon with the camp. Seeing men in gray uniforms moving about the compound, the Americans opened fire from a distance, not realizing they were shelling Serbian POWs. The camp's commandant sent four men—including, by chance, Patton's son-in-law, Lieutenant Colonel John Waters—to alert the American force to its mistake. As the men approached the tanks, an anxious German guard shot Waters in the back. Waters was carried back to the camp and treated by a Serbian medical team.

Negotiations between camp representatives and Captain Baum went forward despite the incident and carried on for several hours. As thousands of American prisoners gathered at the compound's perimeter fence to cheer the task force's arrival, it became clear that there was no way Baum could transport them all back to Allied lines. Baum decided only field-grade officers would be allowed to journey with the task force. The remaining American prisoners were given the option of traveling the fifty miles west back to the American lines by foot, if they so wished. Many wisely opted to stay put until the final liberation. At 20:00 hours, the task force pulled away from the camp. The outward journey had cost Baum more than a quarter of his fighting force. The journey back promised to be just as arduous. There was no moon to light the way. Baum and his men would have to use the lights on their vehicles, meaning they would be easy prey for the German forces stalking the return route.

Several miles from the camp, near the town of Hollrich, the task force's lead tank was hit by a German *panzerfaust*. German troops swarmed the vehicle and maneuvered it into a nearby garden. They aimed its gun down the road and took out three more Shermans in rapid succession. Baum ordered his men to pull back. What remained of Baum's force retreated to a nearby hill, where they spent the remainder of the night. Staring at the four pillars of fire in the near distance, Baum knew their chances of making it back to the American lines alive were slim. Early the next morning, as Baum ordered what remained of his men and machines to move out, the hill rumbled violently to life. Throughout the night, German forces had moved into concealed positions at the base of the hill. They now opened fire from all directions, sending up great columns of blasted earth, obliterating flesh and metal. Baum ordered "every man for himself." The men scattered and ran into the surrounding woods. The Germans quickly rounded up those who were slow or injured. Baum made it into the woods but was shot in the leg and soon captured. He wound up a prisoner in the very camp he'd been sent to liberate. His stay, however, would prove to be a short one. The U.S. 14th Armored Division liberated the camp ten days later, on April 5, 1945.

The rescue operation proved costly in both men and machines. Baum's task force lost all 57 vehicles; 26 of its 314 men were killed. The Americans assumed control of Oflag XIII-B at the war's end. In the camp's northern compound, the U.S. Army interned known and suspected Nazis. It was here Courtney arrived on a damp March afternoon. He was greeted by the camp's American commandant and escorted to a room in one of the compound's stone-built barracks. A small table surrounded by three chairs sat in the center of the room. Courtney took a seat and waited several minutes before two armed guards brought Johann Schneider, shackled at the wrists, into the room.

Courtney studied a file in front of him and reviewed the man's particulars. Schneider had worked as an unskilled laborer, bouncing between farm work and the odd construction job, before joining the SA (the first Nazi paramilitary organization, its members often referred to as "brownshirts") in 1932. He soon transferred to the SS and marched with troops into Austria and the Sudetenland in 1938, and then Poland the following year. Between 1940 and 1943, he served as a chauffeur with the Security Service on the Eastern Front before taking a job as driver with the Gestapo in Munich. Courtney, done reading, looked up and introduced himself. He urged Schneider to share what he knew about the business at hand. All Schneider could do was nod and give his version of events.

At roughly ten o'clock on the night of March 29, Schneider answered a knock on the door of his Munich flat. A uniformed policeman stood in the hallway with a summons from Gestapo headquarters. Schneider got dressed and rode his bike to the office, arriving within the hour. As he entered the building, Schermer met him and ordered him to prepare a six-seated car for a late-night journey. Schneider went down to the garage and checked out a vehicle. As he finished checking the tire pressure and oil levels, Schermer and Geith appeared.

"We drive to police HQ," Schermer said.

At the station, the two men disappeared inside and left Schneider behind the wheel. They emerged fifteen minutes later with two prisoners shackled together at the wrists. They drove back to the Gestapo building, where Geith ordered the prisoners out of the car and led them away to an interrogation cell.

"Be ready to leave," Schermer said when the captives were out of sight. "Make sure you have a machine-pistol with you. This may take a long time, but I'll let you know."

It took the better part of three hours. Not until four-thirty in the morning did Schermer return to the garage.

"On Schäfer's orders, you have to drive in the direction of Ingolstadt," Schermer told Schneider. "It concerns two prisoners who have often escaped. They are air-raid shelter burglars and looters. Should these two escape, then you will shoot on my orders."

Weil and Geith placed the prisoners in the back of the car at gunpoint and sat on either side of them. Schneider assumed his position behind the wheel, while Schermer sat in the front passenger seat. In the east, the first slate moments of daylight were evident above the city's shattered skyline as the car pulled out of the garage. Schneider turned onto the autobahn outside Munich and drove twenty-one miles in the direction of Ingolstadt. The sky had by now sufficiently brightened to a point where headlights were no longer necessary. In the back, the prisoners stared out at a frostbitten landscape, at fields covered in white, and the glistening branches of trees. Eyeing the bleak terrain, Schneider suddenly felt Schermer's hand on his arm.

"Stop," Schermer barked. "Pull up to the right."

Schneider pulled onto the frozen shoulder. As the car slowed to a stop, Schermer turned to the men in the backseat.

"Relieve yourselves," he said.

Weil and Geith got out of the car and led the prisoners down a slight incline into the meadow. Schermer, standing near the passenger door, leaned through the window, motioned to the submachine gun under the driver's seat, and told Schneider to exit the vehicle. Schneider got out, retrieving the gun as he did so. He pulled a magazine from his pocket, jammed it home, and slung the gun over his shoulder. He walked to the rear of the car and leaned against the luggage box. From this vantage point, he had a clear view of the meadow and the prisoners— still chained at the wrists—fifteen feet in front of him. Except for the random bush and tree, there were few places for the prisoners to take cover should they make a run for it.

As Schneider surveyed the scene, he noticed Schermer, standing several feet away, excitedly waving his hands. When Schneider looked in his direction, Schermer pointed at the prisoners and, in a hushed but excited voice, said, "Shoot! Shoot!"

"I looked at him again briefly," Schneider told Courtney, "and then it went through my head. He wants me to shoot the two prisoners here on the spot."

Schneider took aim with the submachine gun and squeezed off six rounds. He saw the two prisoners collapse in the snow and heard Schermer tell him to "stop shooting." In the meadow, Weil and Geith knelt beside the bodies and checked for signs of life. Death having been established, the two men signaled Schermer the job was done.

"Take off the chains at once," he ordered.

Schneider remained by the car, a thin wisp of gray smoke curling up from the gun's muzzle. He stuck the weapon back under the driver's seat and, following Schermer's orders, retrieved a large piece of tarpaulin from a toolbox in the back. Weil and Geith spread the tarpaulin over the two bodies and camouflaged it with fallen fir branches gathered from the base of a nearby tree. Alongside the road, Schermer busied himself collecting the spent shell casings. He ordered Schneider to pull the car fifteen feet forward and scattered the casings about the car's new position.

"If there is a commission of enquiry," he said, "you shot from here."

The remainder of Schneider's story mirrored Weil's statement. He and Schermer went off to notify the proper authorities while Weil and Geith remained with the bodies.

"Schermer told me later that nothing had to be mentioned about this case," he said in conclusion.

Courtney took Schneider into custody and placed him in a cell at Minden. The Americans confirmed they had Eduard Geith in custody, having arrested him on May 5, 1945, and soon turned him over to Courtney. A career police officer before the war, Eduard Geith had joined the Munich Police Force as an auxiliary officer in 1919, shortly after his twentieth birthday. He worked his way up the chain of command, eventually achieving the equivalent rank of assistant senior detective. In January 1938, he transferred to Gestapo headquarters, Munich, and continued his ascent. The war took a personal toll on him in November 1944, when his wife, Magdalene, was killed in an air raid.

Johann Schneider called at Geith's flat shortly after midnight on March 29, 1944, and said he was to report immediately to local Gestapo headquarters. A car was waiting downstairs. The two men arrived at the Wittelsbach Palais less than half an hour later and reported to Schermer. Reading from a teletype, Schermer said that local police had captured two fugitive RAF officers. The men were to be turned over to the Gestapo and, on orders from Berlin, shot. Schermer filed the teletype in a desk drawer and made Weil, Schneider, and Geith swear to secrecy. The men discussed how to execute the order. They decided the best course of action would be to find open country near the edge of a wood and shoot the men near the tree line, making it look as if the prisoners had made a run for it. Geith said that he and Weil advised against using their Walther service pistols, for fear the weapons were not accurate enough.

"Schneider proposed after long hesitation that he would carry out the matter with a machine-pistol," Geith said. "He was certain of himself and would also guarantee there would be no mistake. Schermer agreed to Schneider's solution, and Weil and myself were also content with this solution. Every one of us took an equal part in this plan."

Following the hour-long meeting, Geith said he and Schermer retrieved the prisoners from the local police station and brought them back to the Palais for interrogation. One of the prisoners spoke broken German, while Weil—present in the room—spoke schoolboy English. Their combined language skills enabled the two sides to communicate in an effective, if not efficient, manner. The process, however, appeared to wear on Schermer's nerves. Working his way through one cigarette after another as the prisoners gave their statements, he harried them to keep it brief.

"Nothing," said Geith, "went quickly enough for him."

During the interrogation, Geith said, the prisoners made it clear they were British airmen and provided personal information, a few scant details about the escape, and the towns they had passed through in their bid for freedom. The prisoners signed their statements, which did not survive the war, and were then ordered to strip. Geith inspected the men's armpits; Weil looked elsewhere. The search complete, the prisoners were ordered to dress and were chained together at the wrists. Sometime between five and five-thirty that morning, the airmen were bundled into a car for what they believed was the return journey to Stalag Luft III. Geith and Weil each wore a Walther pistol in a holster on his right hip, with a round loaded in the breech. They sat in the back with the airmen and faced them on two fold-out chairs.

They drove through the northern suburbs of Munich and pulled onto the autobahn. They clocked no more than twenty-five miles before stopping on the right shoulder, alongside a meadow that sloped gently upward into a pine forest. Geith said he and Weil got out of the car and led the prisoners into the field, away from the main road. Once satisfied that passing motorists could not see them, they signaled the prisoners to stop and relieve themselves.

"In my opinion, it could only have been a matter of seconds that the prisoners stood there," Geith said. "Then, there were two short bursts of fire—one immediately following the other. The two prisoners collapsed forward on their knees onto the ground without making a sound. We—Schermer, Schneider, Weil, and I—hurried to the fallen men."

One of the airmen lay twitching on the ground.

"I'll see to that," said Schneider, still clasping the submachine gun, and fired two shots into the prisoner's head.

Geith knelt beside the bodies and undid the chain that bound the two men together. The shackle had been lightly fastened so as not to leave any trace of a bruise. As Geith unlocked the restraint, Schneider removed and pocketed a wristwatch worn by one of the dead officers. The men quickly gathered branches and fir green from the nearby woods and covered the bodies.

"After all this had happened," Geith said, "Weil and I fired a few shots with our service pistols in the direction of the forest, aiming mainly at a telegraph pole in the direction of the wood, so as to leave on it marks of the so-called pursuit shots."

The coroner, summoned to the scene, gave the bodies a quick going over.

"Yes," he said, "there is certainly no more to be done here."

The bodies were loaded into a wagon and taken to the crematorium at the Eastern Cemetery in Munich to be destroyed. Returning to Gestapo headquarters, Geith said, he and his compatriots were "inwardly excited" by Schermer's insistence that an Allied inquiry into the murders would likely follow. They inventoried the victims' personal items back at the office and divvied up a pack of cigarettes found on one of the bodies. Once Schermer filed his incident report several days later in Berlin, Geith considered the matter closed. Schäfer again swore all participants to secrecy and threatened them with death should even the "smallest detail" come to light. Not long thereafter, the Sagan killings made international headlines. Geith, sitting down one evening to read a newspaper in his Munich flat, found British Foreign Secretary Anthony Eden staring up at him from the front page. The article detailed Eden's recent speech denouncing the German explanation that prisoners had been shot while trying to escape.

"I was compelled to agree without question that the animadversions of Mr. Eden conformed to the truth," Geith said. "The explanations of the Offices of the Reich stank and lied on all points."

Geith approached Schermer several days later and voiced his concerns. "This is one hell of a business," he said.

Schermer said nothing and simply walked away. The two men never discussed the matter again. In the wake of the Normandy invasion, as the Allied armies pushed deeper into Germany, Weil told Geith all records pertaining to the murders would be destroyed.

Geith had now reached the end of his story.

"I did not take part in the happenings of my own free will, or out of personal interest," he said. "It was an order for me. I could have refused this order, but I am quite convinced that a refusal would have had the severest consequences. I think I can maintain that no other official would have dared to refuse the order, just as I did not do so, and also did not happen in the case of Weil and Schneider."

He paused, momentarily distracted by some inner disturbance.

"I can give an assurance that in my thoughts I feel the most unhappy man since this happening," he said. "If I have kept quiet so far, which again was a big mistake on my part, then I did this for personal reasons for the sake of my little daughter, the only member of my family still left to me from this tragic war—not least cause of this was also the fact known to me that Schneider possesses a family of many children."

Despite the satisfactory progress his team had made thus far in closing the Munich investigation, Courtney remained frustrated by his failure to locate Munich Gestapo chief Oswald Schäfer. Numerous leads, courtesy of information provided by various inmates who claimed to harbor some knowledge as to the man's whereabouts, had been followed up without success. One such source pointed Courtney's team to the Bavarian village of Utting, where the father of Schäfer's onetime secretary now lived. It was rumored that Schäfer had fathered a child with young Fräulein Lore Hebberling—a rumor the girl's father strongly denied. He said his daughter now worked as an interpreter with the 44th Air Depot, U.S. Army Air Corps, in Schordorf. When questioned several days later, Hebberling confessed to being friends with Schäfer but stressed that their relationship had been strictly platonic. She said she had resigned from her secretarial job seven months before the Americans took Munich and had not heard from Schäfer since. She couldn't say for sure whether the man was even still alive. It seemed to Courtney that the girl had no reason to lie.

The hunt for Schäfer would continue.

EIGHT

A DEATH IN THE MOUNTAINS

Dennis Cochran joined the Royal Air Force in 1940 after a *Luftwaffe* raid on London's East End killed two close friends. The resulting hatred for all things Teutonic fueled a fierce desire to get airborne, which impressed his senior officers—but his war, at least in the skies, proved to be a short one. Enemy fire downed his Whitley bomber in late 1942. Cochran was processed at Dulag Luft, the *Luftwaffe* transit camp through which most Allied airmen passed following their capture. For the young and impatient flying officer, captivity was akin to torture. One might as well have died in battle than languish helpless and prostrate on the sidelines. Not long after his internment, he tried his hand at escape. He and two other prisoners donned German uniforms, acquired through bribes, and armed themselves with wooden rifles made by a fellow inmate. Feeling sufficiently confident, they stomped toward the main gate and presented the on-duty guard with false identity papers. The guard allowed the men to pass through after giving the documents only a cursory glance. Free of the camp, the men split up, with Cochran going off on his own. His two comrades were recaptured almost immediately when they were spotted and recognized at the local train station. Cochran, however, managed to board a train, only to be caught by an alert soldier several hours later. Not long after this brief adventure, Cochran was transferred to Stalag Luft III.

In Sagan, Cochran was known for his quiet, brooding attitude; a solitary figure who kept mostly to himself, often times lost in a book. All the while, he contemplated escape. His desire to break free became all-consuming when he received word of his mother's sudden death in July 1943. Because he spoke fluent German, Cochran was number sixteen in the tunnel on the night of the escape. He planned to travel from Sagan alone and believed a partner would only hinder his progress or put him at unnecessary risk. His RAF uniform was altered to resemble the nondescript clothes of a simple day laborer. Once free of the tunnel, he made his way to the station at Sagan and boarded the 1 A.M. train for Breslau. His objective—like many other escapees'—was Switzerland, which he hoped to enter through Basle on the Rhine. It was an ambitious journey of nearly six hundred miles, but he made good progress. On the afternoon of Sunday, March 26, Cochran was spotted by another escapee sweeping a street in Frankfurt with a group of French laborers. Four days later, he had made it to Lörrach, a city in southwest Germany close to the French and Swiss borders, but his forged travel papers failed to pass inspection at a German checkpoint. Cochran, with freedom visible just across the Rhine, was taken into custody by the *Kripo* and imprisoned in Ettlingen.

Eight weeks later, Cochran's ashes arrived at Stalag Luft III. On the urn was notated the place of cremation: Natzweiler concentration camp.

In August 1944, Britain's Special Air Service launched Operation Loyton. The mission called for operatives of SAS 2 Regiment to drop behind enemy lines in the Vosges Mountains, make contact with the French Resistance, and identify targets for future military action. The agents just happened to land at the same time the Germans were reinforcing the area against advancing U.S. forces. The British operatives—realizing their mission was compromised—wreaked havoc behind enemy lines. They sabotaged German patrols and employed guerilla tactics, making use of the heavily wooded landscape and deep stony ravines that snaked their way through the mountains. Suspecting local residents of assisting the British, the Germans entered the village of Moussey and rounded up every male between the ages of sixteen and sixty. The villagers said nothing under interrogation and were subsequently shipped off to concentration camps. Only 70 of the 210 men and boys ever returned home.

An airdrop in September reinforced the SAS team with additional men and six machine gun–mounted jeeps. German supply convoys and staff cars carrying senior personnel now came under heavy fire. One morning, several jeeps sped through Moussey just as an SS commander called his troops out for inspection. The jeeps' gunmen opened fire with their Browning machine guns and cut down a number of Germans before fleeing into the mountainous terrain beyond the village. So startled was the enemy garrison in town, the commander evacuated 250 of his men out of fear that a much larger British force was on the offensive.

Initially scheduled to last two weeks, the SAS incursion dragged on for two months. The British fought not only the Germans, but encroaching starvation due to dwindling supplies. Of the ninety-one agents who took part in the operation, only sixty eventually made it back to Allied lines. The fate of the missing remained a mystery until July 1945, when military officials in the French Zone unearthed the bodies of thirty British servicemen in the town of Gaggenau. The victims were identified as SAS agents.

Charged with investigating the matter was Major Bill Barkworth of 2 SAS War Crimes Investigation Team. An experienced field operative who spoke fluent German and French, Barkworth traveled to Gaggenau with a dozen agents and established his command post in an old villa near Karlsruhe, where the local Gestapo had based its operations. Barkworth and his team set about canvassing the French internment camps, intent on interviewing former Nazi officials and Gestapo personnel. French disorganization, however, which had thus far hampered the RAF's efforts, plagued the SAS investigation. Corruption also stonewalled the inquiry. It slowly emerged that a number of French officials had released former Nazis from captivity—or expunged their names from camp records—under threat of being exposed as German collaborators.

Barkworth made slow but substantial progress. Through persistent detective work and forceful interrogation, he learned the men were murdered by the SS at Natzweiler concentration camp. Built high in the Vosges Mountains, surrounded by electrified barbed wire, its barracks overrun with lice and typhus, the chimney above its crematorium constantly belching acrid smoke into the mountain air, Natzweiler was the only facility of its kind built on French soil. Between 1941 and 1945, disease, hunger, routine barbarity, and the gas chamber claimed nearly twenty-two thousand lives. It was at Natzweiler that eighty-six Jewish men and women were gassed to provide anatomical specimens for the Jewish skeleton collection, an exhibit the Nazis hoped to display at the planned Reich University of Strasbourg to highlight the physical inferiority of the Jewish race.

Over the course of his investigation, Barkworth interviewed former members of the Karlsruhe Gestapo, now in French custody. One man questioned was forty-year-old Walter Herberg, a law student turned sports editor who joined the Gestapo in 1934. He was now being held in a prison in Wuppertal. Although Herberg knew nothing about the SAS murders, he told Barkworth he had information regarding the shooting death of an RAF officer in the vicinity of Natzweiler. On June 7, 1946, Barkworth forwarded Herberg's name to the Royal Air Force.

McKenna received the news lying in a hospital bed in Rinteln. The investigation had taken a physical toll and forced him to seek treatment for exhaustion. On doctor's orders, he was confined to a bed—a situation not to his liking. Now, with a possible lead into Cochran's murder, he found his circumstance intolerable. Deciding he had rested enough, he snuck out of the hospital one afternoon. Lyon, in on McKenna's plan, waited in a car outside. The two men drove to the prison in Wuppertal to interrogate their suspect. Herberg told McKenna that he had taken leave from work in late March 1944 to visit his parents in Mainz. While out one day in the country—he couldn't recall the exact date—he encountered a number of police officers patrolling a local lane. Herberg asked one officer, who demanded to see his identity papers, what had prompted such a strong police presence in the area. The officer told

Herberg a number of British Air Force officers had recently escaped from a prison camp in Silesia.

Herberg decided to cut his leave short and returned to Karlsruhe two days early. He arrived home to find his telephone ringing. On the end of the line was local Gestapo chief Josef Gmeiner's secretary asking him to report for duty. Gmeiner handed Herberg a teleprint when he arrived at the office. It was addressed to "The Head of the Office of the State Police HQ, Karlsruhe, *Oberregierungsrat* GMEINER." It read:

> By order of the *Reichsführer* SS, the British RAF Officer Cochran, who has been recaptured inside the area of that Department, is to be moved in the direction of Sagan immediately by car. During this move, he is to be shot. The body is to be handed over for crema-tion to the nearest crematorium after having been released by the State Attorney in question. The death certificate is to be sent here. Only a restricted number of persons may have knowledge of the contents of this teleprint. These persons are to be especially bound to silence by hand-clasp.

It was signed, "Müller, *Gruppenführer.*"

"After I had noted the contents of this letter," Herberg told Mc-Kenna, "Gmeiner explained to me that I was to carry out this order. Greatly shocked by this order, I begged him to entrust someone else with it. I was told that I had nothing to do with the matter itself. All I had to do was negotiate with the crematorium and the State Attorney."

"I'm still on leave," Herberg said.

"You'll get another day off for this," replied Gmeiner.

The matter seemed set, though issues of practicality remained. Herberg told Gmeiner the order would be impossible to carry out. No state attorney, he said, would issue a death certificate under such circum-stances. Gmeiner gave the matter some thought and reluctantly agreed. Instead of transporting the prisoner east, in the direction of Sagan, it was deemed more convenient to head west, toward the concentration camp at Natzweiler. The body could be destroyed there without questions being asked. En route, the car would stop and the prisoner would be told to get out and stretch his legs. Otto Preiss, a fellow agent, would pull the trigger and Herberg would see to it that all evidence was consigned to the furnace. Satisfied with the plan, Gmeiner shook hands with Herberg and committed him to the deed. As Herberg left the office, Preiss and driver Wilhelm Boschert walked in for their briefing.

At seven the next morning—March 31—the men piled into a green V170 Mercedes and drove to the prison in Ettlingen. The car pulled into the prison yard shortly after eight-thirty. Herberg, Preiss, and Boschert entered the administrative office and stated their business. A guard retrieved Cochran from his cell. The airman, Herberg guessed, was twenty-one and roughly six feet tall, his frame slender after two years in captivity. The long face was pale and slightly freckled beneath reddish-blond hair. He wore a uniform dyed lilac-violet and free of insignia that might betray him as an officer or soldier. When spoken to, he responded in fluent German.

"You are to be taken to a camp," Herberg told Cochran. "From there, you will be returned with other recaptured officers to Stalag Luft III."

The Gestapo men escorted Cochran out to the car and put him in the backseat alongside Preiss. Up front, Herberg took a map from the glove box and served as navigator while Boschert drove. They took the road out of Ettlingen toward Strasbourg, where they turned in the direction of Natzweiler. Both Preiss and Herberg engaged the airman in casual conversation, Preiss going so far as to offer Cochran peppermints and cigarettes. When Herberg asked about the breakout, Cochran's relaxed manner became one of sudden defiance.

"I can't talk about that," he said. "I gave my word of honor to the British Camp Senior to keep silent on all the circumstances of the escape."

The men drove on without another word. Neither Herberg nor Preiss, reluctant to follow their orders, suggested pulling the car over to allow the airman a brief respite. Instead, they gazed out the window, lost in thought, as the Mercedes followed a winding route up into the

Vosges Mountains. Having now abandoned the map, Herberg left Boschert to navigate the mist-shrouded road on his own. The car eventually reached the crest of a hill stripped of trees. Here, the road led to a compound of squat, single-story buildings surrounded by razor wire. A guardhouse and a large wooden gate crowned in wire marked the entrance to the Natzweiler camp. The sight snapped Herberg and his companions out of their grim reverie. Quickly, Herberg told Boschert to turn the car around and head back the way they had come.

"We've lost our way," Herberg said over his shoulder.

As Boschert sped from the camp, Cochran, oblivious to his captors' intent, failed to realize anything was amiss. A little more than a mile down the road, a small track branched off to the right at a slight incline, cut its way through a field, and disappeared into woods. Boschert took the turn and drove the car 120 feet up the mud- and rock-strewn path before stopping among the trees. Herberg looked over his shoulder, said he needed to relieve himself, and asked Cochran, still handcuffed, if he cared to do the same. The airman said yes, and all four men got out of the car. Herberg stayed near the vehicle as the other men walked Cochran down the path. Not wanting to witness the scene, Herberg turned his back to the group. A minute later, he heard two shots. When Herberg turned around, Cochran was lying on the ground. He could see that one bullet had passed through the airman's right eye. Preiss, standing over Cochran's prostrate form, had fired the second slug through the back of the airman's heart. The men fetched an old motor blanket from the car, wrapped the body, and carried it back to the vehicle. It was sometime between eleven and noon. The body strewn across the backseat, all three Gestapo agents sat in the front and returned to the concentration camp. They arrived minutes later at the camp's main administrative office, a single-story building painted forest green. Inside, Herberg met with the camp's deputy commandant, Adjutant Otto Ganninger.

"We have been unlucky," Herberg said, sticking with the Gestapo cover story. "We had a prisoner who tried to escape and was shot in flight."

Ganninger offered Herberg a knowing smile.

"I am already in the picture," he said without elaborating.

Herberg simply nodded, not caring to know from whom Ganninger got his information. He just wanted to be done with the job.

"Do you now want a death certificate?" Ganninger asked.

When Herberg answered yes, Ganninger led him across the sodden grounds to another wooden barrack, which housed the camp's registration office. Upon hearing Herberg's story, the registrar—a member of the *Kripo*—refused to issue the necessary paperwork on the grounds that the death had occurred outside the camp. Ganninger pressed the issue, but the registrar refused to budge and summoned the camp doctor, who took the same stance. A desperate Herberg explained he was under orders "to produce this death certificate in the highest quarters." His appeal failed to sway either man. While the stalemate ensued, Cochran's body was taken to the camp's crematorium and destroyed in its single oven. Once the ashes were consigned to an urn, Herberg sent a wire from the camp to Gestapo headquarters in Karlsruhe, stating that his mission was complete. He and his comrades eventually left Natzweiler in possession of the urn but not a death certificate.

McKenna slid a pack of cigarettes across the table. Herberg reached for one with a slightly trembling hand and smiled when McKenna offered him a light.

"In Karlsruhe, where I reported by telephone, I think to Gmeiner, I was reproached for not having a death certificate," Herberg said, blue-gray smoke clouding his features. "Whether this was obtained later, I do not know."

"What happened next?" asked McKenna.

Herberg leaned back in his chair and took another deep drag on his smoke. Several days after the murder, he said, he went to the local cinema in hopes of taking his mind off recent events. Halfway through the picture show, a Gestapo agent summoned him from the theater and escorted him to a waiting car outside. How the agent found him was a mystery. The man ordered Herberg into the vehicle and drove him to Gmeiner's flat, where Herberg was told to leave immediately for Berlin. It seemed that Herberg's handling of the Cochran murder had not satisfied Gestapo Chief Müller. Herberg left that afternoon for the capital with several blank sheets of office stationery signed by Gmeiner.

Arriving at Müller's office the following day, Herberg discovered that Gestapo agents from various regional offices had also been summoned for a meeting. Müller chastised all of them for their lack of imagination. Every report filed in connection with the killing of a Sagan escapee claimed that the prisoner had tried to escape during a bathroom break alongside the road. Müller took from Herberg the blank sheets of paper signed by Gmeiner and passed them to his secretary, who fed them into a typewriter. Pacing back and forth, Müller dictated a new report, stating that the car transporting Cochran back to camp had blown a tire. During "an unguarded moment," Cochran leapt from the vehicle and made a dash for the woods while his captors busied themselves with the flat. Herberg and his men had no choice but to open fire, and they downed the airman with two shots. Müller finished dictating, passed the new report to Herberg, and ordered him to return to Karlsruhe and refile the document. Herberg could only nod and do what he had done since the whole sordid episode began: follow orders.

Herberg stared across the table at McKenna and lowered his head. He opened his mouth, but the words seemed to catch in his throat. McKenna felt pity and loathing for this man whose anguish seemed genuine—but the "following orders" excuse served as inadequate defense against a crime so cold and calculated. Was Herberg merely weak-willed and cowardly? Perhaps, for McKenna didn't believe the man to be sadistic. He offered Herberg another smoke and transferred him from the police prison in Wuppertal to the holding facility in Minden. From there, he would be sent to the London Cage.

Herberg's statement opened other avenues of investigation. In his notebook, McKenna now had the name of the gunman, Preiss, and Boschert, the man who drove them to the scene. He also had an eyewitness account of Karlsruhe Gestapo chief Josef Gmeiner ordering Cochran's execution. On June 4, McKenna and interpreter Sergeant J. Van Giessen returned to the prison in Wuppertal and met with Major Barkworth. Did he have any information regarding Ganninger—the adjutant at Natzweiler—or Magnus Wochner, the camp registrar?

Indeed, said Barkworth, taking a manila folder from his desk drawer and passing it to the RAF men. McKenna turned back the cover and stared unblinking at the grisly black-and-white photograph. A man lay strewn across a prison cot, his neck opened in a jagged, glistening wound.

"Ganninger?" asked McKenna.

Barkworth nodded. His team had arrested Ganninger two months prior and interrogated him on April 26. Alone in his cell afterward, Ganninger took a razor from the inside lining of his jacket and sliced his throat. Wochner, also captured, was tried before a military tribunal in May and received ten years for his complicity in the atrocities committed at Natzweiler. McKenna's next step was to find and interrogate Preiss. He journeyed to the American sector and commenced his hunt at Dachau. It was easy, coming to a place such as this, to believe that every German was complicit in what had happened. How could those living in the surrounding village not have known what was going on behind the brick walls and barbed wire? Surely, they harbored some knowledge, an inkling, of the crimes being carried out in their name. And what if they did—what recourse did they have? It seemed to McKenna every simple question gave way to one of greater complexity. Or, maybe the matter wasn't that vexing; maybe people knew but simply didn't care. What did that say about humanity? McKenna pushed the thought away and walked to the administrative office, where he commandeered a desk and read through the inmate files. His search, which took the better part of the day, proved futile.

The following day, he drove to Ludwigsburg, north of Stuttgart. Here, the Americans housed Nazi war criminals at the Flak-Kaserne, which, until the capitulation, had served as barracks for the German Army. The files there held nothing on Otto Preiss. Over the proceeding days, McKenna hit two more camps, including a compound in Mannheim that had once served as a satellite branch of the Natzweiler concentration camp. He eventually arrived at the U.S. internment camp at Darmstadt and found his man in the files. From Herberg McKenna had a physical description of Preiss, and he knew he'd caught him when guards brought the man into the interrogation room for questioning. Preiss was forty years old, completely bald, and slender, with a "round, unhealthy face, dark eyes, dark eyebrows, and a brutal expression." According to his file, he had become a civilian police officer in 1925. He worked in various cities from Baden to Mannheim before being transferred to the Karlsruhe Gestapo in 1939. He initially worked in the press department, before joining Department II E, which specialized in economic sabotage and also handled breach-of-employment matters and cases involving foreign workers. It was in this department that Preiss remained until the end of the war, having achieved the rank of *Kriminalsekretär*, or detective constable.

"I'm an officer with the Special Investigating Branch of the Royal Air Force," said McKenna. "I'm investigating the murder of Flying Officer Cochran, and I believe you have information pertaining to that crime."

Preiss drummed a nervous cadence on the tabletop and seemed reluctant to speak, but relentless prodding soon elicited a confession. He detailed being summoned into Gmeiner's office the day before the shooting and tasked with pulling the trigger. Why he had been selected, he couldn't say, for matters involving prisoners of war fell beyond the scope of his department. There was, however, no point protesting the assignment. "The order has been given and is to be carried out," he remembered Gmeiner telling him. "No discussion is allowed." The facts, as he related them to McKenna, followed Herberg's account closely, though their stories diverged when it came to the actual shooting. When the car stopped in the woods, Preiss said, all four men got out and stayed together. With Herberg and Preiss walking on either side of Cochran, and Boschert bringing up the rear, the men trudged another sixty feet into the woods. Herberg chatted amicably with the prisoner before stopping and turning him toward a tree. He nodded at Preiss, who pulled a 7.65mm Walther from his jacket pocket and fired point-blank into the back of Cochran's head.

"The pistol did not quite touch his head," Preiss said. "The prisoner fell to the ground, and Herberg ascertained that death was instantaneous. As the body of the prisoner was still twitching slightly on the ground, Herberg requested me to fire another shot. I believe that

Herberg used the words *coup de grâce*. I then fired another shot into the region of the heart of the prisoner."

Several weeks later, Herberg ordered Preiss back to the concentration camp to retrieve Cochran's ashes and take them to *Kripo* headquarters in Breslau. From there, they would be taken to Stalag Luft III.

"I declare that I only acted in accordance with orders and not because of my own free will," said Preiss, watching as McKenna scribbled in his notebook. "I do not consider myself guilty, but state however that since the position is now said to be different, I am now incriminated by this matter."

He fell silent, as though pondering a morbid fate.

"This was my first and last execution," he said.

McKenna secured permission from the Americans and took Preiss into custody. He booked him into the prison at Minden, where Herberg still awaited transfer to the London Cage.

Back in his office at Rinteln, McKenna began making a series of calls and learned that the U.S. Third Army was holding Boschert at the No. 2 Civilian Internee Hospital in Karlsruhe. Initially detained by the French, Boschert had broken his spine some weeks prior under mysterious circumstances. The French, apparently done with him, had passed him on to the Americans, who had no particular use for him. On June 26, McKenna and Van Giessen left Rinteln and traveled by jeep, via Düsseldorf, to Karlsruhe. McKenna found the patient, shackled to his bed and lying in traction, reluctant to elaborate on his unfortunate accident but willing to discuss the murder of Flying Officer Cochran. His story followed the same plot laid down by Herberg and Preiss, although he claimed to have been keeping an eye on the car when the other two men walked Cochran into the woods.

"After about half a minute to a minute, I heard two shots from the direction the three men had taken," Boschert said. "Herberg and Preiss came out of the woods carrying the dead body of the prisoner . . . and I saw that he had been shot through the heart and the back of the neck." At the concentration camp, while Herberg haggled for a death certificate, a guard ordered two prisoners to remove the body from the car and carry it to a building on the other side of the compound. Boschert remembered "the building had a chimney like a crematorium. . . . I never saw the dead body again."

McKenna had the Royal Army Medical Corps transport Boschert to a British internment camp near Paderborn. There he would remain until doctors deemed him fit enough for interrogation back in London. With a grim sense of satisfaction, McKenna watched medics load Boschert into the back of an ambulance and pull away. The men who had conveyed Cochran to his grave were now in custody—but the whereabouts of Josef Albert Andreas Gmeiner, their chief, remained unknown. The Americans had no leads to offer, and the Karlsruhe Gestapo had destroyed all their records prior to American forces reaching the city. The French, responding to McKenna's inquiries, came forward and said they were holding Gmeiner in connection with wartime atrocities committed in Alsace Lorraine but were unwilling to turn him over to the British. Only after the RAF promised to hand him back should he be found not guilty in the Sagan case did the French release him into McKenna's custody.

Transferred to the War Criminals Holding Center in Minden, Gmeiner portrayed himself as an unwilling participant in the crime. He said that a few days after the mass breakout from Stalag Luft III, a wired transmission came through to his office from Gestapo *Gruppenführer* Müller in Berlin. Reciting from memory, Gmeiner said the document read, in part:

> By order of the Führer, Der *Reichsführer* SS, and chief of the German Police, has decreed that the English pilots who have escaped from the prisoner of war camp at Sagan are to be liquidated in case of their capture. The executions have to take place because the Englishmen, having escaped, have broken their word of honor! Therefore, it is lawful and necessary!

"Having received the order, it was impossible for me to prevent its execution, although I considered it a crime," Gmeiner said. "My death sentence, at any rate, would have been the unavoidable consequence, and I could not have prevented or altered the fate of the unfortunate prisoner by sacrificing myself and my family. After my arrest, the prisoner would have been executed even before my own death sentence had been effected. There was nothing left for me but to abstain from taking part in the execution of the dreadful deed. To know of the order and not be able to prevent its execution causes me great and depressing spiritual distress."

The war, Gmeiner said, had cost his family everything.

"I became a civil servant to earn at least a minimum living for the maintenance of my family," he said. "Although my income was modest, my wife and I saved a few thousand Marks—denying ourselves all personal enjoyment—for the future of our three children. In April 1944, my wife had to flee with the children from Karlsbad, where we had our family dwelling. She could only take with her what she and the children had on their bodies."

Gmeiner told McKenna everything his family owned had been destroyed. All he possessed were the clothes he currently wore.

"If in my forty-second year," he said, "I have nothing before me after years of very hard work and doing without, and after the complete loss of the modest fruits of my work—and when my family is forced to live on the mercy of relatives—then it is only the thought that I have not to reproach myself for any guilt. I was forced to act as I did, which kept me from taking my life, as was done in a cowardly way by those responsible."

Toward the end of July 1946, McKenna shipped Gmeiner—along with the other Natzweiler conspirators—off to the London Cage. McKenna forwarded the news to Wing Commander Bowes, who, in a progress report to his superiors in London dated August 6, 1946, wrote: "This case can now be regarded as completed."

NINE

SAARBRÜCKEN

Freezing temperatures, anti-aircraft fire, and marauding enemy fighters inflicted a heavy blood toll on Allied aircrews. As the war progressed, and greater swaths of Germany fell under the onslaught of British and American bombs, the citizenry adopted an increasingly dismal opinion of Allied airmen. Members of the Allied air forces heard nightmarish stories of angry citizens hanging captured airmen from lampposts or shooting crash survivors on the spot.

Seven members of one British bomber crew who survived being shot down in February 1945 were captured by German soldiers and taken to a village, where refugees from the city of Pforzheim—recently set ablaze by the RAF—had come seeking shelter. The men were placed under guard in the basement of the local school. They did not remain there for long. An angry mob stormed the premises and dragged the aircrew outside, where a vengeful throng had gathered. They pushed and shoved the airmen down the street and beat them as they stumbled along. Bleeding and bruised, the airmen were forced into a large barn that stood alongside the village church. A single bulb illuminated the barn's interior and revealed nooses hanging from a support beam. One of the airmen—wireless operator and air-gunner Tom Tate—caught site of the makeshift gallows just before entering the barn and made a break for it. He thrashed his way through the crowd and ran as hard as he could, not stopping even when he heard gunfire erupt behind him. He spent the night sleeping in some woods, surrendered the next morning to a group of German soldiers, and eventually wound up in a POW camp. Not until later did he learn that the enraged villagers had shot his crewmates outside the barn. Tate's flight engineer, who escaped only to be recaptured the next day, was beaten by a mob of Hitler Youth and shot in the head by a fifteen-year-old boy who had lost his mother and five siblings in a recent raid.

Shipment to a POW camp held no guarantee of civil treatment, as one airman, shot down over Hamburg in 1942 and imprisoned in Stalag VIII-B in the small Silesian town of Lamsdorf, wrote in a letter home:

> First of all, the fleas are terrible. Fellows find them in their cloths [sic], and their beds swarm with them. I am one of the lucky few who don't seem pestered by the pesky blighters. Naturally, I keep my stuff as clean as poss: and that helps. I pick up 1 or 2 now and again, which cannot be helped. . . . Boy, do we feel uncivilized. . . . Sleeping accommodation is vile. There are 190 of us in the one barrack. A third of that number sleep on the floor. . . . Incidentally, this camp is noted as the worst Stalag in Europe. I can quite believe it. Well, I'm dog tired now, so I'm off to my so-called bed. Will carry on with a few moans in at a later date.

Dulag Luft, the *Luftwaffe* transit camp, lay just outside Frankfurt. Upon arriving at the compound, prisoners were photographed, stripped to their underwear, and subjected to a rigorous search. After providing name, rank, and service number, the men were placed in solitary confinement. They lingered there for up to a week in a cell measuring 10½ feet long by 5½ feet wide. Only the ordeal of interrogation broke the monotony of isolation.

The Germans initially took a gentle approach to questioning and handed prisoners what they claimed to be a Red Cross form. Filling in all the blanks, they said, would allow the airman's family to be informed of their loved one's fate in a timely manner. The questions, however, went beyond the personal basics and sought details on the composition of bomber groups, the strength of air squadrons, and other topics of military importance. Most airmen were quick to identify the ruse, which only stoked the ire of their captors. One RAF flight engineer sat silently as his interrogator went through the form and read the questions out loud. After nearly half an hour, the airman's lack of response led to a sinister threat.

"There are too many people going around France dressed up as airmen and wearing RAF identity discs," the German said. "Unless you tell me more about yourself, I will have you shot as a spy."

"Go ahead and shoot," the airman replied.

The German, struck by his captive's nonchalance, lost his enthusiasm for the threat and sent the airman back to his cell.

The Germans did what they could to make the airmen uncomfortable and weaken their resolve. While in solitary, prisoners were denied the pleasure of cigarettes and the use of basic toiletries. Their dining options also left a lot to be desired. Breakfast was a bleak affair consisting of two pieces of black bread and jam, served with ersatz coffee or ersatz tea, usually "made from various mixtures of hay, carrots, and parched grain." The men hardly fared better at lunch with their midday ration of thin, watery gruel. By dinner, the two pieces of black bread were almost a relief. A common practice employed by the Germans involved cranking up the heat in the solitary cells. The temperatures would reach stifling levels, aided by permanently sealed windows and cement walls lined with heavy insulation. In extreme cases, the metal bed frames would get hot enough to blister flesh. Once the Germans were satisfied they had learned all they could from a prisoner, the airman was moved out of solitary and into a regular barrack, where he awaited transfer to a permanent camp.

The barrack walls were lined with microphones, something the inmates had fun with when they discovered them. "We used to go in these rooms with the microphones," remembered one RAF pilot, "and shout the most horrible lines about our new 15-engined bombers with twenty pilots sitting in a row, and I am sure we shook the Germans on many occasions. Eventually, this game got rather pallid and we connected up the electric-light system and the microphone system and blew-up the whole works. The only thing that happened was that a German, who happened to be listening in at the time, nearly got his head blown off—and the Senior British Officer, who was the 'unfortunate' on these occasions got five days solitary confinement."

Roger Bushell arrived at Dulag Luft in May 1940. In those early days of war, the art of escape was a primitive thing. Prisoners had yet to learn the complex craft of digging tunnels, while the Germans lacked methods of detection to expose such activity. Both sides, however, would prove to be quick studies. Shortly after his arrival, Bushell joined the camp's escape committee, which set about digging a tunnel out from one of the barracks. The intended goal was a dry streambed just beyond the wire. For weeks, the men dug with their hands, clawing at the earth and sweating into long cotton underwear to avoid dirtying their uniforms. They soon passed under the wire and had a mere eight feet to go when they struck an underwater spring and flooded the shaft. The Germans quickly discovered another tunnel started shortly thereafter.

The escape season came to an end with the onset of winter but resumed in the spring of 1941. Digging began as soon as the ground had thawed. The men planned to break out on the first moonless night in June, and they completed the eighty-foot-long tunnel without any major setbacks. Bushell, originally intending to make his break through the tunnel, decided to blitz out on his own. Fluent in German, he believed he sported an above-average chance of making it to the Swiss border. A goat shed sat in the corner of the exercise field, which lay just beyond the compound's barbed-wire perimeter. Bushell's plan was simple: hide in the shed during the day and sneak away after sunset. When the day in question arrived, fellow prisoners distracted the guards by leading the goat into the field and staging a mock bullfight. Bushell took his position in the shed and waited for nightfall, the last few hours spent in the company of the goat, who didn't seem to mind the intrusion.

Bushell snuck away after dark. He made it to the local railway station and purchased a ticket with the few German marks he had managed to scrounge in the camp. He traveled through the night and disembarked the next day in the town of Stühlingen. Thirty yards from the border,

Bushell's luck ran out. Presenting himself as a drunken ski instructor, he tried staggering across the frontier, telling the border guard he was returning home after organizing a local ski event. The suspicious guard insisted Bushell accompany him to the police station. Bushell broke character and ran, prompting the startled German to give chase. The guard drew his pistol and squeezed off several rounds, the bullets missing their mark and kicking up asphalt. Bushell veered round a corner and found himself in a dead-end street. He was promptly arrested and dispatched to Stalag Luft I, a bleak and desolate compound near the Baltic coastal town of Barth, where he remained for several months.

The meager rations and frigid Baltic weather took a harsh physical toll, but the miserable conditions only strengthened Bushell's resolve. He was soon overseeing the construction of a new tunnel, but the Germans transferred the prisoners to another camp before its completion. Men, thirsty and hungry, were herded into railway cars for the nearly two-hundred-mile trip to a compound near Warburg. During the journey, prisoners used a table knife smuggled aboard to cut a hole in the car's floorboards. Bushell—forty pounds lighter since his internment at Stalag Luft I—carefully lowered himself through the hole, the track beneath him a rushing metallic blur. He could feel the wind pulling on him, threatening to suck him under the wheels of the train. He held tight and waited for the train to slow down before dropping himself onto the rails and rolling clear of the undercarriage. Now on the run, he partnered with Czech airman Jack Zafouk and accompanied him to Prague. Their timing proved unfortunate, arriving as they did in the wake of Reinhard Heydrich's assassination.

Hitler ordered the arrest and murder of thousands of Czechs. Friends and neighbors betrayed one another to save their own skin—and so it was the Germans discovered the local family sheltering Bushell and Zafouk. The family paid in blood for its transgression. Zafouk was shipped to Colditz and Bushell eventually arrived at Stalag Luft III with his plan for a great escape in place. Like the final creation an artist is intent on completing, the escape became Bushell's obsession. He oversaw every aspect of the planning with an almost tyrannical zeal. He expected the men executing his plans to accomplish the impossible, whether it be the forging of two hundred travel passes or the tailoring of two hundred civilian outfits. He had no patience for skepticism and doubt.

Just prior to the escape, Bushell partnered with Lieutenant Bernard Scheidhauer, a Frenchman. Scheidhauer was eighteen in June 1940, when France collapsed under the German onslaught. He fled the country by boat to England in what proved to be a harrowing cross-Channel voyage. The boat ran out of fuel mid-crossing and left the Frenchman and his five sailing companions adrift for days. They steadily worked their way through all the food and water on board. On the twelfth day, a Scottish freighter spotted the stranded men, ravaged by thirst, hunger, and exposure. Scheidhauer made a quick recovery and joined the Free French Air Force less than one week later, eventually taking to the skies with No. 131 Squadron. He began flying combat operations over Northern France in the summer of 1942. When his patrols took him over the coastal town of Brest, he would swoop in low and buzz his parents' home, hoping they might realize it was their son waging war among the clouds. He was fighting not only for them, but the redemption of his nation's honor—a matter he held dear. On November 18, 1942, it all came to an end when mechanical problems forced his Spitfire down. Scheidhauer, the controls going slack in his hand, managed to maneuver his plane out to sea toward the English Channel Islands. He landed the stricken fighter on what he believed to be the Isle of Wight. Clambering out of the cockpit, he was approached by local farmers, who informed the young pilot he had actually crash-landed in German-occupied Jersey. Less than an hour later, the Germans had him in custody. His next stop was Stalag Luft III, where he provided the escape committee with intelligence on France.

On the night of the escape, Bushell and Scheidhauer were numbers five and six, respectively, to emerge from the tunnel and disappear into the woods. Disguised as French civilians and traveling by train, they hoped to make it to France and connect with the Resistance. They purchased tickets at the Sagan station for the Berlin-to-Breslau express. From Breslau, they journeyed to Saarbrücken, near the French border. Their train pulled into the city's main railway station on the evening of Sunday, March 26. A police officer approached them on the platform and asked to see their travel papers and identity cards. He glanced at their documents and returned them without comment. Bushell and Scheidhauer thanked the officer in French and turned to walk away.

"Good luck," said the officer in English.

"Thank you," replied Scheidhauer, also in English.

It was a simple—but effective—trap. The two men were arrested and taken to Lerchesflur Prison. Interrogated by the *Kripo*, they claimed to be French businessmen returning home to their families. Not until their captors threatened to shoot them as saboteurs did Bushell and Scheidhauer confess to their true identities. The local police, following protocol, relayed news of the capture to the War Search Headquarters of the Criminal Police in Berlin. The information made its way from there to Gestapo headquarters.

In the early morning hours of Wednesday, March 29, the phone rang at the home of local *Kripo* chief Gustav Dingermann. The caller was Dr. Leopold Spann, head of the Saarbrücken Gestapo, with orders to ready Bushell and Scheidhauer for immediate transfer to Berlin. The order, Spann said, came from the highest quarters. Regardless of its origin, the order struck Dingermann as odd. The *Wehrmacht* or the *Luftwaffe* usually reclaimed captured escapees and returned them to their camps, not the Gestapo. When Dingermann questioned the change of protocol, Spann's voice turned cold. He repeated the instructions and hung up the phone. Dingermann called the prison and asked that the necessary arrangements be made. When he arrived at his office later that morning, he learned that the RAF men had been picked up before daybreak. Several days later, one of Dingermann's officers entered his office and closed the door. He took a seat on the other side of Dingermann's desk and spoke in almost a whisper.

"I heard in confidence from a Gestapo man," the officer said, "that the vehicle carrying the two Air Force officers never arrived in Berlin at all, but that both were shot when trying to escape again."

Dingermann, who suffered from a chronic heart condition, slowly massaged the center of his chest and absorbed the news.

"I seriously do not believe," he said, "that the two of them tried to escape."

Urns bearing the names Bushell and Scheidhauer arrived at Stalag Luft III shortly thereafter. An inscription on the base of each urn identified Saarbrücken as the place of cremation.

———————

At his desk, McKenna took a pull from his glass of whiskey and opened the folder in front of him. The room was dark, except for the small circle of light cast by the green-shaded desk lamp. He dragged a hand across his tired eyes and began reading the document, a statement recently taken from Dingermann. Courtney's team had found him several weeks prior at No. 6 CIC, Moosburg. Once the paperwork cleared, releasing Dingermann into British custody, the RAF had transferred him to the London Cage. He proved to be a cooperative witness and fully explained his involvement in the Saarbrücken affair. The day of the Sagan escape, Dingermann said, Berlin issued instructions laying out the protocol for the handling of recaptured escapees. "What struck me," he told his interrogators, "was the provision that in the case of escaped prisoners being retaken, they were to be immediately interrogated in detail on how they managed to escape and that—until further instructions were given—the recaptured prisoners were to be kept in police custody. There was thus to be no direct handing over to the Wehrmacht as had been usual hitherto in cases of recapture."

Dingermann detailed how Bushell and Scheidhauer had been captured at the main railway station in Saarbrücken. "When informed a few days later that the vehicle carrying the two Air Force officers never arrived in Berlin at all, but that both of them were shot when trying to escape again," he said, "I was very upset."

Dingermann identified Spann as the primary architect of the Saarbrücken murders but could not name the actual gunmen or say with any certainty if Spann himself pulled a trigger. It was doubtful Spann even survived the war. "About three or four weeks ago—that is the end of February and the beginning of March 1946—during my stay at the internment camp at Moosburg, I spoke to Kriminalkommissar Jaffke, who until the end of 1943, had been working at the State Police in Saarbrücken," Dingermann said. "He told me that he had heard Spann, together with about forty to fifty officials of his department, had been killed during one of the large-scale air attacks on Linz, during which the offices there of the Gestapo had been badly hit."

McKenna pushed the statement aside and took another sip of his drink. He would have to confirm Spann's death before striking him off the RAF's list. The Saarbrücken affair was McKenna's case. While he had teams canvassing the American and British zones, the French Zone, which included Saarbrücken, had been deemed McKenna's beat. The French were still struggling to bring order to their house in terms of record keeping. From an investigative standpoint, there were additional considerations. Other than Leopold Spann—a man who might or might not be alive—McKenna had no names in his suspect pool. Early on he realized that the Saarbrücken case would entail a lot of knocking on doors, so to speak. He began a drawn-out hunt for those in the German security services assigned to Saarbrücken in 1944.

The search took him from one prison facility to another. It was an exhausting routine, but one to which he had gradually become accustomed. The investigation had thus far pushed him—both physically and mentally—to an extent he had never experienced before. Some days passed with no more than a few hours' sleep, and his emotional response to the unfolding story of the killings covered the gamut between revulsion and outrage. In a prison camp outside Saarbrücken, McKenna found a man named Josef Lampel, a onetime member of the *Kripo* assigned to Saarbrücken at the time of the Sagan escape. Lampel said a *Kripo* agent named Bender had arrested Bushell and Scheidhauer at the train station. Prior to his wartime service, Bender ran a tobacconist shop in Vorstadtstrasse, Saarbrücken.

"I presume he is still living there," Lampel said.

McKenna checked with local authorities and learned that Bender never returned to Saarbrücken after the war. He forwarded the man's name to war crime investigators in the American and French zones. He scored a hit with the French Security Police. The man was serving twelve years' forced labor at Witlich Gaol, near Trier, for taking part in atrocities committed during the German occupation of Alsace Lorraine. French investigators had taken a statement from Bender, in which he detailed his role in the Saarbrücken affair. Also in French possession were a number of Gestapo documents containing entries relative to the detention and cremation of Bushell and Scheidhauer. At the present time, the French needed the documents for their own investigation and were unable to turn them over to the British. As Scheidhauer was a French national, they had a legitimate concern in the Saarbrücken case.

In early May 1946, French Security Police passed along a statement taken three months earlier from a German police inspector stationed at Saarbrücken during the war. The inspector, a man named Schmoll, said Spann approached him one day in late March 1944 and ordered

An aerial reconnaisance photograph of Stalag Luft III. The white arrow is pointing to the railway station the escapees headed for once clearing the tunnel. **BRITISH NATIONAL ARCHIVES: AIR 40/229**

him to oversee the cremation of two prisoners recently shot while trying to escape. Schmoll made the necessary arrangements with the Neue Bremm torture camp just outside Saarbrücken, where two men he identified as Emil Schulz and Walter Breithaupt delivered the bodies by truck. McKenna added Schulz and Breithaupt to the RAF's wanted list and forwarded the names to investigators in the British and American zones. The U.S. Army traced Breithaupt to his parents' house outside Frankfurt and cleared the RAF to take him into custody. British military police surrounded the house in the early morning hours of October 7. An officer knocked on the front door and told the elderly couple who answered that their son was wanted for questioning in a sensitive matter. They allowed the officer to enter and said Walter was still in bed upstairs. The officer entered Breithaupt's bedroom and found the wanted man sleeping. A startled Breithaupt was handcuffed, dragged outside to a waiting car, and taken to the holding facility at Minden.

At the time of the shootings, Breithaupt was Spann's personal driver and lived in a small room above the maintenance garage behind the offices of the Saarbrücken Gestapo. Shortly after four in the morning on March 29, Spann woke Breithaupt and told him to prepare the car for a journey to Mannheim. Breithaupt forced himself out of bed and checked the tires and engine oil. Satisfied, he pulled the car round to the front of the office and saw *Kriminalsekretär* Emil Schulz standing in the predawn gloom. Getting in the car, Schulz explained that two escapees from Stalag Luft III were being held by the local criminal police and were "to be returned to a camp in the Reich." They drove to Lerchesflur Prison, retrieved the fugitives, and brought them back to Gestapo headquarters, where Schulz shackled the prisoners' wrists. Bushell protested and surprised Breithaupt and Schulz by addressing them in angry German.

"This is not compatible with the honor of an officer," he said.

An apologetic Schulz said he was only following orders and disappeared inside the building. He returned several minutes later with Spann; both men wore their gray SS uniforms. Schulz climbed into the backseat between the prisoners. Spann got in the front and told Breithaupt to start driving. He informed the airmen they were being taken to a prison camp deep in the heart of Germany. From Saarbrücken, Breithaupt drove to Hamburg and picked up the Reichsstrasse. He followed it to Kaiserslautern and merged onto the autobahn in the direction of Mannheim. The road at this early hour was empty, prompting Breithaupt to ride hard on the accelerator.

"Don't drive so fast," Spann said. "We have plenty of time."

Bushell and Scheidhauer remained silent during the journey. Spann eventually ordered Breithaupt to pull onto the grass verge. He told the driver to stay with the prisoners and got out of the car with Schulz. The two men each lit a cigarette, and they stamped their feet in the frigid air. They walked to the rear of the car and stood conversing in close quarters, their voices quiet. Breithaupt, watching them through the back window, saw Spann beckon to him.

"I have received an order by teleprint from Berlin to shoot the prisoners," Spann said matter-of-factly. Seeing the look on Breithaupt's face, he tried to offer words of reason. "Remember what happens to our wives and children during air raids on our cities."

The matter closed to further discussion, Spann returned to the car and told the men to get out and relieve themselves. An indignant Bushell raised his shackled wrists and said he couldn't do anything while handcuffed. Spann agreed and ordered Schulz to remove the manacles. The prisoners got out and stood on the snow-covered roadside, rubbing their wrists to get the blood flowing. Spann and Schulz covered them with pistols in hand.

"Shots will be fired immediately if you try to escape," Spann said.

He gestured with his Walther and made the airmen walk several feet from the roadway, down a slight embankment. Schulz followed close behind, while Breithaupt—standing at the rear of the car— watched from his elevated vantage point. Satisfied passersby on the autobahn could not see them, Spann—standing to the left and slightly behind the airmen—told them to stop and attend to their business. Schulz covered the prisoners from behind and to the right. Bushell and Scheidhauer were unbuttoning their trousers when Spann looked at Schulz and nodded. The two Gestapo men raised their pistols. Spann took aim at the back of Scheidhauer's head. Breithaupt looked away just as Schulz and Spann fired their guns at point-blank range. The two shots "sounded almost like one" to Breithaupt, who turned around to see the airmen lying in crimson-colored snow between some shrubbery. Neither prisoner, in that final moment, made a sound. His weapon still smoking, Spann ordered Schulz to guard the scene and returned to the car for the journey back to headquarters.

"You are not allowed to talk to anyone about what has actually taken place," Spann told Breithaupt as they pulled away from the scene. "Should anyone ask you about the whereabouts of the prisoners, you are to say they've been shot whilst escaping—or while trying to escape."

Breithaupt nodded and listened as his superior dictated further instructions. In the cellar of the Saarbrücken office, there was "a big, coffin-like wooden box" large enough to hold two bodies, Spann said. Breithaupt was to load the box into a truck and retrieve the corpses. Arrangements had been made for their disposal at the "working camp" in the small town of Neue Bremm. Back at the office, Breithaupt did as instructed. He slid the box, with the help of another driver, into the back of a canvas-top truck and returned to the scene of the shooting. He and Schulz loaded the bodies into the box and drove to Neue Bremm, less than two miles outside Saarbrücken, on the southwest fringes of the city.

"What's going to happen to the bodies?" asked Breithaupt.

"They are to be cremated," Schulz replied.

Although not a concentration camp, Neue Bremm was a place of barbaric treatment. The Nazis referred to it as an "expanded police prison," a facility used to break prisoners. The conditions were squalid and the barracks fetid. Inmates were starved to the brink of death, tortured, and oftentimes murdered. For those fated for Auschwitz, Belsen, Buchenwald, and the other larger death camps, Neue Bremm often served as a waypoint before their final destination. Breithaupt and Schulz arrived at the compound late in the morning and were met outside by Schmoll, the police inspector contacted by Spann.

"He pointed out an empty space where we put the case with the bodies," Breithaupt said. The bodies delivered, the Gestapo men returned to headquarters.

As for Schulz, Breithaupt said he knew the man had most recently lived in Saarbrücken, on the corner of Saargemünder and Julius Kiefer Strasse. He described the *Kriminalsekretär*, thirty-eight, as being slim in build and five feet, five inches tall, with medium fair hair. McKenna, Williams, and Van Giessen drove to the Saarbrücken address. It was a run-down apartment building with an exterior scarred by war. The men walked hallways of threadbare carpet and peeling walls, knocking on doors and questioning tenants. Yes, the Schulz family once lived in the building, but they had moved in recent months. Where? Frankenholz, a village just outside Saarbrücken. The investigators traced the family to a small house and were met at the door by Frau Angela Schulz. Through Van Giessen, McKenna stated the purpose of his visit and asked her if she had been in recent contact with her husband. Frau Schulz shook her head and said she had not heard from Emil in several months. A small girl clung to the woman's side as she spoke.

McKenna entered the house and took a cursory glance around but saw nothing to suggest a recent male presence. On the walls, family snapshots showed a smiling middle-aged man, slender in a gray suit and fedora, flanked by two young girls—one of whom still held firm to her mother's dress. Normality, the kind forever captured in the pictures, now seemed a distant thing of the past. With Frau Schulz's permission, McKenna and his team searched the house. The men moved from room to room, opening drawers and emptying wardrobes. McKenna searched a bureau in the bedroom and found, buried beneath some clothes in the top drawer, a neatly folded letter written in German. He passed the paper to Van Giessen, who read the opening line aloud: "My dearest, brave darling, it is a wonderful comfort to me that you and the children are safe." Frau Schulz stood watching in the doorway with tears in her eyes. McKenna took the letter from Van Giessen and quietly asked the woman who wrote it. There was no date or return address, and the signature was no more than a scribble. Her face trembling, the woman said the letter was from a close acquaintance. McKenna did not push the matter. The wife and children were suffering. He pocketed the letter and explained he would have to take it with him. The RAF men left the house and drove away in silence.

Closer examination of the letter's paper stock revealed it to be the type of stationery used in French prisons. The French operated a number of internment camps near Saarbrücken, the closest one being less than ten miles outside of town. McKenna felt some apprehension as he and Flight Sergeant Williams drove through the camp's main entrance. If they found their man here, there was no guarantee the camp's commandant would hand him over to the British. Because of Scheidhauer's nationality, the French might decide they had jurisdiction and refuse to release any suspects connected to the murders. In the commandant's office, McKenna introduced himself and said he was looking for a man named Emil Schulz, wanted for the murder of an RAF officer. McKenna made a point of stressing Bushell's nationality—"South African born, but of British nationality." He showed the commandant the letter found in Frau Schulz's bedroom. The Frenchman examined the document and focused his attention on the illegible signature. He told McKenna it looked as though Ernst Schmidt, a current inmate, had signed the letter. Armed guards brought Schmidt to the office and sat him in a chair.

"I am an RAF officer investigating the murders of British escapees from Stalag Luft III," McKenna said by way of introduction. "I have reason to believe that your name is Emil Schulz and that you have information relevant to this investigation."

The man's face twitched slightly at the mention of Emil Schulz, but he played ignorant. McKenna thought back to the modest house in Frankenholz, the worried wife and upset children. He took the letter from the commandant's desk and passed it to the man known as Schmidt. It took the prisoner only the briefest moment to realize the futility of his situation. He grasped the piece of paper as though it were some treasured artifact and pulled it close. He lowered his head and confessed to his true identity. *"Ich bin Emil Schulz. Angela Schulz is meine Gattin."*

Schulz's statement, for the most part, followed Breithaupt's take on events. After the car pulled to the side of the road, Schulz unshackled the prisoners and let them out of the vehicle. Schulz left the handcuffs on the backseat, pulled a Walther PPK from his coat pocket, and followed the two airmen onto the grass. At that moment, Schulz said, Spann fired several shots.

"I also fired one of these shots in the direction of the bigger officer," Schulz said, referring to Bushell. "I do not know whether I hit him; I saw both officers collapse. Scheidhauer fell on his face. I think Bushell crumpled up, fell somewhat on his right side and, in lying there, turned on his back. On approaching closer, I noticed the dying man was in convulsions."

Schulz knelt beside the writhing airman and took careful aim. He steadied his right hand in the crook of his left elbow, brought the pistol to bear on Bushell's left temple, and pulled the trigger.

"Death," Schulz said quietly, "took place immediately."

McKenna slapped two cartons of English cigarettes on the commandant's desk and said he wanted to take Schulz into custody without delay. The Frenchman eyed the smokes and considered the offering. McKenna, hoping the Frenchman would not broach matters of jurisdiction, nudged the cartons closer. The commandant opened one of the boxes and inhaled the smell of tobacco. He smiled and nodded. An adjutant presented the necessary papers and had McKenna sign his name. Emil Schulz was now a prisoner of the Royal Air Force. McKenna and Williams hurried Schulz to their jeep, eager to leave the French Zone before higher authorities learned of the trade and took Schulz back into custody. Williams drove, his foot heavy on the accelerator; McKenna sat alongside Schulz in the backseat. The car sped through open country toward the British Zone. Their journey took them past the very spot where Bushell and Scheidhauer had been murdered. McKenna told Williams to stop the car and ask Schulz in German if he cared to relieve himself. The prisoner shot McKenna a terrified look and recoiled. "*Nein!*" he screamed. McKenna allowed himself a smile and told Williams to keep driving. The men spent the night in the American Zone and arrived at the Minden holding facility the following morning. Schulz gave another statement, this time in front of an RAF stenographer.

"I had never killed a man before, and haven't killed anyone since," he said. "I tried to get out of this killing. I told Dr. Spann that what he was asking me to do was wrong, but all he said was, 'Just do as I tell you.' He said, 'Remember, this man was a terror-flier. Think of what our wives and children had to suffer in the German cities.' What else could I do? If I'd not done it, someone else would have done it. If we had all refused, we could have been shot. But I have always expected to answer for this . . . this deed I never wished to do. And now, it is the end of the road."

Arrangements were made to transfer Schulz to the London Cage, with McKenna serving as escort. En route, Schulz asked McKenna if he would deliver a letter to his wife. McKenna initially refused, but Schulz's gentle pleading won him over. In truth, McKenna felt pity for the man. He was no Nazi—or at least not a true believer. He was simply another casualty of war caught on the wrong side and swept up in a situation far beyond his control. McKenna thought of the man's wife and children back in Frankenholz. They would never see him again—a fact Schulz acknowledged. McKenna provided the pen and paper. Schulz wrote:

Dear Angela, dear Ingeborg, dear Helga, you dears of mine!

I am already in England now, and, alas, could not say Goodbye to you. I am here as a prisoner because of carrying out an official order in the spring of 1944.

I never on my own initiative acted against the laws of humanity. Had I not taken part, then I would have gone down at that time. I was on guard duty with Ludwig Weiss, who is in hospital in Hamburg. Ask him!

I'm waiting for justice. I only ask to be treated as I deserve and judged according to my position. In that case, I'll be all right. Do what you can for me. You, dear Angela, have courage and live only for the children. I'll do the same.

The snaps of Ingeborg and Helga are my faithful companions. From them I find a lot of consolation and new strength.

If I did not tell you anything it was only because I did not want to worry you unduly. It would have been much, much more difficult for me. How easier it would be to suffer death three times in order to prevent all this happening to you and especially the

children. Ask Rudolf Specht to help you in everything you under-
take for me. He can help you. I shall write again as soon as I can.
Be brave with the children. My regards to my old father, brothers
and sisters. They will stand by you. Greetings to you, dear Mother,
your suffering goes to my heart, it hurts me very much. Give my
regards to my two brothers-in-law who are now in England.
　　Ever your faithful husband, your daddy and your

Emil

McKenna, violating the RAF's "strict rules governing fraternization," delivered the letter to Schulz's wife and gently explained her
husband's situation. Choking on her emotions, Frau Schulz blamed the
Gestapo for her family's circumstance. She and her husband had been
childhood sweethearts. He started his career as a civilian police officer
in 1928 but was posted to the Gestapo ten years later. Following his
transfer, he wore plain clothes to work in lieu of a uniform—something
she found distressing. Why was there a need for such secrecy? "That's
not good," she would tell her husband. "I do not like it, Emil." She now
took the letter with unsteady hands and retreated to another room. She
read it multiple times and committed the words to memory. She was
not allowed to keep it. McKenna sat quietly in the small sitting room
until she emerged, letter in hand, her face twisted in anguish. She slipped
the letter with care back in its envelope and gave it to McKenna, thank-
ing him for his kindness. Realizing there was nothing he could say or
do to ease the woman's torment, he simply wished her well and left her
to grieve.

The weight of the woman's misery proved a heavy burden as he
drove back to Rinteln.

TEN

DANZIG

While the investigation moved forward on various fronts, it remained stagnant on others. McKenna thought of it as a complex machine comprised of multiple systems all working independent of one another, thrumming to their own mechanized rhythm. Some parts moved with greater efficiency than others. McKenna reviewed the case files, cigarette smoke hanging thick and heavy over his desk. The Munich case was all but solved. True, Munich Gestapo chief Oswald Schäfer remained at large, but the actual gunmen were now in British custody. Four of the nine men wanted for killing Squadron Leader Kirby-Green and Flying Officer Kidder in Zlín were in the British military prison at Minden, awaiting trial. Still being sought was Otto Kozlowsky, the Brno Gestapo lawyer who constructed a false account of the killings to present to the Red Cross. Sources in Czechoslovakia had recently told the RAF that Kozlowsky had been arrested in Prague, tied to a lamppost by outraged citizens, doused in gasoline, and set alight. The story had yet to be verified. Gunman Adolf Knuppelberg, it emerged, was freed from a Russian prison camp in 1945. His whereabouts remained a mystery and would continue to do so. Hugo Roemer, the major who passed the order to kill from local Gestapo chief Wilhelm Nöelle to Knuppelberg, also remained elusive.* Roemer's personal driver, Fritz Schwarzer, had been found in Czech custody and was being left to the authorities in that country.

The hunt for Zlín Gestapo chief Hans Ziegler continued. McKenna had the man's picture printed in the *Bavarian Police Gazette*, hoping to generate some leads, but the public failed to respond. The British military continued to monitor the mail of his wife, Therese, as well as his mother and sister, without success. McKenna had confirmed the death of Leopold Spann, head of the Saarbrücken Gestapo and the man who oversaw the murders of Roger Bushell and Bernard Scheidhauer. Following up on the report that Spann had transferred to Linz after the killings and subsequently died in an air raid, McKenna found a certificate in the town records stating:

> In the death records of the Kriminal Polizei office at Linz dates 26.4.45 no. 1470/45 K. N 2155, the profession of Dr. Leopold Spann who died in Linz on 25.4.45 was recorded as "Leader of the Gestapo, Linz." By order of the undernamed authority of administration it was ordered that this description of profession should be altered to the occupation "official."
> Signed: The Official Town Administration.

The Natzweiler case, the murder of Flying Officer Dennis Cochran, had reached a satisfactory conclusion. But for all that was known, so much still lingered in seemingly impenetrable shadow. Four airmen— Squadron Leader James Catanach, Pilot Officer Arnold Christensen, and Lieutenants Hallada Espelid and Nils Fuglesang—had died in Kiel, the gunmen phantom figures without faces or names. Twenty-seven men had died in the Breslau region, but the RAF had yet to make a single arrest in the case. Based on the information readily available to him, McKenna decided at present to focus on the murders of Flying Officer Henri Picard and Flight Lieutenants Edward Brettell, Romas Marcinkus, and Gilbert Walenn in Danzig. They had a few details

---

* Roemer was never heard from again; the Czechs executed Kozlowsky in 1947.

regarding the crime courtesy of Erich Graes, deputy director of the Danzig *Kripo*. Following Graes's statement to Flight Lieutenant Courtney back in January, the RAF had begun searching for Danzig Gestapo chief Dr. Günther Venediger. To the physical description provided by Graes, McKenna had added his own notes based on information acquired during the canvassing of internment camps:

> Deep powerful voice. Clipped manner of speech. Invariably holds his head at an angle and his eyes take on a fixed expression. Good strong teeth. Dark hornrimmed spectacles. Plays piano. May have gone to Wernigerode in the Harz mountains.

Word had recently reached the RAF that a German general, a man named Ritzer, was in contact with Venediger at an internment camp in Neumünster. McKenna dispatched a member of his team, Flying Officer D. J. Walker, to interview the general. Ritzer, when confronted, denied ever communicating with Venediger and said he had simply heard a rumor that the onetime Gestapo chief was in the camp under an assumed name. Walker spent several days interrogating the camp's inmates. When done, he wired McKenna the results of his inquiry: "It is interesting to point out that Venediger was never actually seen at No. 1 C.I.C. It is possible that Venediger never was at the No. 1 C.I.C. and that his 'hearsay' presence in that camp was the result of a previous interrogation in which Venediger may have been mentioned. The mentioning of his name probably started the glorified rumour of his presence among the inmates of the Camp."

Considering the scope of the Sagan investigation, one would have expected more men assigned to the case. As it was, only one wing commander, four flight lieutenants, sixteen noncommissioned officers, and sixteen interpreters on loan from the Dutch armed forces made up the RAF's investigative team. McKenna spent much of his time on the road, traveling between zones of occupation. Conducting a routine canvas of a camp outside Hamburg, McKenna stumbled across a man named Kurt Achterberg, a former deputy in the Danzig Gestapo. Graes, in his statement provided several months earlier, had mentioned Achterberg as someone who might know about the Danzig killings. Guards brought the prisoner to McKenna for questioning. He was a man of rather unfortunate appearance. Unruly brown hair stuck out in all directions above a pair of thick-rimmed glasses, which sat atop a bulbous nose and ears that seemed too large for his head. When the man spoke, he revealed a mouth of irregularly shaped teeth, badly yellowed and capped with gold fillings. His hands were large and his physical frame was impressive. McKenna thought the man would prove more than a handful in a physical altercation.

"One morning in the late summer of 1944, it was during August or September, I stood in the antechamber of Dr. Venediger's office," Achterberg said. "There, Kriminal Secretary Reinhold Bruchardt spoke to me. He had a file under his arm and was apparently on his way to see Venediger. He said to me, 'It has been damned difficult to get the Red Cross to believe that the British officers had been shot whilst escaping.' I was greatly startled by this remark. There was, however, no further discussion between us, as apparently Venediger came along and went with Bruchardt into his office."

McKenna expressed interest in Achterberg's story and urged him to continue.

"I remember at about that time, there was a rumor going around the building of the State Police that Bruchardt had murdered some people," Achterberg said, pushing his glasses up his nose with an oversized finger. "I did not press Bruchardt to give me more details, as I did not want to mix myself up with Venediger's business."

"Venediger's business?" McKenna asked.

"Of course," said Achterberg, as if it all made perfect sense. "Bruchardt was subordinated to Venediger directly. He accepted instructions from Venediger only. It can only be in the Sagan incident that Venediger gave the order for the murder to Bruchardt and, with him, formed the murder squad."

"What do you know about the Sagan case?"

"Until then, all I knew was that in spring 1944 a large number of British RAF officers had escaped from the PW camp in Sagan and that, on account of this, a nation-wide search had been started," Achterberg said. "I did not learn the results of the search, nor the fate of the recaptured officers. I only knew that recaptured prisoners of war were to be handed over by the Criminal Police to the Armed Forces."

"You never heard of any other arrangement?" asked McKenna.

"Never at any time did Bruchardt mention to me that he had received orders to kill captured Sagan officers," Achterberg said. "He also never discussed with me the carrying out of such an order."

Achterberg said he subsequently spoke with a fellow coworker who saw Bruchardt in an office, packing into boxes the personal effects of the four murdered officers. What happened to the possessions Achterberg couldn't say. "Possibly," he theorized, "Berlin got them."

"And what about Bruchardt?"

"He has not yet been captured."

Achterberg told McKenna he was in contact with other incarcerated members of the Danzig Gestapo and *Kripo*, all of whom were allegedly outraged by the murders. If Bruchardt was in custody, someone would have known about it. Achterberg fell silent and pondered some distant point only he could see. McKenna, sensing the man had something to say, urged Achterberg to speak his mind. The big German offered a weak smile, his thick lips parting just enough to reveal a glimpse of yellow teeth. It was, McKenna realized, a look of embarrassment. In a quiet voice, Achterberg said Bruchardt had been having an affair with his wife. He had found out during the war when he stumbled across letters exchanged between the two.

Bruchardt apparently enjoyed and cultivated a reputation for violence. In his office, alongside his desk, he kept a bullwhip soaking in a bucket of water—something he supposedly enjoyed using on prisoners with vicious regularity. He hardly ventured out without a pistol tucked away in a pocket and harbored no fear of physical confrontation. Achterberg told McKenna to find a woman named Frau Blum in Kempten, a town in the southwest of Bavaria where the Nazis operated one of Dachau's satellite camps. Blum, Achterberg explained, was friends with both his wife and Bruchardt. Since the end of the war, Blum had been the mail go-between for Bruchardt and Achterberg's wife, forwarding letters from one to the other when they arrived at her home.

Achterberg did not have an address for the woman but told McKenna she would undoubtedly know where to find Bruchardt.

Kempten was situated in the American Zone, meaning the RAF had to obtain permission from U.S. authorities to take Bruchardt into custody. Several days of bureaucratic headaches, fueled by stifling paperwork and face-to-face meetings, ensued before the necessary clearance was granted. McKenna and Lyon paid a visit to the field office of the United States Counter Intelligence Corps. With the help of two American agents, the RAF men began sifting through files maintained by the U.S. Army, reviewing the names and addresses of local residents. Although monotonous, it paid off several hours later when one of the Americans found the address of Frau Blum. She lived just outside of town. It was past midnight when McKenna and Lyon, accompanied by the two agents and two U.S. soldiers, drove to the address on record. They parked away from the house and approached on foot. The soldiers covered the rear of the house. McKenna approached the front with Lyon and the two agents and banged on the door. The windows remained dark and the house stayed silent. McKenna thumped on the door again but still got no response. Lyon yelled at the house in German and threatened to stand outside all night if necessary. McKenna, his fist poised to knock once more, backed away when he heard a lock turn on the inside. A light came on and the door opened slowly. A middle-aged woman wrapped in a dressing gown stood in the doorway, a look of puzzlement on her face.

"Frau Blum?" asked McKenna.

"Yes."

McKenna pushed his way into the house and threw a cursory glance about the place. There appeared to be no signs of a hasty exit. Through Lyon, he told the woman he was looking for Reinhold Bruchardt. The woman said she had never heard the name before. The mentioning of Achterberg and his wife did nothing to persuade Frau Blum to come clean. McKenna and his team searched the house top to bottom, turning out wardrobes and drawers, upturning beds and furniture. They found nothing. Throughout the investigation, even when facing individuals he considered reprehensible, McKenna had maintained an outward calm. On this particular night, he found his patience lacking. When Blum again denied knowing anyone named Bruchardt, McKenna took the hard line. He turned and spoke to Lyon. "Please tell Frau Blum that she has probably heard a lot about the British officers, and British police officers, and how kind they are to women. Please tell her not to believe it, because some of us here are going to alter the shape of her face unless she is very careful. And I personally am going to take a leading part in this. She is in very great danger of being severely beaten up."

McKenna watched Blum recoil and immediately regretted his course of action, but to backpedal would have served no purpose. He instead allowed the shaken woman to ponder the veracity of his threat. She lowered herself into a chair and spoke in a quiet voice, admitting she knew the man McKenna sought. He lived in a flat at Rathausstrasse 22, in Kempten, under the alias Brandt. McKenna asked the two soldiers to stay and watch over Blum until Bruchardt was in custody. With Lyon and the two American agents, McKenna drove to Bruchardt's flat, which he noted with some irony sat above the local police station. The Americans retrieved tommy guns from the trunk of the car, Lyon a German automatic. McKenna opted not to carry a weapon. Inside the building, he asked the concierge to lead them to Brandt's flat. The man led them up a cramped flight of stairs and down a narrow hallway. Outside the door, the concierge passed McKenna the key and hurried back down the hall.

McKenna put the key in the lock and turned it slowly. The men entered the flat, worked their way in stagnant gloom down a short corridor, and paused outside a bedroom door left slightly ajar. They could hear the sound of heavy breathing from the dark space beyond. McKenna stepped quietly into the room and felt for a light switch on the wall, all the while keeping an eye on the large, dark shape in the bed. When McKenna flicked the lights on, the shape sprang to life. It leapt from the bed and lunged for a small side table in a blur of arms, legs, and flapping sheets. McKenna and his team had only the briefest moment to register the man's immense size before tackling him to the ground. It took all four men to subdue Bruchardt, who flailed and screamed under their collective weight. He eventually calmed down enough to be led from the flat at gunpoint. In the side table's drawer, McKenna found a loaded pistol. Bruchardt spent the night in the local jail. He left with the RAF men the following morning for the two-day journey to Minden, where McKenna booked him into the British holding facility. That night, the prison's deputy commander—pulling heavily from a bottle of whiskey—scanned the inmate registry and noticed the RAF had booked a suspect that afternoon wanted in connection with the Stalag Luft III murders. When McKenna arrived at the jail the following morning, he entered Bruchardt's cell only to find the man beaten almost beyond recognition. The man's face was a grotesque mask of swellings and contusions. Bruchardt refused to say what had happened, but McKenna was quick to find out. A complaint to the head of the War Crimes Investigation Unit later that same day saw the immediate dismissal of the prison's deputy commander.

Bruchardt was a rock. He displayed neither remorse for the crime nor concern for his future. He said he met with Dr. Venediger one spring morning in 1944 and was told four British escapees from Stalag Luft III had been captured near Danzig. Venediger, he said, wanted the prisoners returned safely to Sagan, but matters had not gone "smoothly." Transporting the RAF officers was a detachment of Eastern European soldiers "formerly employed in the border fights in Poland, and who had, as a result of the East Front retreating, found employment at our Dienststelle as additional guard duty." Roughly thirty Ukrainians—"respectively white Russians who were hardly masters of the German language"—made up the guard detachment in question. It was Bruchardt's supposed understanding that somewhere near the neighborhood of Gross-Trampken—some twenty-five miles outside Danzig—the prisoners told their Ukrainian guards they needed to relieve themselves. Let out along the roadside, they made a dash for the nearby trees and were gunned down in their last desperate bid for freedom.

McKenna, disbelieving, said nothing.

"It appeared to me," Bruchardt continued, "as if this incident seemed very unpleasant to Dr. Venediger, because he spoke of possible international conflicts and inquiries. I was to drive out there and look at everything and ask the Ukrainian *Untersturmführer* about the exact facts of the case in order to furnish Venediger with an account and to set everything on the right path."

Bruchardt said he rode his motorcycle to the scene of the shooting and saw two cars parked alongside the road. The guards' commander, leaning against one vehicle, told Bruchardt his men had warned the prisoners they would be shot if they tried to escape. When the officers scrambled for the trees, he and his men opened fire. He admitted with a coy smile to being somewhat drunk at the time and had perhaps been too quick to rely on his weapon.

"When he had led me into the woods for about 100 meters, I saw four corpses lying one next to the other in a line. In various directions leading into the wood, were tracks of bodies having been dragged, at the end of which I saw traces of blood," Bruchardt said. "As the shots had all obviously entered into the backs of the bodies, I had no doubt of the authenticity of the story."

Bruchardt dispatched one of the guards to retrieve a truck and take the bodies to the local Gestapo headquarters, where he debriefed Venediger. The Gestapo chief told Bruchardt to write a report on the incident for Berlin but omit any reference to Venediger having relied on "White Russians" to transport the prisoners. In the report, Bruchardt was to say he had been in charge of returning the RAF officers to Sagan and was forced to shoot them when they tried to escape.

"What purpose would it have served if I refused?" Bruchardt asked McKenna. "It would either have been deemed as a refusal to obey an order during a time of war, or a violation of instructions regarding Secret State Matters. Both would have resulted in the death penalty. I arranged to coffin and cremate the bodies in the crematorium at Danzig-Langfuhr. The urns with the ashes were then sent to Berlin, together with the belongings of the dead bodies."

Based on what Venediger told him, Bruchardt said he believed the remains and personal possessions were destined for England. He claimed not to know of any plan to kill recaptured POWs. Surely, he said, had the Gestapo murdered the British officers in cold blood, the bodies would have been disposed of quietly. He thought nothing more of the matter until some months later when the Sagan affair made international headlines.

"Since the Nuremberg Trials, I have lived in constant fear of being connected with this incident," Bruchardt said. "Now, I am hoping for the speedy seizure of Dr. Venediger so that he can clear me by describing the real facts of the case."

McKenna, confident Bruchardt was one of the Danzig gunmen, arranged for his transfer to the London Cage. All the while, the whereabouts of Venediger remained unknown.

ELEVEN

FINDING SCHARPWINKEL

What the RAF knew of the Breslau murders came from postwar statements by escapees who had passed through the jail at Görlitz before being shipped back to Stalag Luft III. Thirty-five of the seventy-six men who fled through the tunnel found themselves, shortly after their recapture, in the civilian jail at Sagan. Instead of being returned to the camp as expected, they were driven to Görlitz—some sixty miles away—for interrogation at the local Gestapo headquarters. There, all the officers were questioned in regards to the escape. The interrogators, who wore civilian clothing, tried to scare information from the prisoners by threatening them with execution if they failed to answer specific questions.

On the morning of March 30, 1944, Flight Lieutenants S. A. "Dick" Churchill and R. A. Bethell heard cars pull up outside the jail. They peered through the barred window of their cell and saw three cars idling in the frost-covered courtyard below. "Ten civilians of the Gestapo type" emerged from the vehicles and entered the building. They reappeared several minutes later with six prisoners in tow, including Australian Flying Officer Al Hake, who had overseen the escape committee's compass factory at Stalag Luft III. From their vantage point, Churchill and Bethell watched the Gestapo bundle the RAF men into the waiting cars and drive them away. Six urns arrived at Stalag Luft III several days later. A plate on each urn, dated March 31, identified the place of cremation as Görlitz. The Gestapo agents returned on the morning of March 31. Through their cell window, Churchill and Bethell saw a large, middle-aged man they recognized from the day before. One prisoner described this particular agent, who appeared to be in charge of the others, as having a "battered-looking, pugilistic type of face." The Gestapo removed ten prisoners from the jail that morning. Shortly thereafter, ten urns—each stamped with a name, but no date—arrived at Stalag Luft III from the town of Liegnitz, fifty-five miles east of Görlitz.

The dead this time included Czech Flying Officer "Wally" Valenta, head of the escape committee's intelligence section. "You will never escape again," the airman had been informed upon recapture. Likewise, murdered Flight Lieutenant Cyril Swain was told he would be shot. Flying Officer A. Wlodzimierz Kolanowski, also among the dead, had appeared severely depressed following his questioning by the Gestapo. Survivors later remembered him sitting quietly in a corner, refusing to say what had transpired during his interrogation. Flight Lieutenant

The rock marking the spot where the Great Escapers emerged from Harry and fled into the forest. The inscription, written in Polish, reads: "Allied airmen, prisoners of Stalag Luft III, were Great Escape participants."

Brian Evans, also among the ill-fated group, had penned a letter to his fiancée just days earlier:

> You know darling, I still haven't got over the idea that we're going to spend the rest of our lives together. We're going to have even better times, too, than we've yet had. In one of your letters, you said you were going to spoil me when I get home. I'm very anxious to know how you're going to spoil me. I think you deserve a lot of spoiling, too, dearest; in fact, I've got a terrific lot to repay to you. If it weren't for your letters I don't know what I'd do, for they've helped me tremendously, Joan. I've got such a lot of things to say to you, but somehow they just can't be written; they wouldn't make sense. In fact, I don't think this letter reads too well. Hope you can understand what I mean. Letters are unsatisfactory things, aren't they? Remember, I'm coming home soon to look after you, darling. Until then, remember that I'll always love you.

On April 2, officers from the *Luftwaffe* showed up to escort four prisoners back to the camp. By whatever strange reasoning dictated who would live and who would die, Flight Lieutenants A. Keith Ogilvie, Alastair McDonald, Alfred Thompson, and Paul Royle were deemed worthy of survival. For the men still imprisoned in the Görlitz jail, each day became a torturous waiting game. "I remained at Görlitz for eleven or twelve days," one survivor later told investigators. "From about 30 March, a guard would go into a different cell and call out names. These men would then be taken away, and we did not see them again. We thought that they were being taken out for further interrogation, and when they did not return, that they had been sent back to camp."

Trench-coated Gestapo agents drove off with another six prisoners on April 6. Among them were Flight Lieutenants William Grisman and Harold Milford, who were told upon recapture that they would never see their wives again. Flight Lieutenant Alastair Gunn, placed in the back of a Gestapo sedan, was threatened with decapitation. The six urns that arrived at Stalag Luft III several days later bore plates indicating the bodies had been destroyed in Breslau, ninety-five miles east of Görlitz.

The *Luftwaffe* returned another eight men, including Churchill and Bethell, to Sagan on April 6. One week later, the Gestapo picked up Flight Lieutenant James Long, the last of the Sagan escapees held at Görlitz. His ashes were shipped from Breslau and soon arrived at Stalag Luft III.

Solving the Breslau-Görlitz murders hinged on finding Dr. Wilhelm Scharpwinkel, head of the Breslau Gestapo. In October 1944, acting on the orders of his superiors in Berlin, Scharpwinkel assumed command of the Breslau Criminal Police. With the Red Army closing in, his mandate was to ensure that the local populace remained defiant to the end. He summoned his subordinates to a meeting shortly after taking control and told them "the work of the Gestapo is, at the moment, more important than that of the Criminal Police." Present at the conference was Hans Schumacher, a senior police commander irked by Scharpwinkel's presence. Breslau's situation grew increasingly dire in the days and weeks that followed. Residents began fleeing the city en masse, as the sound of artillery fire crept ever closer. By the end of January, with the city well within range of Russian guns, Schumacher ordered all "ailing, elderly, and female members of the office" to evacuate Breslau. Only those deemed healthy enough to serve in uniform and carry out their policing duties stayed behind. That left forty officers to police a population of a hundred thousand.

Scharpwinkel studied the Russian positions on a map in his office. The closer the enemy advanced the more militant he became. In a tense meeting with Schumacher, Scharpwinkel demanded the remaining forty officers be relieved of their policing responsibilities and deployed in a fighting capacity. Schumacher resisted. The officers, he said, had no military training. Scharpwinkel again broached the matter several days later and announced the formation of his own military unit. Despite Schumacher's protestations, he enlisted the forty police officers, agents from the Breslau Gestapo, and the elderly members of the *Volkssturm* (Home Guard), creating a mixed regiment of questionable fighting ability. Scharpwinkel, asserting his authority, placed sixty of the men under Schumacher's command and charged him with preventing the Russians from infiltrating a sector of the city behind the front lines. Without enough ammunition or weapons to go around, the men were ill-equipped for the challenge. It was only a matter of days before Scharpwinkel reclaimed the majority of Schumacher's men and stuck them in the front-line trenches.

An unrelieved seventy hours at the front saw the majority of men succumb to enemy fire and freezing temperatures. An outraged Schumacher confronted Scharpwinkel, only to be accused of cowardice and threatened with execution. Shortly thereafter, Schumacher fell ill with a kidney ailment and was removed from the front line. He never saw Scharpwinkel again.

Schumacher himself conveyed the details of those last desperate days in Breslau to British investigators following his apprehension in February 1946.

"I cannot imagine Scharpwinkel escaped from Breslau," he told an interrogator at the London Cage. "If he is not already dead, he has probably acquired a pay book with a false name. It is also quite possible he is somewhere in Lower Silesia as a civilian."

Although he claimed to know little of the Breslau murders, Schumacher was no innocent bystander. Prior to his transfer to the Criminal Police in February 1943, he had served with a police unit in Kiev and investigated "partisan activity, treason, serious cases of sabotage, and unauthorized possession of arms." Individuals found guilty of such crimes were often shot. Schumacher assumed the role of executioner on more than one occasion. His unit shot anywhere from ten to thirty people a week. Killing was easy, he said, once you had been psychologically numbed to the atrocities on the Eastern Front.

"Frequently, mothers brought their own neglected children and asked for them to be destroyed," he said. "This demand was always refused."

To expedite the liquidation of Communist Party members, Berlin dispatched to Kiev a number of "gas lorries"—mobile gas chambers—with their own attendant staff.

"Death," Schumacher said, "occurred instantaneously and was painless, as an accompanying chemist assured us."

The search for an eyewitness to the Breslau murders eventually led McKenna's team back to the U.S. Army internment camp in Moosburg. There, on May 20, 1946, RAF Flight Sergeant R. M. Daniel questioned the recently apprehended Max Richard Hansel, a former *Kriminal Inspektor* with the Görlitz Gestapo.

"I want you to tell me all you know of this matter, and as we are in possession of a great deal of information already, I would advise you not to attempt lying," Daniel said. "Do you remember a *Grossfahndung* in March 1944 after the escape of a large number of British RAF officers from a prison camp in Eastern Germany?"

"Yes," Hansel said. "They escaped from Sagan."

"And how many officers were recaptured in and around Görlitz?"

"I do not know. I did not hear."

"You do know," Daniel shot back. "Some officers were brought into the Gestapo office at Görlitz. How many were there?"

"Six or seven," Hansel conceded. "I first saw them when they were brought in from the jail in three cars guarded by about twelve men under the command of Dr. Scharpwinkel. I did not know any of the guards. They were from Breslau and may have been *Kripo* or Gestapo."

"What time of day did they arrive?"

"I saw them about 19:30 hours, but I cannot remember the date."

"What happened then?" Daniel asked.

"All the prisoners were taken into my office for interrogation," Hansel said. "I was not there all the time, as I was sent out of the room, but I came in from time to time and I heard some of the questions asked."

"Who carried out the interrogations if you did not?"

"Dr. Scharpwinkel," Hansel replied. "He interrogated the men separately."

Fourteen questions were put to each officer, starting with the basics: name, rank, place of birth, and civilian occupation. These questions the prisoners answered freely, but they fell silent when pressed on more sensitive matters. What targets had they bombed prior to being shot down? What squadron did they belong to? Scharpwinkel, and six of his men who sat in on the proceedings, grew visibly agitated whenever an airman failed to cooperate.

"Who are the persons responsible for organizing the escape?" Scharpwinkel asked each captive. Not one of the men answered. "What are the names of the other escapees?" Again, silence was the only response. Prisoners were stripped of all personal items and locked together in a room with an armed guard at the door. "Take care they don't get away—otherwise something unpleasant will happen to you," Scharpwinkel told the guard, "or something unpleasant will happen to them."

Scharpwinkel turned to address Hansel and the other Gestapo men present, including one Hansel recognized as *Kriminalobersekretär* Lux. He motioned them into an office and closed the door. Taking up position behind the desk, he produced from his tunic a printed order from Berlin. The matter at hand, he said, was top secret (*"geheime reichssache"*). The prisoners were to be taken away and shot. The Gestapo men accepted the news without comment and began immediate arrangements to see the order through. The airmen were bundled into four black cars parked outside the offices at Augustastrasse 31. Shortly after one that afternoon, the vehicles pulled away in convoy, with Scharpwinkel in the lead. Hansel and his driver brought up the rear, with two prisoners in their backseat. They followed the autobahn past the town of Halbau and continued another eight kilometers before coming to a wood. Traffic was light, and only a few cars passed in the opposite direction. The wood grew thick on either side of the roadway. The lead car eventually pulled to the side of the road, and Scharpwinkel got out. The other vehicles followed suit. They had been traveling for two and a half hours.

"Scharpwinkel announced that a short break would be made here," Hansel recalled. "The prisoners were to be sent up to the head of the column and guarded there. I directed the two prisoners from my truck to the front where the others were already standing. The guarding was done by Scharpwinkel's staff, who were equipped with two submachine guns and in SS uniform. As far as I can remember, *Kriminalobersekretär* Lux had one of the submachine guns."

Hansel returned to his car and ate a butter sandwich he'd packed for the journey. The prisoners milled about for several minutes under the watchful eye of their Gestapo guardians, waiting for some sort of order. Finally, Scharpwinkel motioned with his hand, indicating the prisoners were to be marshaled deeper into the woods. Hansel, still eating his sandwich, watched the men disappear among the trees. A machine gun clattered somewhere beyond the tree line. Several sharp cracks of a pistol followed in rapid succession. Hansel got out of the car and ran into the woods, where he found the Gestapo men standing over six bodies. The prisoners lay among the dead leaves, their corpses roughly fifteen inches apart. One of the Gestapo agents turned to Hansel and said the prisoners had tried to escape.

"Did you believe that?" Daniel asked.

"No," Hansel said. "They would have been crazy to try to escape with men armed with machine pistols standing so close behind them. Their chance of getting away was so slight."

Scharpwinkel observed the carnage and ordered Hansel, who was familiar with the local area, to drive to Halbau and telephone the undertaker in Görlitz. Hansel returned to the car and passed the orders along to his driver. It was four o'clock when they pulled away from the crime scene. It took the better part of two hours to get hold of the undertaker and tell him what had transpired. The undertaker, believing RAF officers had been shot while trying to escape, alerted the Görlitz crematorium.

Hansel and his driver returned to the woods to await the undertaker's arrival. Scharpwinkel and most of his party had already departed. Only Lux and three other men remained to guard the bodies. At eight-thirty, two vans from the undertaker's office pulled up to the scene. Three bodies were placed in the back of each vehicle and taken away to be destroyed. Hansel retrieved the ashes from the Görlitz crematorium three days later and brought them to Scharpwinkel in Breslau.

"Who paid the cost of the cremations?" Daniel asked.

"The Breslau office," Hansel said.

Two or three weeks later, Hansel told Daniel, Scharpwinkel summoned him and the other participants to a meeting at the crime scene to coordinate their cover stories. Scharpwinkel told those gathered that the Swiss government had informed London of the killings.

"I wish only that Scharpwinkel may be captured and have his just punishment meted out to him," said Hansel, his tone spiteful. "What he has done to us old officials cannot be made good again."

The same month Hansel detailed what he knew about the Breslau murders, Flight Lieutenant Harold Harrison joined McKenna's team and quickly decided postwar Germany was an inhospitable place. Unlike other members of the team, Harrison was not a policeman by training. He had learned his investigative skills, including the art of interrogation, on the job. Questioning captured members of the Gestapo left him disturbed, repulsed by what he considered to be their arrogance even under the heel of utter defeat. Germany was a nightmare of ruin and desperation, and he knew he had played a small role in rendering it as such. Dropping bombs had not caused him any great pleasure, though he did enjoy flying and took solace in the fact that Bomber Command's actions were justified. It was a point disputed by the Gestapo men he questioned. When Harrison asked how they could mercilessly kill another human being without so much as looking them in the eye, the Gestapo men would invariably ask how Harrison could do the same thing. He discovered that normal civilians harbored similar resentments toward British aircrews. "People would recognize my aircrew brevet and say: 'You must have been on that fire-bomb raid on X or Y. My wife, or my kid, was killed there.' I learned in the end not to start the arid argument that I had killed on the field of combat and they performed cold-blooded murders. The answer always was: 'We were both acting under orders.' I could only wrap the answer up in the beautiful German word *vielleicht*: 'Perhaps . . . take out of it what you will.'"

Harrison learned that traveling about Germany could be a hazardous undertaking. Driving one night, he was startled by a muzzle flash just beyond the trees along the edge of the road. Bullets hammered the side of his jeep but fortunately caused Harrison no harm. Whether it was a deliberate attack against a British airman or simply a random assault, he never found out. Highway banditry was not an uncommon occurrence. "One was shot at," he later recalled, "bricks were thrown and bottles broken on the road." All RAF jeeps in Germany were equipped with a wire cutter—two sharp pieces of angled iron—that sat atop the front of the vehicle like a hood ornament. Unknown culprits had taken to stringing razor wire across the roadways. Such a trap had almost decapitated McKenna while he drove back to base one night. Only the glint of the wire in his headlights saved him at the last possible second from a grisly death. For Harrison, who "tended to look on life as something to be enjoyed," postwar Germany "was a completely depressing experience."

While the newest member of the team acclimated himself to his new surroundings, the Breslau investigation moved slowly forward. There could be no closure to the inquiry, however, without locating Dr. Wilhelm Scharpwinkel. Since McKenna's arrival in Germany the year before, the former head of the Breslau Gestapo had been one of the RAF's most wanted. All McKenna and his men had to go on was rumor and hearsay. No one knew for sure if the man was even still alive. A former fingerprint technician with the Breslau Gestapo, questioned by McKenna's men in early 1946, said he had heard that the Russians had hanged Scharpwinkel. Another survivor of the Breslau siege told Allied investigators the Russians had arrested Scharpwinkel but not killed him. All efforts by the RAF to take the search into the Russian Zone of Occupation had thus far failed. Letters requesting permission had either been denied or ignored. The British attempted to curry favor with Soviet authorities by handing over, in early 1946, "three Germans accused of war crimes against Soviet nationals." Arrangements were also being made to transfer into Russian custody a "large number of Germans suspected of war crimes against Soviet citizens in Norway, together with all available evidence, which they (British investigators) have been at great pains to collect."

Even if permission was eventually granted, dispatching an investigation team to the Soviet sector presented considerable problems, namely in the organizing of food supplies, quarters, and fuel.

Although the search for Scharpwinkel proved to be frustrating, news

from the American Zone in early December shed light on the fate of
Arthur Nebe, the top man sought by the RAF. The onetime *Kripo* chief,
responsible for compiling the Sagan execution list, was indeed dead.
Although fond of Hitler when he first came to power in 1933, Nebe
soon grew disillusioned with the Führer's tyrannical behavior. Nebe
initially kept his doubts to himself, fearing the consequences should
he speak out—but his discontent grew as the Nazis systematically liquidated their political rivals. In 1936, his feelings still a secret, Nebe
was appointed national head of the *Kripo*. Two years later saw the
formation of the Central Security Office, which brought Germany's
policing and security agencies under one roof and the overall command
of Heinrich Himmler. The *Kripo* was made Department V of the new
security organization, and the Gestapo Department IV. Nebe did not
like working in close proximity to Himmler, whom he considered a
contemptuous little man. He now began to voice his misgivings to a
close circle of confederates and expressed his desire to resign. They
urged him to stay on, however, and argued he was ideally placed to
monitor Himmler's activities and catalogue the atrocities carried out in
the name of National Socialism. He remained at his post, performing
his duties, including designating who from among the recaptured Sagan
prisoners would be shot. Four months later, in July 1944, he actively
took part in the bomb plot to kill Hitler and was tasked with assassinat-
ing Himmler. When the plot proved a failure, Nebe fled Berlin and faked
his suicide on the shore of Wannsee Lake, leaving a suitcase full of his
possessions at the water's edge. The ruse failed, and he was soon arrested
and tried. He met his end in March 1945, hanged by piano wire from
a meat hook in Berlin's Plötzensee Prison.

McKenna could now cross the top man off his list, but it brought
him little satisfaction. Although he had paid a price, Nebe would
never answer for his complicity in the killings. McKenna wondered
what Nebe would have said; what argument would he have put
forward as his defense? Why would a man who supposedly opposed
Hitler play a role in such an atrocity? McKenna knew from various
British Intelligence assessments that Nebe had bloodied his hands
before the Sagan murders. Between 1941 and 1942, he commanded

Einsatzgruppen B, an SS death squad in occupied Russia—one of four such squads operating in Eastern Europe. Under Nebe's leadership, *Einsatzgruppen* B slaughtered 46,000 Jews, Gypsies, and others deemed undesirable by the Reich. How would Nebe have explained this apparent dichotomy?

On another investigative front, the search continued for Gestapo *Gruppenführer* Heinrich Müller, last seen alive in Hitler's bunker. Flight Sergeant Daniel tracked down the brother of Müller's onetime secretary Babette Helmut. The brother said his sister had voluntarily surrendered and was now in American custody. It would do no good questioning her, he said, for she knew nothing of Müller's whereabouts. He instead told Daniel to speak with Müller's sister, who ran into the wanted man's wife after the war. Frau Müller said her husband had killed himself as the Red Army fought its way into Berlin. Helmut's brother gave Daniel Frau Müller's address, a street in the Munich suburb of Pasing. Upon driving there, Daniel discovered that the brother had slipped him a fake address. He eventually tracked the woman down to a small house she shared with her mother. Taking into account the reputation of Frau Müller's husband, Daniel showed up at the house with a heavily armed police contingent and raided the premises. They found no evidence of Heinrich. The man's wife seemed hardly concerned with the true nature of his fate. She told Daniel her marriage had not been a happy one and that she took little interest in her husband's business. She had fled Berlin in February 1945 to escape the advancing Red Army. One month later, her husband paid her a brief visit. That was the last time the two had seen each other. Just recently, she said, her father-in-law had received a letter from a woman purporting to be Müller's mistress, claiming the man had killed himself. Frau Müller identified the woman as Anny Schmid and said she lived at Schützenstrasse 4, apartment 3, in the Berlin borough of Steglitz. She also gave Daniel the address of Müller's father, Kolonie 2, Rembrandtstrasse 22, Pasing. That, she said, was all the information she had to give.

Daniel left and went to see the father. A search of the house turned up nothing. Müller's nineteen-year-old son, Reinhardt, a *Wehrmacht* veteran who saw action in the war's final months, now lived with his grandparents. He told Daniel the Americans had imprisoned him at the end of the war. Once they had established that he held no fanatical points of view and was not a threat to the public, they let him go. Like his mother, Reinhardt said he last saw his father in Berlin three months before the capitulation. In early May, a letter from Heinrich arrived postmarked April 28. The letter, the son said, had since been lost. Daniel, through his interpreter, asked Müller senior for the letter he had received from Frau Schmid. The man complied with Daniel's request—but only after some hesitation. As Daniel listened to his interpreter read the letter aloud, he understood why:

My relations have told me of your visits and your nosey questions. During all my thirty-two years, I have never known such a cheek. It is a shame that Heinrich is dead to have to undergo such experiences. H. would be very angry if he knew of your present conduct.

However, I have no wish to quarrel with you, only to give a clear statement of fact. You will forgive me if I do not go into the details of H.'s awful last days . . . because my attitude to you has changed after your recent behavior. I only hope your wife knows nothing of your shady activities. I want to at least keep my faith in H.'s dear loving mother.

You are very curious about his bank account and my allowance.

I could afford to pay for my own holidays and for his leaves as well. As for my fur coats—what are insinuating about my fur coats? I still have the receipts in my possession. The same goes for all your other insinuations.

The whole of the private property including furniture, bank account, etc., were confiscated by the State. What [Heinrich] and I intended to keep after the Russian occupation were one carpet and two photographs, which I wanted to keep as a souvenir, and later as a keepsake for Reinhardt.

As for your fairy tales about your poor wife having to go out as a washerwoman, find somebody else to tell them to. You must

*think that my relations and I were born stupid. Even if your wife
does have to set her hand to earning a living, she has been doing
for only one year what I have been doing all my life. Perhaps you
will bear that in mind, Herr Müller.*

In the same letter, Schmid addressed Müller's mother and offered
condolences for the loss of her son. "We were together until the very
last moments of his life," she wrote, implying she had been there when
Müller killed himself. Daniel, impressed by Schmid's moxie, ordered
continuous surveillance on the woman's flat but decided not to confront
her personally. If her reference to Müller's death was a ploy to throw
off Allied authorities, Daniel doubted she would confess to such a thing
under interrogation.

While the hunt for Müller stalled, McKenna could at least find
solace in crossing another high-profile name of the RAF's most wanted
list. On June 14, 1946, the Russians finally confirmed that they had
Scharpwinkel. Negotiations now began to schedule an interrogation.
The British, wanting "an expert" to handle the questioning, assigned
the task to Captain M. S. Cornish of the Intelligence Corps, an interrogator at the London Cage. In late June, the Ministry of Armed Forces
of the USSR agreed to grant Cornish access. Cornish now scrambled
to get himself a last-minute visa for the trip and debated what to wear.
On July 2, the Foreign Office sent a cipher to its Moscow representative
asking, "Should Captain C. wear mufti or uniform?" The first interrogation took place on August 31, in a sparsely furnished room in the
Building of the Procurator of the Soviet Union in Moscow. Four
German-and-English-speaking Russian officers watched the proceedings. Scharpwinkel, tall and gaunt, his body bent and his hair thin
and gray, sat shackled at a long table. In a corner of the room, a secretary readied herself at a typewriter. The Russians told Cornish that
prisoner intimidation would not be allowed due to Scharpwinkel's frag-
ile health.

Scharpwinkel spoke matter-of-factly and told Cornish he had placed
Lux in command of the Breslau murder squad. He also named two

other men—Knappe and Kiske—and said that they, along with Lux, assumed the role of gunmen. He implicated Max Wielen, claiming the onetime Breslau *Kripo* chief was disappointed that the Gestapo—and not the *Kripo*—had been charged with executing recaptured prisoners. Cornish sent the information back to Lieutenant Colonel Scotland at the London Cage, where the sixty-four-year-old Wielen currently awaited trial. Scotland took the signed statement to Wielen, who had never come fully clean as to his role in the Breslau murders. Scotland hoped Wielen, faced with Scharpwinkel's allegations, would "come across with some admission about his own activities." Wielen read the statement and angrily cast it aside.

"It's a damn swindle," Wielen screamed, "it's lies, all of it! You have fabricated this to put me in an awkward position."

"Look at the signature, Wielen," Scotland said. "See for yourself. That story has been written and signed by Scharpwinkel."

"I don't believe you," Wielen said. "The whole thing is a swindle."

Scotland, fighting to maintain his composure, leaned across the table.

"If you were not the old man that you are, Wielen, and if I were not the old man that I am," he said, "I'd give you a punch on the nose for suggesting I'm swindling you."

The Russians allowed Cornish to interrogate Scharpwinkel twice. The second interrogation took place on September 19.

"I believe," said Scharpwinkel, "that in my district twenty-seven shootings took place."

Shortly after the escape, an order from Berlin had reached Scharpwinkel's office stipulating that six of the British officers recaptured in the Breslau area were to be shot. Lux, said Scharpwinkel, retrieved prisoners from the Görlitz jail "in order to carry out his mission."

"The first six were shot in the neighborhood of Görlitz, the others, I cannot say for certain, in the region of Liegnitz or Breslau," Scharpwinkel said. "After each shooting, Lux reported to me that the order had been carried out. He told me also the approximate locality of the shooting. At the same time, he laid before me the teleprint destined for

Berlin, which went out as Top Secret as directed and which only I was allowed to sign. It contained only the following text: 'The British PW (followed by name) was shot at _____ hours, near (followed by name of locality) while again attempting to escape.' Further details did not interest me, particularly as they were not explicitly asked for from Berlin. Other important work of a police nature prevented me from asking Lux for detailed particulars."

Scharpwinkel said he played observer only to the first six shootings.

"My driver was Schröder," he told Cornish. "The British were brought to the headquarters. As I speak English, I put one or two questions to the prisoners while they were being interrogated: were they married? had they children? etc. Lux explained to the prisoners that by order of the Supreme Military Commander they had been sentenced to death. Then we drove away. When the Reichsautobahn was reached the summary shootings were carried out. Everybody got out. The prisoners were placed in position. It was revealed to them that the sentence was about to be carried out. The prisoners showed considerable calm, which surprised me very much. The six prisoners stood next to one another in the wood. Lux gave the order to fire and the detachment fired. Lux shot with them. By the second salvo, the prisoners were dead."

Based on information provided by airmen imprisoned in Görlitz after the escape, Cornish knew that the first six men shot were Flying Officers Al Hake and Porokuro Patapu "Johnny" Pohe, Squadron Leader Ian Cross, and Flight Lieutenants Mike Casey, Thomas Leigh, and George Wiley.

"As regards my activities and those of all the accused of my HQ, I should like to say I hope that whoever is judging the matter will take into account the condition in Germany, and the fact that soldiers and officials in Germany who had taken the oath had to obey every order," Scharpwinkel said. "Non-compliance would have resulted in court-martial proceedings."

Negotiations began immediately to transfer Scharpwinkel into British custody. If Scharpwinkel was not brought to trial, it would be impossible for the RAF to "account for the murder of 29 out of the 50 British officers concerned." The British, in a show of good faith, turned over to the Russians forty-three Germans formerly employed at the Sachsenhausen concentration camp in Oranienburg, twenty-three of whom "held positions of importance on the camp staff." Established in 1936 some twenty-one miles north of Berlin, the camp was a training facility for SS officers who went on to serve at other camps. It was "intended to set a standard for other concentration camps, both in its design and the treatment of prisoners." Thousands of Red Army prisoners ended up in Sachsenhausen. Of the thirty thousand inmates who died of disease, starvation, and execution, the majority were Russians. Two days before Soviet forces liberated Sachsenhausen on April 22, 1945, thirty-three thousand inmates vacated the camp on a forced march to the northeast. The guards shot those who, weakened by malnutrition and barbaric mistreatment, collapsed. Most prisoners did not survive. The camp now lay in the Russian Zone of Occupation and was being used as an internment facility by the NKVD, who showed little mercy to those under their charge.

After three months of bureaucratic back-and-forth, Soviet authorities informed the British government they could have Scharpwinkel if they tracked down "the former Counselor of the German Embassy in Moscow, Von Walter Hephart, and Engineer Lieutenant Gershkov Michael Vasilievich, who . . . committed a serious crime in the Soviet Union." The Russians refused to elaborate on the nature of the crime. Unwilling to hand the two men over on the basis of such a vague accusation, the British turned down the Soviet request. Consequently, negotiations to extradite Scharpwinkel stalled. The Soviets held on to their prisoner, much to McKenna's frustration. Following his statements to Cornish, Scharpwinkel was hospitalized with pneumonia and pleurisy. It seemed the man would never answer for his crimes—at least not in a British court.

Nothing about the Breslau case was straightforward. Scharpwinkel, in his statement, said he was present only at the execution of the first six prisoners taken from the Görlitz jail. The RAF tracked down

Scharpwinkel's deputy, SS Officer Erwin Wieczorek, whose scarred upper lip twitched when he spoke. He told investigators he remembered Scharpwinkel being present at the shooting deaths of Pilot Officer Sortiros "Nick" Skanziklas and Flight Lieutenants Antoni Kiewnarski and James Wernham. He said Lux and Scharpwinkel retrieved the men from a prison in Hirschberg. The party traveled in four cars, with Scharpwinkel and his driver taking the lead. Although he could not remember the date, he recalled it was an evening in late March, sometime after six. As they drove along a forested road, Scharpwinkel's car came to a slow stop in the middle of the lane. Wieczorek, in his car, watched Scharpwinkel's driver exit the lead vehicle and check under the hood. Scharpwinkel also got out and said they were having engine trouble. He ordered everyone out of the cars and demanded that the prisoners stand between the second and third vehicles in the convoy. Wieczorek wandered up to Scharpwinkel's car, where the driver still toiled beneath the hood. In a quiet tone, he told Wieczorek that Scharpwinkel had instructed him to stage the breakdown. The driver pretended to work on the engine for another ten minutes or so, as Wieczorek watched over his shoulder. The sound of screaming and machine-gun fire startled Wieczorek and drew his attention down the line of cars. The glare of headlights made it hard to see what was happening. He and the driver ran to where the shots had been fired and witnessed a scene of pandemonium.

"The officials were running around excitedly," Wieczorek said. "I saw a number of officials running around on the field adjoining the road, and they were shining torches on dark shadows which were lying in the field. The last car turned round and set off at great speed towards Hirschberg. I heard somebody report to Scharpwinkel, 'They are all dead.'"

Wieczorek was taken into British custody and charged with complicity in the killings. His capture proved only a small victory. The Russian refusal to hand over Scharpwinkel was not McKenna's only frustration with the Breslau investigation. Most of the gunmen—identified by Scharpwinkel in his statements to Cornish—were dead, killed in battle during the final days of the war. Information reached McKenna via an informant that one executioner, a man named Laeufer, had committed suicide. McKenna was skeptical. Through an associate who last saw Laeufer two days before the German surrender, McKenna learned that the man was eager to reunite with his wife and child. Laeufer's wife lived in Berchtesgaden and said that the last she had heard, her husband was making his way home. In the event, Laeufer never showed up and was now presumed to be hiding under a false name. Even more frustrating for McKenna was the death of *Kriminalobersekretär* Lux, the chief executioner. Two eyewitnesses traced by McKenna's team confirmed that Lux had died fighting in Scharpwinkel's unit in Breslau. McKenna was bitterly disappointed. More than half the Sagan escapees had died at the hands of men who would never answer for their deeds.

Four years after the event, the RAF tracked down Scharpwinkel's driver, Robert Schröder, who said his superior witnessed the shooting of the ten officers taken from the Görlitz jail on March 31. The prisoners— Flight Lieutenants Edgar Humphreys, George McGill, Cyril Swain, Charles Hall, Patrick Langford, and Brian Evans, and Flying Officers "Wally" Valenta, A. Kolanowski, Robert Stewart, and Henry Birkland— were loaded into the back of a military transport truck. On the Sagan road, halfway to the camp, the truck pulled over so the men could relieve themselves. The weather that night was frigid. Scharpwinkel, riding with Schröder in the lead vehicle, got out of the car and walked to where the officers stood on the shoulder of the road, stomping their feet in an effort to keep warm. Dr. Gunther Absalon and Lux, armed with machine guns, stood nearby with their weapons at the ready. "The lorry stood forty meters behind me," Schröder said. "I was sitting alone in the car when I suddenly heard shouts followed immediately by a mad firing of machine pistols. I jumped out of the car and ran to the rear. Behind the lorry lay the prisoners scattered on the ground. Some of them were right on the road, others were on a slope nearby, but they were all close together. When I had asked one of the officials what had happened, he said that some of the fellows had tried to escape and that they had all caught it."

Schröder's statement confirmed the RAF's long-held suspicion that Absalon "not only investigated the escape from Stalag Luft III but had participated in the shootings."

By the end of 1946, McKenna and his team had yet to nail down any solid leads on Absalon's whereabouts. If alive, he most likely had a new identity and corresponding papers.

TWELVE

ALONE

In the days that followed the murders, prisoners at Stalag Luft III loitered about the camp bulletin board in the freezing drizzle and studied the list of names. The grim roll call hung alongside a poster declaring, "To All Prisoners of War: The escape from prison camp is no longer a sport." The rain and damp had by now smeared many names on the list, but among those still legible was twenty-three-year-old Flight Lieutenant Anthony Hayter's. Numerous attempts by the RAF to ascertain Hayter's fate had only met with disappointment. No urn bearing his name ever arrived at the camp. The absence of any information meant the RAF had no point of reference upon which to build an investigation.

Prior to the war, Hayter indulged his love of sports on the squash and tennis courts—but his true passion lay in the clouds. When Hayter was nine, his stepbrother took him up in a biplane. The exhilarating speed and the wind against his face, the towns and people a distant vision below, ignited a love affair with flying. He joined the peacetime RAF in 1938 and began his pilot training the following year. In April 1940, the RAF sent him with No. 57 Squadron to Northern France, where he flew his first combat operation on May 10. Flying reconnaissance over the Dutch-German frontier, Hayter's Blenheim was attacked by three Messerschmitts. He threw the bomber about the sky in a desperate effort to evade enemy fire. The Messerschmitts stayed on his tail, guns blazing, but were forced to give up the chase when their fuel ran low. Hayter managed a safe return to base despite his bomber having 237 holes in the wings and fuselage. Shortly thereafter, he returned to Britain and was sent to Scotland to serve with Coastal Command. Again, luck seemed to be on his side. Prior to a practice flight, a Wellington bomber collided with Hayter's Blenheim on the runway. One of the Wellington's propellers sliced into Hayter's plane and severed his navigator's arm. Hayter pulled the wounded man from the flaming wreckage and saved the navigator's life. The RAF eventually stationed Hayter in the Middle East with No. 148 Squadron, a Wellington unit. He survived a crash landing in the desert in early 1942 when one of his plane's two engines gave out. On April 24, 1942, his bomber went down over Sicily. He escaped the crash without injury but was quickly seized by the Germans. He arrived at Stalag Luft III one week later.

For months, McKenna's team stumbled blindly along, groping at the faintest of leads in Hayter's case, with disappointment always being the end result. Only recently, in August 1946, had information emerged that might point to a resolution. In the London Cage, Lieutenant Colonel Scotland had decided to interrogate for a second time Walter Herberg—charged in the killing of Flying Officer Dennis Cochran—to see if any pertinent information had come to his mind since his last interrogation. At the behest of his captors, Herberg again recalled Cochran's murder in detail and, as Scotland had hoped, divulged something new. Herberg said that after the killing, he was ordered to the Central Security Office in Berlin to report Cochran's murder to Gestapo Chief Müller. While there, he saw other Gestapo officials who he presumed were visiting on similar business. This he had mentioned in his previous statement, but he now recalled having recognized a man named Heinrich Hilker, an agent with the Strasbourg Gestapo.

It was the first time in the investigation anyone had mentioned Strasbourg. All the RAF knew about Hayter following the breakout had come from surviving escapees who reported last seeing him traveling in the direction of Mülhausen, which would have taken him near Strasbourg. The information from Herberg was relayed to Bowes, who cautioned McKenna the development "should be treated with reserve." Then, in February 1947, French Army investigators shared with the British a document discovered after the war in the archives of the German Gendarmerie Detachment of Mülhausen, near the Rhine. The document did not reveal who murdered Hayter, but it did provide details of his arrest:

Detachment of the Mülhausen   Zillisheim, 31st March 1944

Gendarmerie at Zillisheim

Daily Log Book Reference 46/44

To the HQ of the Gendarmerie at Mülhausen/Alsace

Subject: Arrest of the escapee English Captain (Air Force) Anthony Hayter.

Reference: Blitz-Fs. Breslau Number 4817 dated 25 March 1944, search for 80 escaped British Air Force Officers.

On 27 March 1944, at about 8:30 a.m., the escapee [Flight Lieutenant] Anthony Hayter was stopped by the 3 Home Guard men Alfred Herrmann, Jakob Herrman and Ferdinand Wacker on the road between Mülhausen and Altkirch, and his papers were checked. Whilst checking his papers, the above-mentioned Home Guard men noticed that he was a foreigner and that the papers purported to be those of a Danish national. The Home

Guard men had the strictest order to take every foreigner to the Gendarmerie Detachment and, for this reason, the suspicious foreigner was taken to the Gendarmerie Detachment at Zillisheim.

When I checked his papers more closely, I noticed that the pass he had was false, that it had several office stamps of different colours and that it purposed to be made out at the Police Headquarters at Leipzig. The photograph was unsatisfactory and Leipzig was spelt with a 'ch' at the end.

When I put it to the escapee that he had false papers, he admitted to be a Captain in the English Air Force who had escaped from Sagan on 24 March 1944. I then arrested the escapee and notified the Gendarmerie at Mülhausen. Soon after that, the escapee was taken to Mülhausen and brought before the officer in charge of the Gendarmerie there.

Names, addresses and personal data of the 3 Home Guard men who arrested the escapee and brought him to the Headquarters Detachment are as follows:

1. *Alfred Hermann, farmer, born 22.9.1906 in Zillisheim, who was in charge of the patrol.*
2. *Jakob Hermann, farmer, born 21.2.1904 in Zillisheim, Home Guard man.*
3. *Ferdinand Wacker, electrician, born 19.1.1915 in Zillisheim.*

The N.C.O. i/c of the Detachment of Gendarmerie
Signed, Welter
Meister of the Gendarmerie

Welter, the document's author, was in French custody and awaiting trial on war crimes. "It would be very useful," read a hand-scribbled note in French at the bottom of the document, "to know whether the English Colonel Hayter is still alive in order to get from him more precise information as to what happened after he had been arrested in the manner described above."

Over the proceeding weeks, McKenna's men made extensive inquiries in and around Strasbourg. Agents who served in the local *Kripo* and Gestapo at the time of the killing were located in area prisons with the help of the French *Departement des Crimes de Guerre* and interrogated without result. Among those questioned was *Obersturmführer* Julius Gehrum, a man who took apparent pride in his role as "executioner for the Strasbourg Gestapo." With at least twenty confessed murders to his name, Gehrum told Flight Lieutenant Harrison that had orders been received for the shooting of any person by the local Gestapo, he would have been the triggerman. Harrison voiced his disgust at the man's willingness to kill. When done with his statement, the Nazi asked Harrison—a former navigator with Bomber Command—if he had flown against Dresden. Harrison answered in the affirmative. The city, bombed by the Americans and British on February 13–14, 1945, suffered a fiery holocaust that all but wiped out the ancient capital of Saxony and killed an estimated fifty thousand people. Why, Gehrum wanted to know, had Harrison taken part in the raid? Harrison answered that if he had not flown the operation, he would have been court-martialed for disobeying orders. The German, satisfied, flashed Harrison a grim smile. The RAF man balked. Yes, he acknowledged a certain legitimacy in the other man's point, but the two scenarios could hardly be considered the same. One was an order to commit murder, cold and ruthless; the other, to execute a strategic operation of war. Indeed, obeying orders was only a legitimate defense if one could properly argue that the order was lawful.

Reaching out to the Americans for any leads, Harrison learned that former Strasbourg Gestapo Chief Alfred Schimmel was being held in War Crimes Cage 29 at Dachau. Schimmel told Harrison during interrogation that he was appointed chief in May 1942 but resigned the following year. Consequently, he knew nothing about the Hayter affair. Harrison traveled to Paris and reviewed Schimmel's personnel file on record with CROWCASS (Central Registry of War Criminals and Security Suspects), which revealed he had stayed with the Gestapo until May 1944. When confronted with this evidence, Schimmel said he had lied previously out of fear he might be charged in connection with the mass murders of paratroopers in the Elzas.

"Shortly after the end of the war," he said, "rumors were heard in Munich that mass-shootings had taken place and that arrests—especially in Gestapo circles—could be expected."

His lie exposed, Schimmel said he was summoned to Berlin on official business in early March 1944 and remained there for three weeks. When he returned from his trip, he learned from one of his deputies that an agent named Heinrich Hilker had been dispatched on a "special mission" to Breslau. He had left two days before Schimmel's return, escorting "a man caught on the frontier during the *Fahndung*." Hilker returned three days later but said little of his recent expedition. His reluctance to discuss the journey piqued Schimmel's curiosity. When questioned directly, Hilker insisted his mission had involved nothing out of the ordinary. In the days that followed, Schimmel said, he grew increasingly suspicious when rumors in the office suggested the airman had "been shot by Hilker whilst trying to escape."

He claimed to know nothing of any official order from Berlin demanding the execution of recaptured airmen. After leaving the Gestapo, he heard from various sources that Hilker had assumed command of a sabotage unit comprised of operatives from the the intelligence service of the SS. Hilker was shot while fighting in the Vosges Mountains and taken to Baden to recover. Schimmel said a former Gestapo colleague told him he had seen Hilker's false identity papers, which made him out to be seven years younger than his actual age and identified him as a furniture packer.

"In the beginning of 1945, Hilker's wife had a second baby and Hilker tried to get her to Neufeld, near Zaban," Schimmel said. "He did not succeed, and he sent her back to her parents in a village near Karlsruhe."

Schimmel described Hilker for inclusion on the RAF's wanted list:

Height 1.90 M., slim build athletic, pale face, dark hair turning gray, age 42-44, heavy smoker and drinker, clean shaven, no glasses, speaks with a pronounced dialect from Karlsruhe, no peculiarities.

Done with Schimmel, Harrison drove to Strasbourg to examine records at the city's crematorium. He found nothing relating to Hayter's murder. "All the entries are in name form," he wrote in a report, "except for a number of serials, which denote the cremation of bodies from the Anatomical Section at the Natzweiler Concentration Camp. These bodies were brought in by the Gestapo and were in batches; no single body having ever been brought in by the Gestapo. The two men at the crematorium in March 1944 had no recollection of any single body being brought in wearing foreign underclothes or articles of foreign clothing." In the Prison Militaire, Strasbourg, Flight Sergeant Williams found and interviewed a man named Rudolf Peters. Peters joined the local Gestapo in December 1941 and attained the rank of *Kriminalsekretär* with Department IIB, which dealt with civilians who helped POWs on the run. Peters said the head of this department was *Kriminalkommissar* Max Dissner, who in turn reported to Schimmel. It was a morning in late March or early April 1944, Peters said, when Schimmel summoned him to a meeting. Gathered in Schimmel's office were Dissner and an agent from the local *Kripo*. A young man in civilian clothing, his face thin beneath an unruly mop of blond hair, sat in a chair and faced Schimmel across the expanse of a large desk. Peters guessed him to be no more than twenty-eight years old. Schimmel thrust a finger in the man's direction and told Peters, "That's an English Air Force officer."

"In my presence, the Air Force officer was asked a few questions by both Schimmel and the *Kripo kommissar*—both of whom spoke a little English," Peters said. "The Air Force officer gave short replies and refused to give any information. I was then ordered by Schimmel to take the man to my room for the time being."

Schimmel and the *Kripo* agent again attempted to interrogate the prisoner in Peters's room. The airman would only admit that he had recently escaped from Stalag Luft III in Sagan. All questions aimed at

determining how the men escaped and how they obtained civilian clothing and travel papers met with stubborn silence.

After forty-five futile minutes, Schimmel ordered Peters to place the
airman in a cell downstairs. Peters and the *Kripo* agent marched the
officer to the holding area below and locked him behind a cast-iron
door. Later that day, at about three in the afternoon, Peters happened
to glance out the window near his desk into the courtyard below and
saw his immediate supervisor, Max Dissner, get into a waiting car with
Hilker and the airman and drive away. He approached Dissner that
evening and asked where they had gone. The prisoner's suitcase was
still sitting in Peters's room. Dissner, in a foul mood, told Peters to mind
his own business.

"Stop asking questions I cannot tell you anything about," he
snapped.

Peters did not push the subject, and he retired to his quarters for
the evening. Half an hour later, Dissner entered the room and retrieved
the airman's suitcase, which contained only dirty laundry. The Gestapo,
Peters told Williams, did not file any official paperwork regarding Hayter's capture. He knew nothing more about the matter.

It was clear from Peters's take on events that Schimmel had lied
in his second statement to RAF investigators. Harrison and Williams returned to Dachau to interrogate him again. Shown Peters's
handwritten statement, Schimmel now confessed to knowing more
than he had originally let on. Yes, he had been away from Strasbourg
at the time of Hayter's arrest, but he returned to find the airman in
custody. Soon thereafter, a communiqué arrived from Müller in Berlin demanding that the prisoner be executed. Schimmel said he
phoned Müller to protest. His superior was adamant the airman die
and accused Schimmel of being "soft." Schimmel said Müller threatened
him with death by firing squad if he failed to carry out the order. Schimmel hung up the phone and pondered his next move. He could always
take the airman by car to the Swiss border and allow him to escape.
Schimmel said he seriously considered the matter and even entertained
the idea of disappearing into Switzerland himself to escape the

repercussions from Berlin. Thoughts of his wife and children, however, made him drop any such notion. Instead, he dispatched two men— Hilker and Dissner—to drive in the direction of Natzweiler concentration camp, kill Hayter somewhere nearby, and have the body destroyed in the camp oven. The killing was initially planned to take place on Good Friday—but committing the act on such a holy day troubled Schimmel, who decided to have the airman shot a day earlier, on Maundy Thursday.

The men took Hayter away by car and returned the following day. They told Schimmel they drove Hayter to a heavily wooded area less than a mile from Natzweiler. They walked him to a point beyond the tree line and told him to relieve himself. Dissner distracted the airman with casual banter. Hilker, standing behind the prisoner, pulled a Walther from his overcoat and fired point-blank into Hayter's temple. They lugged the body back to the car and drove to the camp. The body was incinerated and the ashes placed in an unmarked urn and shipped back to Stalag Luft III.

The Americans handed Schimmel over to the British, who shipped him off to the London Cage to await trial. The focus now shifted to finding Hilker and Dissner. The Special Air Service traced Frau Mathilde Hilker and questioned her. A woman hardened by circumstance, she surrendered no ground and professed to know nothing about her husband's current whereabouts. Her interrogators, convinced she was lying, approached the U.S. Counter Intelligence Department in Karlsruhe and asked that her mail be monitored. Local inquiries about town turned up a family named Brenck at Humboldtstrasse 25, who had taken Hilker in at war's end and helped him nurse a gunshot wound to the left shoulder. Nearby lived Hilker's mother, who assumed her son to be dead or in hiding.

It would be another twenty years before investigators could close the book on the Hayter case. Not until May 11, 1948, did the RAF catch up with Dissner, living in Hamburg under an alias. He was arrested without incident and taken to the British war crimes prison in Minden. In his cell, he fashioned a noose from a torn piece of bedding and hanged himself before his interrogation. West German authorities eventually tracked Hilker down in 1966 and put him on trial for Hayter's murder. He was acquitted two days before Christmas and went a free man.

THIRTEEN

THE ORDER OF THE BLOOD

In the days following the mass breakout, the Gestapo delivered four urns to Stalag Luft III, each adorned with a single Roman numeral in place of a name and location of cremation. The consecutive numbering on the urns, I to IV, suggested that the four victims had died together. A method of elimination determined the urns most likely belonged to Squadron Leader James Catanach, Royal Australian Air Force; Pilot Officer Arnold Christensen, Royal New Zealand Air Force; and Lieutenants Hallada Espelid and Nils Fuglesang of the Royal Norwegian Air Force. No one knew their decided course of action after fleeing the tunnel. Indeed, a shroud of mystery obscured everything about the killings.

As a young boy, James Catanach charmed friends and family with his easy smile and relaxed humor. He enjoyed athletics and adventure, spending his summer vacations exploring the rugged brush of Victoria's Mount Macedon and the volcanic terrain of Hanging Rock. It was a hunger for excitement that prompted him at eighteen to join the air force when war broke out in Europe. Before shipping off, Catanach gave his cousin a treasured family heirloom, a broken antique pocket watch. "Take care of it," he said, "and I'll fix it for you when I come home."

He arrived in England in April 1941 after completing his flight training in Australia and Canada. Posted to No. 455 Squadron—the first Australian bomber squadron—he soon developed a reputation for his steel composure and brazen flying. It was not uncommon for his Hampden bomber to return from an operation ravaged by flak. On the night of March 13, 1942, Catanach and his crew took off for the killing skies over Cologne, Germany's fourth-largest city, behind Berlin, Hamburg, and Munich. There was no moon as the 135 bombers winged their way across the North Sea. Catanach and his crew passed through the European coastal defenses without incident and turned on course for the final run to the target. The leading aircrews dropped green and red flares and incendiary bombs to adequately mark the target area.

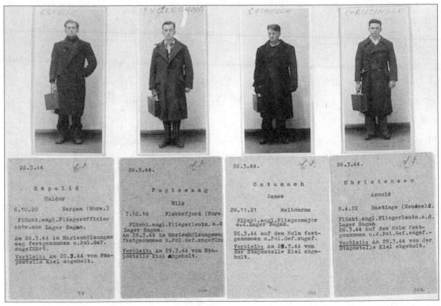

Photographs of Lieutenants Hallada Espelid and Nils Fuglesang, Squadron Leader James Catanach, and Pilot Officer Arnold Christensen taken by the *Kripo* shortly after their arrest in Flensburg. **BRITISH NATIONAL ARCHIVES: WO 235/431**

Searchlights canvassed the sky as Catanach steadied the Hampden on its attack run and followed the slight alterations to the course suggested by the bomb aimer in the nose of the aircraft.

Bombs finally gone, dropped into a sea of fire, Catanach turned the Hampden for home. As he put distance between his bomber and the target, a piece of flak punctured the Hampden's nose and smashed its way into the cockpit, wounding Catanach and leaving him partially blinded. "Boys," he said calmly into his mic, "I think we'd better be getting home now." For his bravery and skill, Catanach was promoted to flight lieutenant less than one month later. In June, he was awarded the Distinguished Flying Cross and became, at the age of twenty, the youngest squadron leader in the RAAF. His squadron had by now transferred from Bomber to Coastal Command as a torpedo-bomber squadron. He and his crew spent two months training in their new role, patrolling the North Sea and attacking enemy shipping when the opportunity presented itself. In September 1942, the squadron flew to Murmansk in Russia on a special mission to target German warships preying on Allied Arctic convoys. The planes took off from Scotland on the night of September 4. Over Vadso, with only an hour flight time remaining, anti-aircraft fire struck Catanach's Hampden, taking out an engine and puncturing a fuel tank.

Losing altitude, Catanach was forced to bring the bomber down on a flat expanse of open wilderness. The uninjured crew climbed out and encountered a group of soldiers dressed in white winter gear devoid of any military markings. It was just their misfortune that the men were members of a German patrol. Catanach and his crew, promptly captured, were shipped almost immediately to Germany. By September, the young Australian, still only twenty, found himself behind the wire in Stalag Luft III. Not long after his arrival, he met another twenty-year-old pilot, Pilot Officer Arnold Christensen of the Royal New Zealand Air Force.

Like Catanach, Christensen was eighteen when he joined the service. He earned his wings and commission in 1942 and arrived in Britain in March of that year. For one who had always loved learning, the island's ancient architecture and monuments to history proved to be a source of endless fascination. He spent his first couple of months flying single-engine fighters with an operational training unit, before being posted to No. 26 Squadron. He hardly had time to settle into his new surroundings. On August 19, six days after his arrival on base, Christensen took off on a reconnaissance flight over Dieppe. It was his first operational flight against the enemy. More than six thousand soldiers—mostly Canadians supported by the Royal Navy—had stormed the Dieppe beaches that morning with the aim of temporarily seizing the port. Christensen and his wingman flew the last two sorties of the day and thundered low over the beach in their Mustangs to assess the field of battle. For twenty minutes they circled overhead while maneuvering through flak and small-arms fire from enemy troops below. Several rounds found their mark and struck both aircraft. The men turned their fighters for home, but Christensen's wingman went down in the English Channel. Christensen struggled to maintain altitude—but to no avail. As the engine began stuttering and the nose dipped toward the water, Christensen bailed out. He landed in the Channel uninjured, inflated his emergency dinghy, and climbed aboard. He remained adrift for two days before washing ashore on the French coast, where German soldiers soon captured him. He then joined the ranks of other inmates at Stalag Luft III.

Christensen's family was of Danish lineage. In captivity, he exchanged letters with loved ones in Denmark. When Roger Bushell's X-Organization launched preparations for the mass breakout, Christensen joined the committee's intelligence section. Its task was to gather information on all parts of Europe that might prove useful to escapees on the run. Christensen collected intelligence on Denmark. Gathering information for the committee on Norway was twenty-four-year-old Lieutenant Hallada Espelid, who had escaped to England by boat when the Germans invaded his home country in April 1940. He joined the Royal Norwegian Air Force the following year and was flying Spitfires with No. 331 Squadron by 1942. On August 27 that year, while he was on a reconnaissance operation over Dunkirk, flak struck Espelid's Spitfire and forced him down in the Pas de Calais. The Germans captured him as he staggered from the wreckage. After arriving at Stalag Luft III, he met Lieutenant Nils Fuglesang, a fellow countryman who had also fled to Britain in the war's early days and wound up flying Spitfires for the Royal Norwegian Air Force.

Fuglesang's war came to an end on May 2, 1943, while flying his eighty-fifth sortie. Over Flushing, he engaged a Focke-Wulf 190. The enemy aircraft charged Fuglesang's Spitfire in a frontal attack. Cannon fire set Fuglesang's machine ablaze. In the smoke-filled cockpit, he struggled only briefly with the controls before realizing the fighter was lost. He bailed out and came down in a field, not far from where a German Army unit happened to be training. Soldiers were soon marching him off at gunpoint.

McKenna charged Flight Lieutenant Lyon with the Kiel investigation, which commenced in earnest in September 1946. Lyon, accompanied by interpreter Van Giessen, arrived in the city with little to go on. No witnesses, no named suspects. From the Intelligence Division of the BAOR (British Army of the Rhine), Lyon had with him a copy of the Kiel Gestapo's "battle order," a comprehensive listing of names and ranks. A considerable number of those listed were already in camps scattered throughout the British Zone. It fell on Lyon to work his way through the list and identify those who had played a direct role in the killings.

On his first day, he stopped by the city's crematorium and questioned the long-serving keeper. Arthur Schafer seemed not the least bit surprised when confronted by an officer in the dark dress blues of the Royal Air Force. He told Lyon four members of the local Gestapo had delivered four corpses to the crematorium one evening in late March 1944 and demanded they be destroyed. The agents refused to identify the victims, saying only that they were French spies arrested near Flensburg and shot while trying to escape. From his desk drawer, Schafer produced for Lyon a leather-bound volume and turned to a particular page. The date and time of the cremation were noted: 29 March 1944 at 18:30 hours. Three quarters of the way down the page, on consecutive lines, Schafer had penned the Roman numerals I through IV. Because the cremation of an individual without proper identification or police authorization was forbidden, a member of the town's administration at the time had called the Gestapo in Berlin. An official on the phone told the town clerk that the Gestapo did not require permission to conduct its own business. The clerk hung up and dialed the local police. He was surprised when the police chief said he wanted nothing to do with the matter.

"The corpses were cremated," Schafer said. "Two officials remained almost until the end of the cremation, and about one week later the urns were taken away by two Gestapo officials. The urns had no names, no dates, no cremation number, but only the figures from I to IV. I asked where the urns were going to be taken, and the officials told me they were to be sent to Berlin."

"Did you know the officials who brought the bodies to you?" Lyon asked.

"No," said Schafer. "I didn't know their names, but I might be able to recognize them. Two were in civilian clothes and two were in uniform. The official who acted as chief wore four stars on his SS uniform, so he must have been a *Sturmbannführer* or an *Obersturmbannführer*. This man ordered everyone around."

Schafer described an individual roughly five and a half feet tall, thirty-five years of age, a man of stocky—but powerful—build, with dark brown or blond hair atop a well-rounded face. Lyon made note of the specifics and asked Schafer if anything else came to mind. The keeper thought momentarily before remembering one final point. He said a Russian laborer working at the crematorium saw the bodies before they were consigned to the furnace. He whispered in Schafer's ear that he believed the dead men, based on their dress, to be British Russian said he knew an officer of the Empire when he saw one.

Schafer gave Lyon the name of the local undertaker, who still lived in town. Wilhelm Tischendorf remembered the night in question and told Lyon two Gestapo officials stopped by his house that evening and said there were four bodies lying in a field outside Kiel, near the Rotenhahn Public House. One of the Gestapo agents, when asked, told Tischendorf the deceased were British airmen who had recently taken part in the mass breakout from Stalag Luft III. Tischendorf ordered two workers to retrieve the bodies and take them to the crematorium.

"I cannot remember the date and times very clearly because all my documents were destroyed during air attacks in August 1944," he said. "I do know, however, that the bills for the transport and two coffin supports were paid by the Gestapo after several requests for payment."

The following day, Lyon and Van Giessen drove to Flensburg. The road out of town took them past the Rotenhahn Public House and the site of execution. Lyon stared out at bucolic fields and sagging barns, at meandering hedgerows and dark woodlands. Had he been ignorant of this landscape's recent history, he might have considered the scenery idyllic. Instead, he pondered his fellow officers facedown, bleeding out in the mud. They reached Flensburg in the late afternoon and sought out the headquarters of the local criminal police. Chief Paul Linke, head of police operations in Flensburg since 1927, ushered the two men into his office. He said all police departments throughout Germany received notification of the Sagan breakout on the afternoon of March 25, 1944. That night, four men—believed to be escapees—were arrested as they made their way through town. Linke said he personally interrogated the men, all of whom confessed to being British Air Force officers. The men willingly revealed their names, the time of their escape, and the route they had traveled once free of the camp.

"Concerning the escape proper, as well as the possession of false identity papers and the money they carried," Linke said, "they refused to provide detailed information."

The men were photographed and their personal details registered on an index card. Linke got up from his desk and walked to a large filing cabinet. He rifled through a drawer, pulled four cards from a folder, and handed them to Lyon. Each card bore a black-and-white mug shot in the top left-hand corner. A record number and name was typed alongside each photograph:

99/44   Halder Espelid
100/44   Nils Fuglesang
101/44   James Catanach
102/44   Arnold Christensen

"Where were they captured?" asked Lyon.

"In the built-up area of the town, in groups of two," Linke said. "Espelid and Fuglesang were arrested on the Marienhelzungsweg, and Catanach and Christensen on the Helm. I cannot state the names of the persons who at that time arrested them. The records have since been destroyed."

Berlin was duly notified of the arrests. Four days later, on March 29, Linke received word by telephone that the Gestapo would be taking the men into custody. *Sturmbannführer* Johannes Post of the Kiel Gestapo arrived at the police prison that afternoon, signed the necessary release papers, and squired the men away in a black sedan. Linke assumed the men were being returned to the camp. Not until later, when the killings hit the headlines, did he learn the truth.

Although Lyon now had a suspect to pursue—Johannes Post—the task of identifying the man's associates remained. Over the weeks that followed, Lyon tracked down two women formerly employed as typists by the Kiel Gestapo who were present when the four RAF officers were interrogated. Both confirmed Post as having conducted the questioning, but they could not identify the other Gestapo agents in the room at the time. A canvassing of internment camps in the British Zone began. At a compound in Hemer, Lyon questioned Herman Clausen, a former officer with the Security Police in Kiel. Clausen said he knew that the local Gestapo had taken four RAF men into custody but did not learn their fate until after the war. From his former senior officer, interred in the same camp, Clausen learned that Post and another man named Oskar Schmidt had removed the prisoners from the police prison in Flensburg. Inmate Erich Mueller, who once oversaw matters of security involving foreign laborers for the Flensburg Gestapo, corroborated the story.

"Officially," said Mueller, "I had nothing to do with the case, but I know that these four officers were taken away from Flensburg by members of the Kiel Gestapo a few days after their arrest. I have heard from comrades of mine that Post, Oskar Schmidt, *Kriminalassistent* Jacobs, and a few more Kiel officials carried out the transportation."

Additional combing of the camps and inmate interviews yielded the names Hans Kaehler and Franz Schmidt. Two more men, Artur Denkmann and Wilhelm Struve, were identified as being the drivers who most likely chauffeured Post and his associates about. Four of the men—Kaehler, Jacobs, and Franz and Oskar Schmidt—were currently interred at the Allied prison camp in Neuengamme. On the afternoon of October 6, 1946, Lyon and a squad of armed RAF police officers showed up at the camp to take the men into custody. The officers retrieved the Germans from their barracks but did not disclose the reason for their arrests. The four men each glanced in Lyon's direction and observed his RAF uniform as they climbed at gunpoint into the back of a military transport truck. With a grim expression, one prisoner turned to another and uttered, *"Dies sieht schlecht aus"* ("This looks bad"). The men were transferred to the holding pen in Minden, where interrogations immediately got under way.

During individual questioning, the suspects told Lyon that Kiel Gestapo chief Fritz Schmidt summoned them to his office on the afternoon of March 29, 1944, and read a teleprint from Berlin, demanding the four RAF officers recently captured in Flensburg be shot. The order was signed by Kaltenbrunner and Müller. The men were "sworn under penalty of death and degradation of their families to absolute secrecy about the whole affair." The agents traveled to Flensburg to retrieve the prisoners. The RAF men were placed in two cars, driven to the killing field just outside of town, and gunned down. The bodies were placed side by side near a hedge and left there for the local undertaker's men. That evening, they were taken to the Kiel crematorium and destroyed. Not until two weeks later did Walter Jacobs collect the urns and deliver them to the Flensburg *Kripo* for shipment to Sagan. Several months later, Fritz Schmidt summoned all participants to his office and warned them a Red Cross Commission would likely be investigating the incident. The gunmen returned to the crime scene to coordinate their stories and reconstruct the RAF officers' alleged escape attempt. Near the end of the war, as the Allies advanced on Kiel, Schmidt and Post fled the city and vanished into the post-conflict chaos.

Only Franz Schmidt, when questioned by Lyon, confessed to actively participating in the murders.   He stood several feet behind one of the RAF officers and put a bullet in the back of the man's head. He knew the prisoners were British POWs when he pulled the trigger, but there were orders to obey. Lyon sent Schmidt back to his cell with a notepad and a pencil and told him to write a full statement. Shortly thereafter, a guard checking on the inmates made a gruesome discovery. Peering into cell no. 11, he saw Schmidt, the man's shirt wrapped around his neck in a makeshift noose, hanging from a ventilation grate high in the wall. The notebook's blank pages lay scattered beneath the man's dangling feet. It appeared he had stood on a chair—the cell's only furnishing besides a cot—knotted the other end of his shirt through the bars in the grate and kicked the chair out from underneath him. The guard fetched Lyon, who, cursing, ran to the cell, grabbed Schmidt by the legs, and tried to ease the tension in the noose. The guard produced a knife, cut through the shirt, and helped Lyon lower Schmidt to the floor. Lyon placed his fingers on Schmidt's neck but felt no pulse. The prison doctor arrived with a large hypodermic needle in hand and plunged it through the chest bone, right into Schmidt's heart. "*Schlechter mann, schlechter mann*"—("Bad man, bad man")—the doctor said to himself as he worked feverishly to revive the prisoner.

Lyon got to his feet and watched the doctor wage a losing battle. The color had already drained from Schmidt's features. For several frantic minutes, the doctor remained hunched over the prisoner's prostrate form, before surrendering to the inevitable. Franz Schmidt was dead. A disgusted Lyon left the cell and ordered guards to retrieve Oskar Schmidt and Jacobs for further interrogation. Both men, as they had done during the first round of questioning, claimed they couldn't bring themselves to fire and stood a good six or seven yards back from the prisoners when Franz Schmidt and Post shot the men at point-blank range. Oskar Schmidt detailed how one of the fallen officers tried to get back on his feet, only to be shot in the head by Post. The following morning, Schmidt said, he was summoned to Chief Fritz Schmidt's office and reprimanded for not following orders.

"He told me that he would merely believe I missed my target, such was his regard for my family," Schmidt said. "He said he would accept such an excuse, otherwise he would have to report the matter to the SS *Polizeigericht*. I uttered my disgust about the shooting and Post's behavior, but Schmidt interrupted by ordering me to leave his room."

Sweating in the interrogation chair, Jacobs also played innocent. He, too, expressed his revulsion at Johannes Post's brutality and the shooting of the wounded officer. He claimed to have been so disturbed by the callousness of the act that he turned his back on the whole bloody scene. He said he then heard Post shoot the remaining three RAF men in the head one last time for good measure.

"I wish to emphasize that I am willing to swear upon the fact that I myself did not shoot," he said. "My conscience did not agree with the shooting at all, and I most definitely condemn it. I regret to have been obliged to take part in the shooting."

Kaehler, however, said the two Schmidts and Jacobs—along with Post—were directly behind the RAF men with Walther pistols in their hands and willingly took part in the killings. Post, he said, took considerable pleasure in the act.

"All of the prisoners fell forward on the ground after the shots were fired," Kaehler said. "Post noticed that one of the executed men, namely the one who, according to my memory, was lying on the extreme right of the group, still moved. Post shouted at me that I should fire a shot on this still-living man and, seeing my hesitation, took the carbine out of my hands and fired a bullet into the head of the prisoner. This shot made one single head wound from which blood and brain came protruding."

For each interrogation, Lyon arranged on the table between himself and the prisoner photographs of the four murdered men. Kaehler pointed to the picture of James Catanach and told Lyon he specifically remembered the young airman because of his proficiency in German.

"I can just as well recall the prisoner Fuglesang," said Kaehler, picking up another mug shot. "I remember him because of the gaudy woolen socks that he was wearing."

He detailed attempts by the Kiel Gestapo to cover up the crime and thwart any ensuing investigation by the Red Cross. He concluded with a familiar refrain.

"I wish to finish this statement," he said, "by emphasizing the fact that I myself did not fire one single shot from either the carbine issued to me or the duty pistol in my possession."

Lyon made arrangements to transfer the men to the London Cage, where Lieutenant Scotland's interrogation techniques would undoubtedly elicit full confessions. Before being shipped to Britain, Oskar Schmidt volunteered one final statement and conceded, perhaps to garner goodwill, that he may have fired one of the fatal shots.

"If Kaehler says that I shot, it is possible that in the shock of the moment I was not conscious of having done so," Schmidt said. "I am, however, still of the opinion that I never shot."

In the days that followed, Lyon tracked down the two drivers. Wilhelm Struve had returned to his hometown of Preetz after the war. Denkmann was confined by illness to a hospital bed in Kiel. Lyon placed an armed guard at his door until he was well enough to be transferred to Minden. Struve told Lyon he drove Oskar and Franz Schmidt, Jacobs, and three of the British officers to the killing field in a six-seat Adler. Denkmann drove Post, Kaehler, and Catanach in a Mercedes 231. Struve said he pulled in behind Post's car at the intended spot and watched the two Schmidts and Jacobs escort the prisoners from his backseat into a meadow on the opposite side of the road. When the men disappeared behind a hedgerow, Struve drove his car a short distance down the road to stop passing traffic. As he opened his car door to get out, he heard the sound of gunfire. The shots seemed to occur simultaneously, resulting in "one loud detonation." Struve drove back to the meadow. Oskar Schmidt approached the driver's side window, pointed at the hedgerow, and said, "They are lying there." A quick glance over the hedge revealed four bodies side by side in the damp grass. Post and

Denkmann returned to Kiel, Struve said, while the others stayed put until the undertaker retrieved the corpses an hour later.

"On the return journey," Struve said, "I learned from conversation in the car that Post had acted once again with particular brutality, for which he was already known. Apart from this, Oskar Schmidt mentioned that Post intended to go to the theater that same day."

Lyon now turned his full attention to locating Post and Fritz Schmidt. A progress report on the Kiel investigation sent to the provost marshal of the Air Ministry on November 18, 1946, declared: "*Sturmbannführer* Schmidt and *Kriminalkommissar* Post, both men of very bad reputation, are still at liberty. . . . The evidence obtained as to the identity of the four officers, the manner in which they were murdered and the Gestapo officials responsible for the murders is conclusive. When Schmidt and Post are located, this particular angle to the case will be complete." Lyon launched his manhunt in Hamburg. Winter had by now set in and pushed temperatures well below zero. All he had at his disposal for getting around Germany was a canvas-topped jeep, which he now took to, wrapped in multiple layers of clothing. "I believe this was the most-bitter winter of the century," Lyon later noted. "Fuel for heating was almost non-existent, and the undernourished Germans were dying like flies. In Hamburg, the authorities constructed what they called heating halls where people could go to warm up. Between Christmas 1946 and March 1947, the temperature in Germany never rose above zero." Lyon traversed the country in conditions he called "appalling" to pursue whatever leads came his way.

Temperatures in Germany dropped that winter to thirty below zero. The conditions proved fatal for roughly twelve thousand people who lacked food and shelter. Circumstances hardly improved for those with a roof over their heads: many had insufficient coal and fuel to heat their homes. "Whenever I think of the winter of 1946 to 1947," one German would later write, "I always recall the glitter on the walls and in the interiors of houses, that I must have seen a hundred times in German homes and which resembled the sparkly sheen of the unpolished side of a granite block. It was the glitter of a wafer-thin layer of white frost, an icy blast of damp; the frozen moisture in the atmosphere created by men, sweat, coughing and breathing; men whose clothing was sometimes soaked through with snow, and who dried out slowly when they got home."

Lyon's hunt in these miserable conditions took him to Denmark, where he hoped to interview former Gestapo agents imprisoned in Aalborg, in the far north of the country. The trip almost proved his undoing. "I shall never forget that drive," he wrote. "Although there was only one main road to Aalborg, it became almost untraceable. The snowstorm increased until it was something out of Scott of the Antarctic. The road was utterly deserted, and I do not remember passing or being passed by any other vehicle the whole way. The surrounding landscape appeared utterly desolate. The surface of the road was solid ice, and the snow was beginning to deepen on it. To top everything, well before the halfway mark, the windscreen wiper packed up and I was forced to lower the windscreen. The lights on the jeep were not too good, and it was extremely difficult to make out where the roadway ended and the ditches and fields at the side began. I remember thinking to myself, 'Dickie, my boy, if you ditch this jeep, you're bloody well going to freeze to death.'"

Lyon drove through the night with both hands clamped tightly on the wheel. Almost frozen to his core, he reached Aalborg after what seemed endless hours on the road. He visited several internment camps and interviewed a number of captured Gestapo officers, none of whom had any worthwhile information to share. Frustrated, before returning to Germany, he drove to Copenhagen. There, a policeman friend introduced Lyon to a young, blond actress of statuesque build and considerable charm. "After the rigors of the winter," he later wrote, "and an accumulation of unclaimed leave, this meeting resulted in my return being delayed rather longer than had been originally scheduled."

He arrived back in Germany several days later, adequately refreshed and ready to resume the hunt. At Neuengamme, he located a former Gestapo driver named Baumann who had traveled briefly with the two wanted men after the war. He told Lyon that Post and Schmidt, fleeing the advancing Allied armies, arrived in Flensburg on May 2, 1945, and used their contacts in the SS to land jobs with the German Customs Police. Post went to work under the alias Pohlmann; Schmidt went by Schmundt. The men were posted three days later to a customs office in Kappeln. They remained employed as customs officials for the better part of a month before deciding to move on. Each man possessed identity papers under his false name. They acquired a yellow Ford V-8 truck and drove to Hamburg, where they filed a movement order with local custom officials. According to the order, the men planned to travel to Itzehoe, roughly thirty miles northwest of Hamburg. They arrived in Itzehoe at three-thirty on the afternoon of June 12. Baumann, who had accompanied Schmidt and Post on their travels, now parted ways with the two men. He landed a job as a farm laborer just outside the town, where a war crimes unit eventually picked him up. From that point forward, the whereabouts of Post and Schmidt remained a mystery. Both men had mentioned their desire to use the Ford to establish a truck rental business in the Russian Zone.

Schmidt grew a mustache in an effort to avoid capture. He was thirty-eight, with a stocky build, thinning hair, and a wrinkled forehead. Although Baumann said he last saw Schmidt wearing the uniform of a customs official, he did possess civilian clothing, including a garish leather coat with a thick fur lining that often attracted stares from passersby. Schmidt, who prior to the war had been a lawyer, was single and had little family. His father was dead, but his mother was believed to be living near the Bodensee, a lake at the northern foot of the Alps. Baumann told Lyon her address could be obtained from one of Schmidt's former shorthand typists, who lived in Kiel. Post, the same age as Schmidt, was more physically imposing: broad of shoulder, with a heavy walk more akin to stomping. He was married with three children, ages four to eight, but the union was not a happy one. Post had long enjoyed the company of Marianne Heidt, his shorthand typist from Gestapo headquarters in Kiel, and had little to do with his family. Baumann said there was still a chance Post maintained contact with his mistress. The woman's father worked as an inspector with the War Damage Office in Kiel and lived at Hanastrasse 8. One of Heidt's girlfriends also lived nearby. Either one of them, Baumann said, might know where to find her.

It was here Lyon's hunt came to an end. In April 1947, his discharge orders came through and he was shipped back to England for demobilization, leaving McKenna to pick up the trail. Despite the information Baumann had passed along, the search for Post and Schmidt proved to be a frustrating one. McKenna, with armed backup, raided the house of Heidt's parents. They were shaken, but cooperative, and said they hadn't heard from their daughter in some time. They gave McKenna a snapshot of Marianne and Post on a skiing holiday in the Harz Mountains. The pair made for an attractive couple, fit and smiling, with snowcapped trees crowding the background. Also from the parents, McKenna obtained the addresses of those Heidt considered friends and acquaintances. In Kiel, the RAF stormed several houses and turned up correspondence that suggested Heidt might be found in the Wesermünde area. In Hamburg, McKenna interviewed Frau Inge Stege, Heidt's cousin. Stege told McKenna that Heidt had spent three weeks at her house in August 1945 but left without providing a forwarding address. Three months later, a man showed up on Stege's doorstep and inquired as to Heidt's whereabouts. When McKenna asked Stege what this random caller looked like, she described a man who matched Johannes Post's physical description. In the event Stege spoke with Heidt again, the man had left a mailing address: Kiel Post Office, Box no. Jo.P. Intrigued by the initials, McKenna contacted 91 Field Security Section, Kiel, and asked them to intercept anyone who accessed that particular box at the post office.

That night, McKenna studied the picture of Post and Heidt on their skiing holiday. He was struck by Post's apparent normalcy: the hint of a smile, the relaxed posture of a man enjoying several days away from it all. It was a dichotomy he had encountered multiple times throughout the course of the investigation: how could someone capable of such barbarity be normal in other aspects of his life? It was a question that he, as a police officer, often pondered. Hitler's executioners had wives and children; they expressed concern for their family and loved ones, yet displayed a total disregard for the fathers, brothers, and sons of others. How did one compartmentalize such differing mind-sets? McKenna knew he would never wrap his brain around it. As the war neared its end, the Nazi regime had only grown more barbaric, liquidating at a frantic rate those it deemed subhuman. The average German citizen was also made to suffer. War-weary Germans who did not display adequate enthusiasm for the Nazi cause, who expressed their lack of faith in final victory and refused to fight, were executed. Three months before the German surrender, Kaltenbrunner effectively gave all local police commanders free rein to murder. "From all police offices," he wrote in a February 1945 order, "[I] expect the highest state of readiness, responsibility, robust action, no hesitation. Ruthlessly eliminate any defeatism in one's own ranks with the harshest measures." The German military was not immune to Nazi brutality. Fanatical SS men lingered behind the front lines and shot soldiers whom they believed to be deserting. In Berlin, where the Red Army was closing in, the SS made a public display of those it deemed defeatist, shooting such people in the street or hanging them from trees with signs around the necks of the deceased identifying them as cowards.

On the Western Front, following the Normandy invasion, there had been acts of barbarity that went far beyond the scope of traditional warfare. Indeed, along with the Sagan murders, the British were investigating a rash of war crimes perpetrated against Allied soldiers in France. Details had crossed McKenna's desk as part of the routine information swap that such investigations entailed. One document listing various crimes made for disturbing reading:

June, 1944—A Canadian prisoner of war who was being marched through Caen saw the bodies of British soldiers lying in rows beside the road. He was informed by the Germans that all had been wounded and then tanks had been run over them to kill them. (Reported by the eye witness who subsequently escaped.)

June, 1944—A party of one Canadian officer, 23 Canadian other ranks and two British other ranks were shot at Chateau d'Audrieu by members of the 12th S.S. Reconnaissance Battalion of the 12th S.S. Panzer Division (Hitler *Jugend*). (The facts of this case have been established by a Court of Enquiry convened by Supreme Commander Allied Expeditionary Force).

July, 1944—A British fighter pilot made a forced landing at Champs Rabats and broke his leg. He was found by a German officer who shouted at him, "You swine, you are still alive," and shot him. (Reported by a German prisoner of war who was an eye witness.)

July, 1944—24 American soldiers in a crater were surrounded by S.S. troops. They were ordered by an S.S. officer to surrender and throw down their arms. This they did. The S.S. officer then shot all 24 himself. (Reported by a German prisoner of war who was an eye witness.)

August, 1944—A party of 8 prisoners of war from the S.A.S. Regiment were taken to a wood near Noailles by German soldiers in charge of two S.S. officers and one Gestapo official. Sentence of death was read out and the German escort opened fire. (Reported by two of these prisoners of war who escaped.)

How had so many succumbed to such murderous fanaticism? That was a question the investigation would never answer. Some of the men questioned by McKenna and his team said they only pulled the trigger to save their families from the torturous SS. Was this a valid excuse? McKenna did not believe that Emil Schulz, most likely to hang for killing Roger Bushell, was a monster. Nevertheless, he shot an unarmed man in the back of the head. A husband and father could not be faulted for wanting to protect his family, but that did not legitimize murder. So what alternative did that leave? It was an uncomfortable question.

Based on Baumann's information, McKenna found Fritz Schmidt's mother living in a small house near the Bodensee. The setting seemed a world removed from the shell-shocked cities and crowded internment camps McKenna had come to know so well over the previous months. Frau Maria Schmidt—"very old and and an imbecile"—smiled when McKenna mentioned her son's name. She seemed to have no inkling of her son's wartime activities and could only tell McKenna she had last seen him three weeks ago. She was unsure when he'd be home for another visit. McKenna—sitting in the woman's living room, looking at the glistening mountain vista beyond the window—suspected Schmidt's visits home were now a permanent thing of the past. He thanked the woman for her time and left. The search for Schmidt would continue for another two decades.

The weeks slowly passed without leads on Schmidt or Post. All the while, demobilization thinned the ranks of the investigation team. By May 1947, the RAF had one wing commander (Bowes), one squadron leader (McKenna), one warrant officer, and three Dutch interpreters assigned to the case. The investigation had now taken on a "spasmodic" quality, the result—McKenna explained in a progress report—"of information given to various officials in the countries visited, who, from time to time, obtain information on persons still wanted in connection with these murders."

Indeed, the investigation appeared to be winding down. The RAF—since launching its inquiry in September 1945—had tracked down 329 suspects, twenty-three of whom were directly complicit in the Sagan murders. Two of those individuals—Seetzen and Franz Schmidt—were dead by their own hand, and one—Friedrich Kiowsky—was in Czech custody. Currently, twenty-one suspects sat in cells in London and Minden awaiting trial. The British, hoping to charge and try Scharpwinkel, were still negotiating his release with the Russians. Venediger of the Danzig Gestapo remained on the run, as did Munich Gestapo chief Schäfer. The hunt for Hans Ziegler, head of the Gestapo in Zlín, continued. His seventy-two-year-old mother was traced to a house at Katzmeyerstrasse 71 in Munich, where she lived with her daughter and three-year-old grandson. Flight Sergeant Daniel raided the premises but found no physical evidence suggesting Ziegler had been there recently. The mother and daughter were questioned in separate rooms, the younger woman making no secret of the hatred she felt toward her interrogators. If she had information, she refused to part with it. Her husband, a former Gestapo agent, now languished in an Allied internment camp. The mother tried to placate Daniel and his interpreter and told them she had last seen her son three weeks prior. Daniel asked his interpreter to speak with the grandson, who sat playing in another room under the eye of a military policeman. The boy, when questioned, said Ziegler had come to visit the previous Sunday—a mere four days ago. Ziegler's mother said nothing when Daniel pressed her further. Where, Daniel asked, was her son? The woman insisted she didn't know.

With no strong leads to go on, it was now a waiting game. McKenna spent his days working the phone and traveling to various internment camps to check on recent arrivals. On May 19, 1947, the commandant of the holding facility in Minden called McKenna and told him the North West Europe War Crimes Unit had just brought in a man named Johannes Pohlmann. A witness had recognized Pohlmann—working as "a haulage contractor" in the town of Celle—as Johannes Post. He was arrested "in connection with the murders of 300 people at the notorious A.E.L. Nordmark Concentration Camp" near Kiel. Formal charges had yet to be filed. The man was still insisting a case of mistaken identity had been made. McKenna traveled to Minden on May 21 to see the prisoner for himself. After checking in with the facility's commandant, he walked to cell no. 4 and peered through a spy hole in the cell door. The prisoner was sitting on a small cot, staring in McKenna's direction, his features haggard. McKenna pulled from his tunic the picture he had of Marianne Heidt and Johannes Post on their skiing holiday. True, the face was thinner—but the eyes and prominent chin left no doubt. He peered into the cell once more and knew the search for Johannes Post was at an end.

He placed an urgent call to the head of the North West Europe War Crimes Unit and obtained permission to interrogate the prisoner. A guard unlocked the cell door and stood watch as McKenna dropped the photograph on the man's lap. Pohlmann hardly glanced at the image.

"That's me," he said, neither surprised nor disturbed. "I am Post." McKenna asked the guard to bring an interpreter to the cell. Post, his cover blown, freely admitted to knowing all about the Kiel murders and added with apparent pride that he was in command of the execution squad. McKenna listened as Post detailed the murders of Catanach, Espelid, Fuglesang, and Christensen. Post mentioned, with some amusement, how Catanach balked when told he would soon be shot, and Post described the young airman's puzzlement when he realized Post had not been joking. "Why?" had been the last word Catanach uttered, according to Post, who shot him through the back without dignifying that simple and desperate question with a response. The bullet pierced the airman's heart. Over the course of the investigation, other suspects had expressed—even if untrue—remorse for their actions. They acknowledged that their deeds were wrong. McKenna now sat looking at Post, waiting to hear some word of regret—but none was forthcoming.

"How could you do such a thing as this?" McKenna finally asked. "How could you be so inhuman?"

McKenna listened to the translator convey the question to Post.

"Inhuman! I was dealing with sub-humans," Post spat, "yet I always gave them a full night's warning before I shot them, so that they could prepare to meet their fate. For the glory of the Führer, I have killed any number of sub-humans. I have liquidated non-Aryans, gypsies, vagrants, Jews, and politically unreliables. The Führer has shown his appreciation by personally awarding me the highest political decoration in the realm. For the glory of the Führer, I only regret that I have not killed more. People like you. I wish I had had the chance to wipe out more people like you, who have left our cities in ruins and killed our women and children. These terror-fliers I disposed of were of no more good to the Reich than to all the other sub-humans whom I sent on their journey to Heaven for the glory of the Führer, who has presented me with the Order of the Blood."

McKenna, his hunt all but over, left the cell sickened. The RAF charged Post with murder the following month, after the Nordmark case went nowhere. With Fritz Schmidt the only man wanted in connection with the Kiel murders, McKenna and Bowes considered the matter closed. On June 30, 1947, Bowes penned a report to SIB headquarters in London:

> It has now been established where all [50] RAF officers were murdered and, in most cases, the names of the Gestapo officials involved. At Hamburg on the 1st July, 1947, the trial will commence of 18 accused Gestapo officials in connection with the murder of these officers. Two others have committed suicide following their arrest; the death of another has been definitely established; one has been executed by the Czech authorities and another is held in custody by them and will almost be certainly sentenced to death for war crimes against Czech nationals. One is still at the London Cage and Wilhelm Scharpwinkel, chief of the Gestapo at Breslau and organizer of the murder squad responsible for the death of 29 of those officers, is held by the Russians at Moscow. So far, all efforts to effect his transfer to British custody have been unsuccessful, but it is still possible that he will be handed over and stand trial for his part in these murders. In all, 25 actively concerned in the death of these officers have been accounted for.

Bowes read what he had written and made a few minor changes before adding the closing line: "This can be considered the final report on this case."

FOURTEEN

REMEMBRANCE

There were thirty-eight men still being sought by the RAF. Throughout July and August 1947, McKenna met with occupation authorities in the American, British, and French zones, distributing more than ten thousand photographs of the wanted men. Among those still unaccounted for were former Munich Gestapo chief Dr. Oswald Schäfer and onetime head of the Zlín Gestapo Hans Ziegler. McKenna traced Schäfer's wife to an address in the town of Braunfels. Lisalotte Schäfer told McKenna she had neither seen nor heard from her husband in two years and believed he was dead.

The photographs were disseminated throughout the Allied armies and agencies investigating Nazi atrocities. The U.S. Army published the photos in *Rogue's Gallery*, a widely circulated sheet profiling those being sought for war crimes. The new wave of publicity led to Ziegler's apprehension in late 1947. He was shipped to the London Cage to answer questions regarding the Kirby-Green and Kidder murders. On the night of February 3, 1948, a guard looking into Ziegler's cell saw the man lying dead on the floor in a pool of blood. The tin dinner tray he used to slice his throat lay beside him.

Eighteen defendants in the Sagan case went on trial at the British Military Court in Hamburg on July 1, 1947. Presiding over the trial were a

major general, three army officers, and three representatives of the Royal
Air Force. Charges against all eighteen men were read into the record:

(i)   "Committing a war crime in that they at diverse places in Ger-
       many and German-occupied territory, between 25 March,
       1944, and 13 April, 1944, were concerned together with SS
       Gruppenführer Müller and SS *Gruppenführer* Nebe and other
       persons known and unknown, in the killing in violation of the
       laws and usages of war of prisoners of war who had escaped
       from Stalag Luft III.

(ii)   Committing a war crime that they at diverse places in Germany
       and German-occupied territory, between 25 March, 1944, and
       13 April, 1944, aided and abetted SS *Gruppenführer* Müller
       and SS *Gruppenführer* Nebe and each other and other persons
       known and unknown in carrying out orders, which were con-
       trary to the laws and usages of war, namely, orders to kill
       prisoners of war who had escaped from Stalag Luft III."

Additional charges of murder were leveled against the defendants
for their role in the killings of individual POWs. Emil Schulz and Walter
Breithaupt were charged with killing Squadron Leader Roger Bushell
and Lieutenant Bernard Scheidhauer; Alfred Schimmel was charged
with shooting Flight Lieutenant Anthony Hayter; Heinrich Boschert,
Josef Gmeiner, Walter Herberg, and Otto Preiss were charged in the
death of Flying Officer Dennis Cochran; Eduard Geith, Johann Schnei-
der, and Emil Weil were charged in the shooting deaths of Lieutenants
Johannes S. Gouws and Rupert J. Stevens; Walter Jacobs, Oskar
Schmidt, and Wilhelm Struve faced murder charges in the deaths of
Lieutenants Hans Espelid and Nils Fuglesang and Pilot Officer Arnold
J. Christensen; Erich Zacharias was charged in the slayings of Flying
Officer Gordon Kidder and Squadron Leader Thomas Kirby-Green;
Artur Denkmann, Hans Kaehler, and Johannes Post were charged with
shooting Squadron Leader Catanach, Pilot Officer Christensen, and
Lieutenants Espelid and Fuglesang.

The first two charges, faced by all defendants, were charges of conspiracy to commit murder. The chief defendant, Max Wielen—the former head of the Breslau *Kripo* who sounded the national alarm following the escape—was brought to trial on these charges alone and was not charged with participating in any particular killing. Wielen was the only *Kripo* official in the defendant's dock; the other seventeen men represented six regional Gestapo offices. All eighteen defendants pleaded not guilty. The prosecution's underlying argument was simple: "Owing to the *Grossfahndung* (the nation-wide search), notified to every police headquarters, all policemen in Germany must have known that prisoners of war were at large and that therefore the accused, being members of the Gestapo, could not be heard to say that they did not know the identity of the prisoners they went out to kill."

The defense had a much tougher case, as it had to prove the defendants were unaware of their victims' identities or the illegality of their actions. Lawyers representing Post wanted to call character witnesses who would testify that the ardent Nazi had once saved a British airman from an outraged mob. Post bluntly refused. "I could not have been a National Socialist for so many years," he said, "and suddenly put in affidavits from Communists or Jews or freethinkers." The main foundation of the defense's case, however, was "the plea of superior orders"— orders the defendants were powerless to disobey. The defense argued that, "according to laws prevailing in Germany at the time of the offense," orders issued by Hitler were legal; disobeying them was not. International law, however, deemed the following of such orders to be illegal. "International law," defense attorneys proclaimed, "must not place the subject in an insoluble dilemma where he has only two possible courses of action, both of which are criminal, thus leaving him 'no way out.' In order to be able to say that a person has committed an offense, there must be an alternative course open to him, which does not constitute an offense."

Post testified to this issue while on the stand.

"My attitude is quite clear," he said. "If I received an order as I received it then—that is, if I had been told by order of the Führer four

British prisoners are to be shot—this would be a violation of international law, but for the officer who carried it out it would be an entirely legal action. I will prove this. We live in an authoritarian state headed by a Leader, and there can be no doubt that an order given by an authoritarian Head of State is law."

The argument lacked obvious merit in the eyes of the court. While it could be argued that countless Germans assumed what Hitler said to be law, there was no "statute or decree . . . to the effect that a spoken command of the Head of the State had legal force, or as some counsel suggested, replace the finding and sentence of a court of law." Furthermore, the prosecution, in countering the plea of superior orders, cited the case of the *Llandovery Castle*, "a British hospital ship which was sunk by a submarine" during the First World War. The submarine's commander, Lieutenant Helmut Patzig, ordered his men to kill all the survivors. Torpedoes sunk two of the ship's three lifeboats and killed all on board. Patzig and two of his lieutenants were eventually arraigned on war crimes. Patzig fled Germany and escaped prosecution, but his two subordinates were tried and found guilty. "Patzig's order does not free the accused of guilt," said the Sagan prosecutor, quoting the court's findings in 1918. He referenced the *German Military Penal Code*, which states that a subordinate who obeys an order he knows to be an "infringement of civil or military law" is "liable to punishment."

Multiple other arguments put forward by the defense came up short, including one that stated only combatants—and not civilians—could commit war crimes. The prosecution countered by reading into the record an excerpt from chapter 14 of the *Manual for Military Law*: "The term 'war crime' is a technical expression for such an act of enemy soldiers and enemy civilians as may be visited by punishment or capture of the offenders." Despite the shortfall of various defense arguments, the prosecution's case wasn't necessarily clear-cut, relying, as it was, "on the uncorroborated evidence of an accomplice or of accomplices and that one accused cannot corroborate another." In short, the defendants could only be convicted on the corroborative statements of their onetime comrades if the court was convinced "that the evidence given was true." The defendants took the stand in their own defense and expressed in their testimony everything from remorse to pride in their actions. The interrogation tactics employed at the London Cage were also put on trial. On the stand, Erich Zacharias claimed that he confessed to the killings of Thomas Kirby-Green and Gordon Kidder only after Lieutenant Colonel Scotland tortured him by shoving an electrical probe up his rectum.

Taking the stand to refute the defendant's account, Scotland said he neither tortured Zacharias nor sought a murder confession from the man. What he wanted, he testified, was "information on Gestapo hot-iron methods of torture in Czechoslovakia." Scotland said Flight Lieutenant Lyon had at one point visited the London Cage to interrogate Zacharias, something Scotland acquiesced to with a measure of reluctance. In questioning the prisoner, Lyon learned that Scotland had made Zacharias strip to the waist and kneel for hours on a cement floor. Beaten down, Zacharias confessed to murdering the two RAF men.

"I can only die once. I will tell you the truth," he said. "The officers were murdered. I am sorry. They were handcuffed. They did not try to escape. The officers were killed under Ziegler's orders."

Now, on the stand, Scotland said he was angered by the confession.

"I did not want Lyon to be successful," he said.

"Why not?" asked Frau Dr. Oehlert, defense counsel for Zacharias.

"I thought that the torture story was a very much more important one from Zacharias than a confession of shooting guilt," Scotland said. "If I had a confession of shooting, I could not get a confession of torture."

Oehlert grilled Scotland on the methods employed at the London Cage.

"Surely, as a British soldier," she said, "you are familiar with the types of Army punishment?"

"The only army in which I have served for any length of time is the German Army," Scotland testified. "I do not know the punishments in the British Army."

"When were you a member of the German Army?"

"I served in the German Army from 1903 to 1907."

"Have you ever heard of the punishment of cleaning up a room with a toothbrush?" Oehlert asked.

"It sounds very stupid," said Scotland. "I have not heard of it."

"I am very surprised that you, with four years' service in the German Army, do not know anything about that," said Oehlert, her tone incredulous. "Would you be astonished that my client alleges that such singular punishments were given in the London Cage?"

Scotland kept a straight face: "Yes."

Oehlert told the court that Zacharias complained of being severely beaten on several occasions while at the London Cage. He also accused guards of denying him food for days at a time and depriving him of sleep. Oehlert asked Scotland if he cared to address the accusations. Scotland's response lacked conviction. "If that were true," he said, "he should have made a complaint and we would have done something about it."

Other allegations of torture at the Cage put forward during the trial included incidents of hair pulling and electrocution. One defense lawyer accused Scotland of telling Nazi prisoners they would die at the end of a rope and their wives "would become common property" in Siberia. Scotland dismissed them all as "manufactured tales" and worried the accusations of torture would soon overshadow the trial and "the brutal fate of those fifty RAF officers."

Zacharias, called once more to the stand, now said his confession at the Cage had been a lie—an attempt on his part to actually spare the reputation of the German people. Asked by his attorney to explain, he said, "I did not make this statement upon oath, so I did not regard it as too important. I left quite important facts out, of which the most important was the Sagan Order, the fact that the killings had to take place on higher orders, which I assumed to be Hitler. . . . Secondly, I felt that because of the interests of my own colleagues and because of the reputation of the whole German people, I really could not make such a damaging revelation as this reference to Hitler's orders to kill the fifty."

It was a creative, if not pathetic, defense; one destined for failure. As for Scotland, he would continue to defend his interrogation methods. "It was to be expected," he later wrote, "that the world should be intrigued by the success with which we had persuaded substantial numbers of Nazis criminals not only to confess their role in murder plans, but also to write the detailed story of the events surrounding the crimes and the activities of their own colleagues. . . . But how was it all done? What were the secret methods employed to obtain such confessions? There was no mystery. It was no easy task, but there was no mystery. Consider the situation of our German guests at the London Cage. . . . They were eager enough to tell sufficient of their story to demonstrate their individual blamelessness. Many, however, committed the fatal error of underestimating our intimacy with German habits, personalities and language, as well as the facts of the Sagan outrages."

While other defendants on the stand acknowledged taking part in the Sagan murders, they sought to justify their participation. Otto Preiss, who shot Dennis Cochran through the back of the head, said he did not consider himself guilty. He was only acting under the orders of a superior officer. Heinrich Boschert—also charged in the Cochran murder—said he never considered himself a typical Gestapo thug, despite the fact he always took pride in wearing his Gestapo uniform. The prosecutor questioning Boschert voiced his incredulity. "It is only when you lose the war," he said, "that you become a timid little mouse." Eduard Geith, of the Munich Gestapo, said depression had plagued him since he took part in the murders of Lieutenants Johannes Gouws and Rupert Stevens. Adopting a unique strategy, Albert Schimmel—the Strasbourg Gestapo chief who had Flight Lieutenant Anthony Hayter shot the day before Good Friday—played the religion card. Two church officials testified on his behalf, detailing for the court the man's piousness and devotion to God. Indeed, on the stand, Schimmel said he spiritually struggled with his role in the crime and considered ignoring the orders from Berlin. He knew such an action, however, would be met with dire consequences.

"Why did you not carry out this killing yourself?" the judge advocate, presiding over the trial, asked Schimmel. "That would have made one less person in the secret, would it not?"

"No," Schimmel said. "I could not do this."

"And you salved your conscience by making another man do it, is that it?"

"The execution of this order," said Schimmel, "was just as difficult for me as passing on the order to another official."

While many of the defendants said they feared their families would be shot if they disobeyed orders, not one of them could ever recall hearing of an incident where the wife and children of a Gestapo officer were executed by the state. On September 3, 1947, the eighth anniversary of the outbreak of war, the court rendered its verdicts. Not surprisingly, all were found guilty. Wielen was the only defendant found guilty of the first two charges, mainly conspiring with Müller and Nebe in the planning of the fifty murders. The other seventeen defendants were found guilty of actually carrying out the killings. In determining the verdicts, the court pondered two questions: What role did the accused play in the actual shootings? And did they know the victims were prisoners of war? Standing in the dock, the defendants listened to the court pronounce their fates.

Emil Schulz, Walter Breithaupt, Alfred Schimmel, Josef Gmeiner, Walter Herberg, Otto Preiss, Emil Weil, Eduard Geith, Johann Schneider, Johannes Post, Hans Kaehler, Oskar Schmidt, Walter Jacobs, and Erich Zacharias were all sentenced to hang. Gestapo drivers Artur Denkmann and Wilhelm Struve received ten years imprisonment for their role in the Kiel murders. Heinrich Boschert was sentenced to hang for his involvement in the Dennis Cochran murder, but his sentence was later commuted to life imprisonment. Max Wielen, for his involvement in planning and concealing the murders, received a life sentence.

On October 17, 1947, one month after the trial, Soviet authorities sent word to the British government that Dr. Wilhelm Scharpwinkel—the man who oversaw the murders of more than half the Sagan escapees—had died in a Moscow prison. Four months later, on February

27, 1948, at Hameln Gaol in Westfalia, on gallows built by the British Army's Royal Engineers, the fourteen Sagan murderers went to their deaths at the end of a rope.

Ten months later, Breslau Gestapo officers Erwin Wieczorek and Richard Hansel went on trial for their involvement in the murders of twenty airmen. Also in the dock was Reinhold Bruchardt, onetime member of the Danzig Gestapo, who claimed a Ukrainian execution squad had murdered Flight Lieutenants Gordon Brettell, Romas Marcinkus, and Gilbert Walenn, and Flying Officer Henri Picard. Wieczorek was found guilty and sentenced to hang, but the verdict was later overturned based on the fact that he had not actually pulled a trigger. Hansel was acquitted. Bruchardt's death sentence was later commuted to life in prison after the British government announced a temporary suspension of the death penalty. Eight years into his imprisonment, Bruchardt was released under general amnesty.

Kiel Gestapo member Johannes Post stands in the dock in a Hamburg courtroom during his murder trial. He was found guilty and sentenced to hang for murdering Lieutenants Hallada Espelid and Nils Fuglesang, Squadron Leader James Catanach, and Flying Officer Arnold Christensen.

———

Members of the upper Nazi hierarchy complicit in the Sagan killings who did not successfully go underground escaped justice via self-inflicted gunshot wounds and cyanide pills. In the case of *Kripo* Chief Arthur Nebe, he was executed by his own people. Himmler killed himself not long after British troops captured him in May 1945. Ernst Kaltenbrunner—Himmler's deputy at the Central Security Office—and Wilhelm Keitel, head of Germany's armed forces, were both tried and found guilty at Nuremberg. They were sentenced to death and went to the gallows on October 16, 1946. Hermann Göring, also scheduled to hang, poisoned himself the night before the execution.

———

Decommissioned out of the RAF, McKenna returned to England and his job at the Blackpool Borough Police on January 1, 1948. For their work on the Sagan case, McKenna and Wing Commander Bowes—who remained in the service—were awarded the Order of the British Empire. Four months later, in May 1948, the Russians sent word to the British government that Dr. Gunther Absalon, head of prisoner security in the Sagan region and participant in the Breslau murders, had died in a Soviet prison the previous October.

In September 1948, Foreign Secretary Ernest Bevin announced that the British government would no longer prosecute war crimes. Bowes wrote a letter to the provost marshal of the RAF, urging that those still being sought in connection with the Sagan murders be tried if captured. His efforts were in vain. Consequently, a number of Gestapo men wanted at one time by the RAF escaped justice. Munich Gestapo chief Dr. Oswald Schäfer came out of hiding in 1950 and never answered for the murders of Lieutenants Gouws and Stevens. Dr. Gunther Venediger of the Danzig Gestapo emerged from the Russian Zone in 1952. A German court acquitted him two years later on charges he murdered four RAF officers. Bowes fiercely pursued the matter, prompting a judicial review of the case. Venediger consequently received a two-year prison sentence. Likewise, Fritz Schmidt—the former Kiel Gestapo chief—eventually wound up in front of a German court in 1968, only to receive two years in prison for his role in the deaths of Squadron Leader Catanach, Pilot Officer Christensen, and Lieutenants Espelid and Fuglesang.

Although sentenced to life in prison, Max Wielen was released in October 1952 "by British authorities as an act of clemency." He was sixty-nine and in failing health.

For McKenna, tracking down the killers had always been about justice—not revenge. It was an airman's "duty to avoid capture" and his "duty to escape" should he ever be caught. After the war, McKenna expressed his thoughts on the matter, saying those who broke out of Stalag Luft III "didn't see escaping as a sport—and when they used the word 'duty,' they did so with typical British reserve and a degree of embarrassment. Those murdered men were doing no more than what they accepted as being their duty, and it seemed to me—and the chaps working with me—that to be murdered in cold blood for doing one's honorable duty as a serviceman must always be unacceptable to any decent human being. We saw it as being our duty to find the miscreants and thereafter bring them before a court of law."

McKenna died at the age of eighty-seven on Valentine's Day 1994, having never sought publicity for his pivotal role in the Great Escape story.

The work of the RAF's Special Investigating Branch was nothing short of remarkable when one considers the conditions and circumstances under which it conducted the Sagan investigation. With no crime scene, physical evidence, or actual eyewitness accounts to the fifty murders, McKenna and his men launched their inquiry in utter darkness. They had every reason to fail and little prospect of success, but sheer determination and dogged detective work yielded results perhaps not even McKenna initially thought possible. The RAF ultimately identified seventy-two men who played an active role in the Great Escape murders. Of those seventy-two individuals, twenty-one went to the gallows, seventeen received prison sentences, six were killed in wartime, seven killed themselves, five defendants saw the charges against them dropped, three had their sentences eventually overturned, one turned material witness, and another remained free in East Germany.

Not all seventy-two men were fanatical Nazis brainwashed by Hitler's deluded ambitions. Many were simple family men who returned home each evening to their wives and children. When questioned by McKenna and other RAF investigators, a good number expressed dismay over what they had been ordered to do. Even if such remorse was sincere, one cannot forget that for every airman gunned down alongside a desolate road, there were families in England, Australia, New Zealand, Canada, and a handful of other countries, left to suffer a grievous loss. In the end, justice adequately served those complicit in the killings.

In planning the mass breakout from Stalag Luft III, Roger Bushell hoped to "harass, confuse, and confound the enemy." He achieved just that, if only for a short time. The Germans assigned one hundred thousand

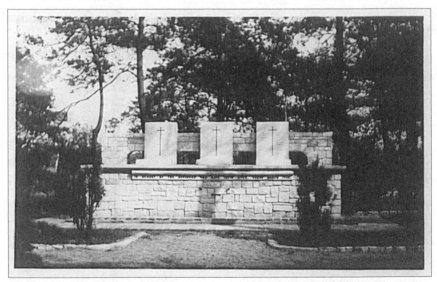

The stone memorial to the fallen fifty, as photographed by the RAF in 1946, built by inmates at Stalag Luft III shortly after the Great Escape. **BRITISH NATIONAL ARCHIVES: AIR 40/2487**

men to the Sagan search. Although any impact it may have had on the German war effort was negligible at best, the Great Escape was a symbolic victory—an act of outrageous defiance and a triumph of ingenuity. But was it worth the lives of fifty men? Perhaps that's a question only those who took part in the event could have answered.

A part of Germany during the Second World War, Sagan today is in eastern Poland. It is still possible to visit the site of Stalag Luft III. Nature is slowly reclaiming the area. All that remain are the stone foundations of the barracks and other buildings that once comprised the camp. In 2010, the Royal Air Force built a replica of Hut 104—the barrack block from which tunnel "Harry" extended—near the camp site. Stretching from where the real hut once stood, a gravel pathway marks the length, width, and location of the actual tunnel. A large rock now sits at the spot where the seventy-six escapees emerged just shy of the tree line beyond the camp wire. A simple inscription on the rock reads, "Allied airmen, prisoners of Stalag Luft III, were Great Escape participants." At the rock's base, some visitors leave fresh flowers— vibrant life and color in an otherwise bleak landscape. It's a fitting tribute to the men whose story will continue to touch both young and old for generations to come.

ACKNOWLEDGMENTS

The book is done; I now have six notches scratched into the barrel of my fountain pen. On the research front, I want to thank the staffs at the British National Archives and the Imperial War Museum for their assistance. Thanks to Stephen R. Davies, former RAF Police officer turned author, for his willingness to lend a hand. My longtime agent Ed Knappman passed away during the writing of this book. He was a great guy who always worked tirelessly on my behalf. He is missed. Thanks to Roger Williams of the Publish or Perish Agency, who took over from Ed, for his continued support. In the UK, I want to thank Rachel Calder for her representation.

At Penguin, I owe a great debt to Natalee Rosenstein for her interest and enthusiasm for the project. Many thanks are also due to Robin Barletta for shepherding the manuscript through the publication process. Thanks to Rick Willett for combing the manuscript for typos and other mishaps.

On the personal side, heartfelt thanks go to Simon Blint, Dan Hoffman, Brian Reiser, and Ryan Sawyer for their years of friendship. As always, I must bestow a special note of thanks upon Tony, Phil, Mike, Steve, and Peter for the music. I was thirteen when I decided I wanted to be an author. From the very beginning, my parents—Bill and Susan—offered nothing but support and words of encouragement. I will always be grateful for their love and friendship. The great Max Hastings once wrote, "Only writers' families know how painful it is to live in a house in which a book is taking shape." Katie, my wife, has spent much time as a "writer's widow" since we met. For her patience and endurance, words alone cannot express my gratitude. Our beautiful son, Spencer, was born during the writing of this book. He has turned our lives upside down in the most fantastic way. Endless love and thanks go to both of them for providing a wonderful home in which to live and work.

THE FIFTY

Flying Officer Henry J. Birkland (Canadian): Recaptured in Breslau region. Last seen alive in Görlitz jail on March 31, 1944. Cremated in Liegnitz, date unknown.

Flight Lieutenant E. Gordon Brettell (British): Recaptured on train in Schneidemühl on March 26, 1944. Died March 29, 1944, and cremated in Danzig.

Flight Lieutenant Lester J. Bull (British): Captured on the Silesian Czechoslovak border. Died March 29, 1944, and cremated in Brüx.

Squadron Leader Roger J. Bushell (British): Recaptured at Saarbrücken. Died March 29, 1944, and cremated in Saarbrücken.

Flight Lieutenant Michael J. Casey (British): Recaptured near Görlitz. Died on March 31, 1944, and cremated in Görlitz.

Squadron Leader James Catanach, DFC (Australian): Recaptured in Flensburg on March 26, 1944. Died three days later and was cremated in Kiel.

Pilot Officer Arnold G. Christensen (New Zealand): Recaptured in Flensburg on March 26, 1944. Died three days later and was cremated in Kiel.

Flying Officer Dennis H. Cochran (British): Recaptured on German border near Lörrach. Died March 31, 1944, and cremated at Natzweiler concentration camp.

Squadron Leader Ian Cross (British): Recaptured near Görlitz. Died on March 31, 1944, and cremated in Görlitz.

Lieutenant Hallada Espelid (Norwegian): Recaptured in Flensburg on March 26, 1944. Died three days later and was cremated in Kiel.

Flight Lieutenant Brian H. Evans (British): Recaptured in Breslau region. Last seen alive in the prison at Görlitz on March 31, 1944. Cremated in Liegnitz, date unknown.

Lieutenant Nils Fuglesang (Norwegian): Recaptured in Flensburg on March 26, 1944. Died three days later and was cremated in Kiel.

Lieutenant Johannes S. Gouws (South African): Recaptured on a train south of Munich. Died March 29, 1944, and cremated in Munich.

Flight Lieutenant William J. Grisman (British): Recaptured in Sagan region. Last seen alive in the prison at Görlitz on April 6, 1944. Cremated in Breslau, date unknown.

Flight Lieutenant Alastair D. M. Gunn (British): Recaptured in Sagan region. Last seen alive in the prison at Görlitz on April 6, 1944. Cremated in Breslau, date unknown.

Flying Officer Albert H. Hake (Australian): Recaptured near Görlitz. Died on March 31, 1944, and cremated in Görlitz.

Flight Lieutenant Charles P. Hall (British): Recaptured in Breslau region. Last seen alive in the prison at Görlitz on March 31, 1944. Cremated in Liegnitz, date unknown.

Flight Lieutenant Anthony Hayter (British): Recaptured on road between Mülhausen and Altkirch on March 27, 1944. Died on April 6 and was cremated at Natzweiler concentration camp.

Flight Lieutenant Edgar S. Humphreys (British): Recaptured in Breslau region. Last seen alive in the prison at Görlitz on March 31, 1944. Cremated in Liegnitz, date unknown.

Flying Officer Gordon A. Kidder (Canadian): Recaptured on the German-Czech border near Zlín on March 28, 1944. Died the following day and was cremated in Moravaska Ostrava.

Flying Officer Reginald V. Kierath (Australian): Captured on the Silesian Czech-Slovelt border. Died March 29, 1944, and cremated in Brüx.

Flight Lieutenant Antoni Kiewnarski (Polish): Recaptured in Hirschberg. Died on March 30, 1944. Place of cremation unknown.

Squadron Leader Thomas Kirby-Green (British): Recaptured on the German-Czech border near Zlín on March 28, 1944. Died the following day and was cremated in Moravaska Ostrava.

Flying Officer A. Wlodzimierz Kolanowski (Polish): Recaptured in Breslau region. Last seen alive in the prison at Görlitz on March 31, 1944. Cremated in Liegnitz, date unknown.

Flying Officer Stanislaw Z. Krol (Polish): Recaptured in Oels, and last seen alive there on April 12, 1944. Cremated in Breslau, date unknown.

Flight Lieutenant Patrick W. Langford (Canadian): Recaptured in Breslau region. Last seen alive in the prison at Görlitz on March 31, 1944. Cremated in Liegnitz, date unknown.

Flight Lieutenant Thomas B. Leigh (British): Recaptured near Görlitz. Died on March 31, 1944, and cremated in Görlitz.

Flight Lieutenant James L. R. Long (British): Recaptured in Sagan region. Last seen alive in the prison at Görlitz on April 13, 1944. Cremated in Breslau, date unknown.

Flight Lieutenant Romas Marcinkus (Lithuanian): Recaptured on train in Schneidemühl on March 26, 1944. Died March 29, 1944, and cremated in Danzig.

Lieutenant Clement A. N. McGarr (South African): Recaptured in Sagan region. Last seen alive in the prison at Görlitz on April 6, 1944. Cremated in Breslau, date unknown.

Flight Lieutenant George E. McGill (Canadian): Recaptured in Breslau region. Last seen alive in the prison at Görlitz on March 31, 1944. Cremated in Liegnitz, date unknown.

Flight Lieutenant Harold J. Milford (British): Recaptured in Sagan region. Last seen alive in the prison at Görlitz on April 6, 1944. Cremated in Breslau, date unknown.

Flight Lieutenant Jerzy T. Mondschein (Polish): Recaptured on the Silesian Czechslovak border. Died March 29, 1944, and cremated in Brüx.

Flight Lieutenant Kazimierz Pawluk (Polish): Recaptured in Hirschberg. Died on March 30, 1944. Place of cremation unknown.

Flying Officer Henri A. Picard (Belgian): Recaptured on train in Schneidemühl on March 26, 1944. Died March 29, 1944, and cremated in Danzig.

Flying Officer John Pohe (New Zealand): Recaptured near Görlitz. Died on March 31, 1944, and cremated in Görlitz.

Lieutenant Bernard Scheidhauer (French): Recaptured at Saarbrücken. Died March 29, 1944, and cremated in Saarbrücken.

Pilot Officer Sortiros Skanziklas (Greek): Recaptured in Hirschberg. Died on March 30, 1944. Place of cremation unknown.

Lieutenant Rupert J. Stevens (South African): Recaptured on a train south of Munich. Died March 29, 1944, and cremated in Munich.

Flying Officer Robert C. Stewart (British): Recaptured in Breslau region. Last seen alive in the prison at Görlitz on March 31, 1944. Cremated in Liegnitz, date unknown.

Flying Officer John G. Stower (British): Captured on a train outside Sittau. Last seen alive in the prison at Görlitz on March 31, 1944. Died and cremated that same day; place of cremation unknown.

Flying Officer Denys O. Street (British): Recaptured in Sagan region. Last seen alive in the prison at Görlitz on April 6, 1944. Cremated in Breslau, date unknown.

Flight Lieutenant Cyril D. Swain (British): Recaptured in Breslau region. Last seen alive in the prison at Görlitz on March 31, 1944. Cremated in Liegnitz, date unknown.

Flying Officer Pawel Tobolski (Polish): Last seen alive on April 2, 1944, when he was transferred from Berlin to jail in Silesia. Cremated in Breslau, date unknown.

Flying Officer Ernst Valenta (Czechoslovakian): Recaptured in Breslau region. Last seen alive in the prison at Görlitz on March 31, 1944. Cremated in Liegnitz, date unknown.

Flight Lieutenant Gilbert W. Walenn (British): Recaptured on train in Schneidemühl on March 26, 1944. Died March 29, 1944, and cremated in Danzig.

Flight Lieutenant James C. Wernham (Canadian): Recaptured in Hirschberg. Died on March 30, 1944. Place of cremation unknown.

Flight Lieutenant George W. Wiley (Canadian): Recaptured near Görlitz. Died on March 31, 1944, and cremated in Görlitz.

Squadron Leader John E.A. Williams (Australian): Captured on the Silesian Czechslovak border. Died March 29, 1944, and cremated in Brüx.

Flight Lieutenant John F. Williams (British): Recaptured in Sagan region. Last seen alive in the prison at Görlitz on April 6, 1944. Cremated in Breslau, date unknown.

Sources: Air 40/2278/016, Air 40/2487/020-039, Air 40/2488/003-005, 032-035, Air 40/2492/004.

A SURVIVOR'S TALE

Squadron Leader Laurence Reavell-Carter's bomber was shot down over the Kiel Canal on the night of June 26, 1942. He took part in the "Great Escape," but surrendered to save the life of another escapee when a sentry stumbled across "Harry's" exit. This is the statement he gave to RAF investigators after the war:

On the night of 24/25 March 1944, I attempted to escape from the North Compound of Stalag Luft III (Sagan) by means of the tunnel known as "Harry." I was number seventy-five and was followed by Flight Lt. A.K. Ogilvie and Flight Lt. M.M. Shand. I was wearing a wind-breaker jacket, which I had made in the camp. Underneath this I wore Army battle-dress. I carried a LI-LO* for the purpose of enabling me to cross rivers. I had been supplied with false identity papers, purporting that I was a Hungarian worker, and had maps, compass, food concentrate, chocolate, raisins, etc.

On leaving the tunnel at about 0500 hours just before dawn, I received the "all-clear" signal on the rope from Flight Lt. Langlois. I followed the rope, passed Langlois, and joined Flight Lt. Bethell. He

---

* An air mattress.

then left with his party, and I awaited the arrival of the other eight members of my party. A few minutes later, I was joined by Flight Lt. A.K. Ogilvie. Flight Lt. M.M. Shand emerged from the exit a few moments later and was crawling along the rope towards me. At this moment, a sentry on patrol outside the fence began to approach the exit of the tunnel. I then signaled on the rope to Shand to be still. When the guard got closer to the exit of the tunnel, he appeared to notice the track through the snow caused by the escapers crawling in the woods. In the interval, Shand resumed crawling and the guard raised his rifle in the direction of Shand and shouted. I thought that the guard was about to shoot Shand, so I jumped from my place of concealment in the wood and shouted to the guard in German, "Do not shoot!" He then fired a shot in the air and began to call for assistance. I advanced towards the guard continuing to shout to him in German. In the meantime, Ogilvie and Shand escaped into the woods without the guard being aware of the fact.

A few minutes later, an N.C.O. arrived from the guard room and took Langlois, Squadron Leader McBride, Royal Canadian Air Force, who was caught just as he was about to emerge from the tunnel, and myself back to the guardroom. There, I destroyed my maps, papers, etc., in the fire. The camp commandant, Oberst Von-Lindeiner, the Abwehr Officer, Major Broli, and the Lager Officer, Haputmann Pieber, arrived and began to question us. Major Broli wanted to know how many had escaped. When we refused to tell him, he said, "That will be so much worse for you."

At this stage, Von-Lindeiner, who had gone into another room, returned and appeared to be in a terrific rage. He was virtually incoherent in his speech and did mention that the Gestapo would have a hand in the affair. Pieber told me that we would never be allowed to return to the compound. We were then placed in a room in the guardhouse, where we remained for about two hours. We were then taken to the cells in the Vorlager [solitary barracks] and placed in separate cells. We were not allowed to have any heating, food, or washing facilities. Those conditions were enforced for two days, and we were told by one of the guards that it was the commandant's orders. At the end of that time, normal cell conditions applied, and at the end of the week we were sentenced to twenty-one days detention. This was to include the time already spent in the cells. On 15 April, we were released into the North Compound.

ESCAPE ACTIVITIES

From January 1941 until March 1942 at Stalag Luft I (Barth), I was engaged on the construction of four tunnels. All were discovered prior to completion. About June 1943 in the North Compound, Stalag Luft III, I devised a scheme of getting out of the camp. Over a period of weeks, I instituted the practice of collecting all wastepaper, etc. This was stacked in sacks and taken out of the camp into the Vorlager of the East and Center Compounds by horse-drawn wagons. My scheme was to get into a sack, which would be tied, and to be taken out of the camp with the sacks of waste paper. On the road between the gate of the North Compound and the entrance to the East and Center Compounds, I would cut my way out of the sack, jump off the wagon, and escape into the woods which were close to the road at this point. The distance between the gates was about 200 yards.

The scheme was approved, but I was not to use it as I am too big. It was decided that Flight Lt. Carter, Royal New Zealand Air Force, and Lt. Spires, United States Army Air Force, should be allowed to attempt to escape by this method. On the selected day, these two men were placed in sacks and loaded on the wagon under my supervision. I was assisted by [Flying Officer] Dennis Cochran, Royal Air Force, (now deceased). The wagon left the compound, and Carter and Spires escaped on the way to the main camp as planned. Carter was recaptured on the Island of Rugen about a week later. Spires was recaptured near the camp.

LIBERATION

I was liberated by Allied Forces near Lübeck on 5 May 1945 and sent to Rheine. From there, I was sent by air to the U.K, arriving on May 8.

Source: Statement by Squadron Leader Laurence Reavell-Carter, M.C., 49 Squadron. Air 40/2491/150-153.

BIBLIOGRAPHY

The Royal Air Force SIB case files now kept at the British National Archives in Kew, London, were the primary source of information for *Human Game*. Files specifically referred to and quoted in the text can be found catalogued in the following folders:

Air 40/2272: Progress reports in respect to Stalag Luft III investigation: results of effort to trace wanted German personnel. September 1945 through August 1947.

Air 40/2278: Murder of [Flight Lieutenant] Hayter and interrogation of associated German personnel.

Air 40/2279: The Kiel murders: enquiries and interrogation of persons involved. September 1945 through January 1947.

Air 40/2286: Reports on action taken in the British Zone to trace Germans wanted for interrogation. September 1945 through August 1946.

Air 40/2287: Reports on action taken to trace Germans wanted for interrogation. January 1946 through December 1946.

Air 40/2487: General papers (Sagan Memorial Book and suspect statements).

Air 40/2488: Progress reports, nos. 1–60. 1945.

Air 40/2489: Progress reports, nos. 61–120. 1946.

Air 40/2490: Progress reports, nos. 121–180. 1945.

Air 40/2491: Progress reports, nos. 181–240. 1946.

Air 40/2492: Progress reports, nos. 241–300. 1946.

Air 40/2493: Progress reports, nos. 301–368. 1946.

FO (Foreign Office) 371/57595: Sagan murder case: interrogation of Dr. Scharpwinkel in Moscow.

Cab 66/56/4: The Committing of Acts of Violence Towards British Prisoners of War. Memorandum by the Secretary of State for War.

BOOKS

Though RAF case files provided the vast majority of information for *Human Game,* a number of books were relied on in the telling of this story. Two books were of considerable help. *Exemplary Justice* by Allen Andrews provided anecdotal material, while *A Gallant Company* by Jonathan F. Vance was a great source of biographical information on the "Great Escapers." The books consulted and referenced are as follows:

Andrews, Allen. *Exemplary Justice.* George G. Harrap & Co., Ltd., 1976.

Bessel, Richard. *Germany 1945.* Simon & Schuster UK, Ltd., 2009.

Brickhill, Paul. *The Great Escape.* Faber & Faber. 1951.

Burgess, Alan. *The Longest Tunnel.* Naval Institute Press, 1990.

Carroll, Tim. *The Great Escape from Stalag Luft III.* Mainstream Publishing Company (Edinburgh), Ltd., 2004.

Davies, Stephen R., *RAF Police: The Great Escape Murders.* Woodfield Publishing, 2009.

Durand, Arthur. *Stalag Luft III: The Secret Story.* Louisiana State University Press, 1988.

Gill, Anton. *The Great Escape: The Full Dramatic Story with Contributions from Survivors and Their Families.* Headline Book Publishing, 2002.

Hastings, Max. *Armageddon: The Battle for Germany 1944–1945.* Alfred A. Knopf, 2004.

MacDonald, C. A. *The Killing of Reinhard Haydrich: The SS "Butcher of Prague."* Da Capo Press, 1998.

MacDonogh, Giles. *After the Reich: The Brutal History of the Allied Occupation.* Basic Books, 2007.

Nichol, John, and Tony Rennell. *Tail-End Charlies: The Last Battles of Bomber Command.* Viking, 2004.

Rolf, David. *Prisoners of the Reich: Germany's Captives 1939–1945.* Leo Cooper, Ltd. 1988.

Ryan, Cornelius. *The Last Battle.* Simon & Schuster, 1966.

Scholey, Pete. *Who Dares Wins: Special Forces Heroes of the SAS.* Osprey Publishing, 2008.

Scotland, A. P. *The London Cage.* Evans Brothers, Ltd., London, 1957.

Vance, Jonathan F. *A Gallant Company: The Men of the Great Escape.* Pacifica Military History, 2000.

Online Articles and Resources

Landsman, Mark. "Property and the Banality of Memory." *Cabinet Magazine,* issue 10 (Property, Spring 2003): http://www.cabinetmagazine.org/issues/10/banality_memory.php.

Meyhoff, Andreas, and Gerhard Pfeil. "Garmisch-Partenkirchen's Uncomfortable Past." *Spiegel Online International,* January 22, 2010: http://www.spiegel.de/international/germany/0,1518,673241,00.html.

"The Massacre at Lidice." Holocaust Education and Archive Research Team: http://blog.holocaustresearchproject.org/2008/12/10/the-lidice-massacre.aspx. (Referred to in the Source Notes as "The Massacre at Lidice.")

Sachsenhausen-Oranienburg, Germany, Jewish Virtual Library: http://www.jewishvirtuallibrary.org/jsource/Holocaust/Sach.html. (Referred to in the Source Notes section as "JVL.")

Struthof: Site of the former Natzweiler concentration camp: http://www.struthof.fr/index.php?id=1&L=1. (Referred to in the Source Notes section as "Natzweiler.")

Task Force Baum and the Hammelburg Raid: www.taskforcebaum.de/index1.html. (This was the primary source of information on the Oflag XIII-B rescue operation detailed in Chapter 7, "Munich," and is referred to in the Source Notes section as "Domes and Heinlein.")

Report of the International Red Cross: Oflag XIII-B. Prepared by Military Intelligence Service War Department: www.taskforcebaum.de/oflag13/report1.html. (Referred to in the Source Notes section as "RC.")

Parliamentary Debates, HC 19 May 1944, vol. 400, cc437-9: Officer Prisoners of War, Germany (Shooting): http://hansard.millbanksystems.com/commons/1944/may/19/officer-prisoners-of-war-germany-shooting.

Parliamentary Debates, HC 23 June 1944, vol. 401, cc477-82: Officer Prisoners of War, Germany (Shooting): http://hansard.millbanksystems.com/commons/1944/jun/23/officer-prisoners-of-war-germany-shooting

News Articles and Periodicals:

Charlesworth, Lorie. "2 SAS Regiment, War Crimes Investigations, and British Intelligence: Intelligence Officials and the Natzweiler Trial." *Journal of Intelligence History* 6, no. 2 (Winter 2006).

Janowitz, Morris. "German Reactions to Nazi Atrocities." *American Journal of Sociology* (September 1946).

"Goebbels invites attacks on fliers." *New York Times,* May 27, 1944.

"German Prisoner Recaptured." *London Sunday Times,* May 14, 1946.

"Britain condemns 2 in Gestapo." *New York Times,* November 7, 1948.

Untitled. *New York Times,* October 25, 1952.

"Ex-Death Camp tell story of Nazi and Soviet horrors." *New York Times,* December 17, 2001.

"The love story that inspired The Great Escape." *Telegraph* (UK), September 26, 2004.

"The secrets of the London Cage." *Guardian* (UK), November 12, 2005.

"Major Henry Druce" (Obituary). *Telegraph* (UK), February 7, 2007.

"He shot the hero of the Great Escape in cold blood. But was this one Nazi who didn't deserve to hang?" *Daily Mail* (UK), October 24, 2009.

Transcripts and Unpublished Manuscripts

Law Reports of Trials of War Criminals: Selected and Prepared by the United Nations War Crimes Commission, vol. XI. His Majesty's Stationary Office (London), 1949.

Private Papers of L. H. Harcus. Imperial War Museum, London.

Diary of Master Engineer Robert James Goode. Imperial War Museum, London.

Documentary Films

Clarke, Steven, dir. *Great Escape: The Untold Story.* A Granada Production, 2001.

West, Steve, dir. *The Great Escape: The Reckoning.* Electric Pictures, Brook Lapping Productions, and Screen Australia, 2009.

PREAMBLE: THE GREAT ESCAPE

1 Stalag Luft III location and security details. Gill, pgs. 53, 54; Brickhill, pg. 27; Carroll, pgs. 59–60, 61.

1 Different colored soils and the need for a long tunnel. Gill, pg. 54; Carroll, pg. 60.

1 Size and construction of barracks and their distance from the fence. Carroll, pgs. 60, 61.

2 Barracks built on stilts and concrete pilings. Carroll, pg. 61.

2 Germans sink subterranean microphones. Air 40/2486/031.

2 Canine units and weather conditions. Carroll, pgs. 60, 62.

2 "main camps." Carroll, pg. 59.

2 Roger Bushell arrives at Stalag Luft III. Brickhill, pg. 19.

2 Bushell shot down and captured. Brickhill, pgs. 3–4; Gill, pg. 14; Vance, pg. 12.

3 Bushell's biographic details from birth to being shot down. Gill, pgs. 11–14.

3 Bushell's escape from the train, being betrayed in Prague. Brickhill, pgs. 8–9; Gill, pgs. 10, 44.

4 Bushell assumes command of X-Organization, takes advantage of seasoned escapers. Brickhill, pg. 20; Gill, pg. 75.

4 Locations of the tunnels. Gill, pgs. 106–107.

4–5 Concealing the tunnels. Gill, pgs. 111–112, 114; Brickhill, pgs. 34–36.

5 "a standard pastime at Stalag Luft III." Air 40/2487/009.

5 The role of the "duty pilots." Gill, pgs. 108, 137–138.

5 The process of digging a tunnel. Brickhill, pg. 79.

5–6 Conditions in the tunnel. Brickhill, pgs. 79, 80.

6 "Digging was the worst . . ." Brickhill, pg. 80.

6 Fanshawe and his "trouser bags." Brickhill, pg. 41; Gill, pg. 125.

6 Walenn and the work of "Dean and Dawson." Carroll, pgs. 110–112; Gill, pgs. 59–60, 146–147.

7 "Made in Stalag Luft III." Gill, pg. 150.

7 The work of Plunkett's cartographic team. Gill, pg. 93.

7 "a bed-stead and mattress, knife, spoon . . ." Air 40/2286/034.

7 Inventory list of items used to build the tunnels. Air 40/2286/034.

7 Lighting the tunnels. Gill, pg. 120; Pumping fresh air into the tunnels. Brickhill, pgs. 50–51.

8 "While bombed-out German civilians had to do their utmost . . ." Air 40/2286/034-035.

8 "heavy earth vibrations." Air 40/2286/031.

8 Laborers working the coal stores are responsible for microphone noise. Air 40/2286/031.

8–9 Discovery and destruction of Tom. Gill, pgs. 140–141, 144; Carroll, pgs. 138–139.

9 Building Harry. Andrews, pg. 46; Gill, pgs. 122–123, 155, 158, 166.

9 The date set for the escape. Burgess, pg. 123.

9–10 Lottery to go through the tunnel, and final preparations. Andrews, pgs. 53–54; Gill, pg. 163; Burgess, pg. 124.

10 Rate of men through the tunnel. Carroll, pg. 211; Escape's slow process and various mishaps. Andrews, pg. 54; Gill, pgs. 179–180, 184, 185.

10 Outside temperature sinks to thirty below zero. Carroll, pg. 211.

10 Prisoners 101 to 200 are ordered back to their bunks. Burgess, pg. 135.

10 Only fifty men have so far managed to get away. Carroll, pg. 212.

11 The first men out of the tunnel. Burgess, pgs. 129–130.

11 Guard discovers tunnel exit. Gill, pg. 187.

11 Chaos following the tunnel's discovery, prisoners are rounded up outside. Gill, pgs. 188–190; Brickhill, pgs. 199–200.

11 Prisoners spend nearly three hours standing outside; seventy-six men escaped. Brickhill, pg. 200.

PROLOGUE: SUNDAY, MARCH 26

13 Hitler calls a meeting with Göring, Himmler, and Keitel. Air 40/2487/011.

13 Göring and Keitel clash over prisoner responsibility. IMT, pg. 2; Westhoff statement. Air 40/2487/131.

14 Breslau Kripo initiate national hue and cry. Law Reports of Trials of War Criminals: Selected and Prepared by the United Nations War

Crimes Commission (referenced from here on as UNWCC), pg. 35; Men being siphoned off to search for escapees. Westhoff statement. Air 40/2487/131.

14 "It is incredible . . ." Carroll, pg. 243.

15 "irrespective of whether it is an escape . . ." *Stufe Römisch III* order. Air 40/2487/045.

15 "The persons recaptured are to be reported . . ." *Stufe Römisch III* order. Air 40/2487/045.

15 Responses to Red Cross, case-by-case handling for American and British prisoners. *Stufe Römisch III* order. Air 40/2487/045.

15 Details of *Aktion Kugel*. The Operation *Kugel* Order. Air 40/2487/049; Mathausen affidavit. Air 40/2487/050.

15 "more than half the escapees." UNWCC, pg. 33.

15 Himmler proposes that fifty escapees be shot. UNWCC, pg. 39; Andrews, pg. 57.

16 "The frequent mass escapes of officer prisoners . . ." UNWCC, pg. 33.

16 *Kripo* charged with handing prisoners over to the Gestapo. UNWCC, pgs. 33–35.

16 Wielen summoned to Nebe's office in Berlin. Wielen statements. Air 40/2488/014 and Air 40/2487/150.

16 Nebe's office and red leather furniture. Wielen statement. Air 40/2488/016-017.

17 "You look tired . . ." based on paraphrased conversation in Wielen statement. Air 40/2487/150.

17 "was very angry." Wielen statement. Air 40/2487/150.

17 Wielen declines to accept responsibility. Wielen statement. Air 40/2487/150.

17 "looked extremely tired . . ." Wielen statement. Air 40/2487/150.

17 Breslau *Kripo* ordered to hand prisoners to Breslau Gestapo. Wielen statement. Air 40/2488/014-015.

17 Wielen arranges meeting with Scharpwinkel. Wielen statement. Air 40/2487/151.

17 "I shall do this personally." Wielen statement. Air 40/2487/151.

17 Thirty-five escapees imprisoned at Gorlitz. Air 40/2487/022.

17–18 Details of recaptured escapees arrive in Nebe's Berlin office. Merten statement. Air 40/2487/076.

18 "You have heard about the Führer Order . . ." Merten statement. Air 40/2487/076.

18 Nebe starts sorting through the index cards. Merten statement. Air 40/2487/076.

18 "He is so young . . ." Merten statement. Air 40/2487/076.

18 "He is for it." Merten statement. Air 40/2487/076.

18 Nebe swaps one card for another and hands stack to Merten. Merten statement. Air 40/2487/076.

18 "Now quickly, the list!" Merten statement. Air 40/2487/076.

18 Merten misstates the location of prisoners. Merten statement. Air 40/2487/077.

CHAPTER 1: "THOSE ARE MY ORDERS"

19 "I have to acquaint you with a top secret matter." UNWCC, pg. 43.

19 "It is an order from the Führer . . ." UNWCC, pg. 43.

19–20 Post's biographical details. Air 40/2287/036; Air 40/2279/007-008.

20 Details and planning of operation under Post's command. Oskar Schmidt statement. Air 40/2279/026.

20 "Anyone not complying . . ." Oskar Schmidt statement. Air 40/2279/026.

21 Catanach and Christensen catch 3:15 to Berlin. Gill, pg. 186.

21 Route the men traveled following the escape. Andrews, pg. 72; Information pertaining to their arrest. Linke statement. Air 40/2279/008-009.

21 Four airmen interrogated and placed in police prison; Berlin notified of capture. Linke statement. Air 40/2279/008.

22 Type of cars driven. Struve statement. Air 40/2279/022.

22 Gestapo agents have lunch in Flensburg, drive to prison. Oskar Schmidt statement. Air 40/2279/026.

22 Handcuffed prisoners escorted out to waiting cars and driven away in convoy. Kaehler statement. Air 40/2279/014.

22 Post points out Kiel landmarks. Andrews, pg. 230.

22–23 Exchange between Post and Catanach is taken from Post's testimony at trial. Quoted in Andrews, pg. 230.

23 Post anxious to make theater performance, drops tickets off at mistress's apartment. Kaehler statement. Air 40/2279/014.

23 Route driven to killing field; change in Post's demeanor. Kaehler statement. Air 40/2279/014.

23 Post marches Catanach into field, shoots airman. Kaehler statement. Air 40/2279/014.

24 Oskar Schmidt tells airmen to get out and relieve themselves. Oskar Schmidt statement. Air 40/2279/027.

24 Prisoners react upon finding Catanach's body in the grass. Oskar Schmidt statement. Air 40/2279/027.

24 "Shoot them!" Kaehler statement. Air 40/2279/015.

24 Airman survives initial shooting. Jacobs statement. Air 40/2279/020; Oskar Schmidt statement. Air 40/2279/027.

24 "He is still alive . . ." Oskar Schmidt statement. Air 40/2279/027.

24 Post and Kaehler leave the scene of the crime. Oskar Schmidt statement. Air 40/2279/027.

24 "He was not mine . . ." Jacobs statement. Air 40/2279/021.

24 "And so did mine." Jacobs statement. Air 40/2279/021.

25 Post arrives at undertaker's. Kaehler statement. Air 40/2279/015.

25 Leather coat and long boots. Tischendorf statement. Air 40/2279/039.

25 "I need you to collect some prisoners . . ." Based on paraphrased conversation in Tischendorf statement. Air 40/2279/039.

25 "What prisoners are they?" Tischendorf statement. Air 40/2279/039.

25 "French. Shot whilst trying to escape." Tischendorf statement. Air 40/2279/039.

25 Tischendorf asks Kaehler about the prisoners. Tischendorf statement. Air 40/2279/039.

25 "They're British airmen." Based on paraphrased conversation in Tischendorf statement. Air 40/2279/039.

25 "Are they the same seventy-six airmen . . ." Based on paraphrased conversation in Tischendorf statement. Air 40/2279/039.

25 "I shall have a car ready to leave . . ." Based on paraphrased conversation in Tischendorf statement. Air 40/2279/039.

25 Details of the drive back to the meadow. Boll statement. Air 40/2279/037; Salau statement. Air 40/2279/038.

26 Boll sees three men standing in field. Boll statement. Air 40/2279/037.

26 Bodies stacked two to a coffin. Salau statement. Air 40/2279/038.

26 Two corpses had bullet wounds to the head. Boll statement. Air 40/2279/037.

26 "If the Russians get here . . ." Salau statement. Air 40/2279/038.

26 Gestapo arrives at the crematorium with bodies to destroy. Schafer statement. Air 40/2279/041.

26 "Here are four corpses to be cremated." Schafer statement. Air 40/2279/041.

26 "Do you have the necessary documents?" Based on paraphrased conversation in Schafer statement. Air 40/2279/041.

26 "Berlin has ordered it." Schafer statement. Air 40/2279/041.

26 "You will not make any entries." Based on paraphrased conversation in Schafer statement. Air 40/2279/041.

26 Bodies to be registered only with Roman numerals I-IV. Schafer statement. Air 40/2279/041.

27 "The corpses are those of prisoners . . ." Based on paraphrased conversation in Schafer statement. Air 40/2279/041.

27 Schafer notes the victims' clothing. Schafer statement. Air 40/2279/041.

27 Jacobs takes possession of the urns. Jacobs statement. Air 40/2279/020-021.

27 "Everything in order?" Based on paraphrased conversation in Tischendorf statement. Air 40/2279/039.

27 "Yes." Tischendorf statement. Air 40/2279/039.

27 "What kind of bodies were they?" Based on paraphrased conversation in Tischendorf statement. Air 40/2279/039.

27 "They were all shot from the back." Based on paraphrased conversation in Tischendorf statement. Air 40/2279/039.

27 Nothing more is said about the incident. Tischendorf statement. Air 40/2279/039.

27 "harass, confuse, and confound the enemy." Carroll, pg. 2.

27 Massey biographical details. Carroll, pg. 73; Gill, pg. 96; Brickhill, pg. 23.

28 Fate and whereabouts of those still on the run a mystery. Carroll, pg. 255; Brickhill, pg. 223.

28 Pieber tells Massey the *kommandant* has "terrible" news. Brickhill, pg. 224; Gill, pg. 221.

28 The camp's rumor mill; Massey escorted to Braune's office. Brickhill, pg. 224.

29 The exchange between Massey and Braune is quoted in Brickhill (pgs. 224–226), Gill (pgs. 221–223), and Carroll (pgs. 225–256). The dialogue differs only slightly in each account. I have quoted the conversation reported by Brickhill, as he was an inmate in Stalag Luft III at the time of the escape.

30 "Please do not think the Luftwaffe . . ." Brickhill, pg. 227.

30 Massey calls a camp meeting. Brickhill, pg. 227; Gill, pg. 223; Numbers tallied. Andrews, pg. 59.

30 Massey's repatriation. Gill, pgs. 224–225.

30 List of dead is posted; Swiss Protecting Power visits the camp. Air 40/ 2488/036.

31 Breakdown of victims' nationalities. Air 40/2488/003.

31 "a full and immediate report." Parliamentary Debates, House of Commons. May 19, 1945, vol. 400. Columns 437–439.

31 Number of victims climbs to fifty, ashes arrive at camp. Air 40/ 2488/036.

31 "No orders have at any time been given . . ." Parliamentary Debates, House of Commons. June 23, 1945, vol. 401. Columns 477–482.

31 "His Majesty's Government must, therefore . . ." Parliamentary Debates, House of Commons. June 23, 1945, vol. 401. Columns 477–482.

CHAPTER 2: COLD CASE

32 McKenna rents room from widowed officer, reviews files. Andrews, pg. 45.

32 McKenna's biographical details. "Sherlock Holmes." *Blackpool Gazette,* February 28, 2007.

33 McKenna joins RAF's Special Investigating Branch after completing thirty operations. *Blackpool Gazette,* February 28, 2007.

33 McKenna tasked with reviewing case files. Andrews, pg. 45.

33 Details of escape found in government report on the incident. Air 40/ 2488/029-042.

33 Bergsland, Muller, and Van der Stok's escape routes. Gill, pgs. 206, 216–218.

34 Task of identifying thousands of German POWs still incomplete. Air 40/2488/041-042.

34 Naming of Wielen, Scharpwinkel, and Nebe. Air 40/2488/038-039.

34 Majority of prisoners captured in Breslau area and imprisoned in Görlitz. Air 40/2488/032; Number of murdered men (27). Air 40/ 2487/024.

34 The various challenges posed by the investigation: seventeen months since the crime, Gestapo destroying papers, agents on the run with

false identities, Germany carved up among the Allies. Air 40/2488/041-042.

35 "In view of these difficulties . . ." Air 40/2488/042.

35 McKenna voices doubt about case. Burgess, pg. 226.

35 "There appears to be little more evidence . . ." Air 40/2488/041.

35 McKenna assigned the case. Burgess, pg. 226; Andrews, pg. 76.

36 McKenna and Williams leave for Germany on September 3, 1945. Andrews, pg. 79.

36 McKenna afraid of the water. Andrews, pg. 36.

36 Absalon strips Lindeiner-Wildau of his command. Based on information in Air 40/2487/014-015 and Air 40/2487/110, which includes references to Lindeiner-Wildau's pro-British sentiments.

36 "Nineteen of the escaped officers . . ." Air 40/2487/020.

37 "200 grams of black bread and one liter of watery soup." Wolter statement. Air 40/2488/008.

37 Inmates tried before a special court. Wolter statement. Air 40/2488/008.

37 "Presumably, it was Absalon . . ." Air 40/2487/020.

37 "a good sort of commandant . . ." Air 40/2487/014.

38 Lindeiner-Wildau's humane treatment of prisoners. Translation of German report. Air 40/2488/093.

38 Names added to the Central Register of War Criminals and Security Suspects. Andrews, pg. 79.

38 "The first task . . ." Air 40/2488/046.

39 "If it is found possible . . ." Air 40/2488/046.

40 23,000,000 people. MacDonogh, pg. 250; "a staggering 93 percent." MacDonogh, pg. 255.

40 McKenna contacts relevant authorities during the first few days of the investigation. Andrews, pgs. 88, 89; Investigation progress report: September 25, 1945. Air 40/2488/057.

41 Prisoners at Görlitz informed they would not see loved ones again; ten inmates taken away on March 31 and cremated at Liegnitz. Air 40/2488/033.

41 Humphreys and Stewart shot down. *Blackpool Gazette,* February 28, 2007; Vance, pg. 186.

42 "camps and concentration areas." Investigation progress report: September 25, 1945. Air 40/2488/057.

42 McKenna's assessment ten days into investigation. Andrews, pg. 93.

43 Absalon's parents in Düsseldorf. Investigation progress report: September 25, 1945. Air 40/2272/108.

43 Parents' address in Düsseldorf. Investigation progress report: September 25, 1945. Air 40/2272/108.

43 "We have not heard from him . . ." Based on paraphrased conversation detailed in investigation progress report: September 25, 1945. Air 40/2272/108.

44 "Yes. She lives in Düsseldorf." Based on paraphrased conversation detailed in investigation progress report: September 25, 1945. Air 40/2272/108.

44 Frau Absalon's address. Investigation progress report: September 25, 1945. Air 40/2272/108.

44 Frau Absalon left to care for two young children and mother. Air 40/2488/026; Andrews, pg. 95.

44 Wife received letter from Absalon in February. Investigation progress report: September 25, 1945. Air 40/2272/108.

44 "Relations between my husband and myself . . ." Based on para-phrased conversation detailed in investigation progress report: September 25, 1945. Air 40/2272/108.

44 "If I do hear from him again . . ." Based on paraphrased conversation detailed in investigation progress report: September 25, 1945. Air 40/2272/108.

45 "well groomed and smartly dressed." Air 40/2488/026.

45 Details of the Battle of Breslau. Bessel, pgs. 39–40.

45 Details of Belsen. Ryan, pg. 328; Andrews, pgs. 90–91; BBC News.

45 Displaced persons from Breslau. Andrews, pgs. 97–98; Bessel, pg. 272.

45 McKenna acquires a list of Breslau refugees in Rinteln. Burgess, pg. 232.

47 McKenna spends an unproductive day in the rain. Burgess, pg. 232; Andrews, pg. 98.

47 McKenna's nightmare. Documentary *Great Escape: The Reckoning.*

48 McKenna hits the streets for second day of questioning. Burgess, pg. 232; Address in Rinteln. Lonsky statement. Air 40/2488/075.

48 McKenna invited into woman's house to wait. Burgess, pg. 233.

49 Lonsky speaks English. Andrews, pg. 99.

49 Lonsky's military and police background. Lonsky statement. Air 40/2488/075.

49 "In this way, I got to know Dr. Gunther Absalon . . ." Lonsky statement. Air 40/2488/075.

49 "Whilst I was in the Military Police . . ." Lonsky statement. Air 40/2488/075.

49 "We were to take them . . ." Lonsky statement. Air 40/2488/075.

50 "There was a Dr. Scharpwinkel . . ." Lonsky statement. Air 40/2488/075.

50 "I remained in the Military Police . . ." Lonsky statement. Air 40/2488/075.

50 Lonsky wounded at Breslau. Lonsky statement. Air 40/2488/076.

50 "I had a good knowledge . . ." Lonsky statement. Air 40/2488/076.

50 "Approval was given . . ." Lonsky statement. Air 40/2488/076.

51 "Since the capitulation . . ." Lonsky statement. Air 40/2488/076.

51 "I met him in Rinteln recently . . ." Lonsky statement. Air 40/2488/076.

51 "I saw Dr. Absalon on occasions . . ." Lonsky statement. Air 40/2488/076.

51 Mercier survives Breslau, is questioned by the Russians. Kah statement. Air 40/2489/008.

52 Mercier eventually makes his way to Hamburg and tries to establish himself in the wine business. Kah statement. Air 40/2489/008-009.

52 Informant calls the police to say Mercier is staying at guest lodge. Burgess, pg. 236.

53 Mercier taken into custody, tries to escape, refuses to answer questions. Burgess, pg. 237.

53 Kah number twelve on RAF's Wanted List. Investigation progress report: October 30, 1945. Air 40/2488/095.

54 Kah offers up Seetzen. Investigation progress report: October 30, 1945. Air 40/2488/095; description of Seetzen. Air 40/2488/059.

54 Raid to take Seetzen into custody. Andrews, pg. 104.

54 Seetzen swallows cyanide capsule. Andrews, pg. 104; Kah interrogation. Air 40/2488/107.

CHAPTER 3: VENGEANCE

56 The story of Russian soldiers taking away Scharpwinkel was relayed to McKenna by Hubertus Zembrodt. Zembrodt statement: Air 40/2488/073-074.

56 Zembrodt's wartime experiences. Zembrodt statement. Air 40/2488/073-074.

56 "The Russians also arrested . . ." Zembrodt statement. Air 40/2488/073.

56 "The arrest at the hospital . . ." Zembrodt statement. Air 40/2488/074.

57 Dr. Rudolf Diels. Investigation progress report: October 10, 1945. Air 40/2488/086.

57 "Nebe was regarded as a most interesting prisoner . . ." Additional information to supplement particulars contained in "Consolidated Wanted List." Air 40/2488/088.

58 "Believed dead but not yet confirmed." Investigation progress report: November 17, 1945. Air 40/2488/138.

58 "Believed killed or taken by the Russians." Investigation progress report: November 17, 1945. Air 40/2488/138.

58 Kah held for interrogation by British Army. Investigation progress report: October 10, 1945. Air 40/2488/086.

58 The account of McKenna's journey to Berlin and his encounter with the Russians is taken from a firsthand account printed in Andrews, pgs. 109–110.

61 "I think you are prepared to help us with information." Kah interrogation. Air 40/2488/105.

61 "Yes, Germany has lost the war . . ." Kah interrogation. Air 40/ 2488/105.

61 "If you do not tell us the truth . . ." Kah interrogation. Air 40/ 2488/107.

61 "I want to help you voluntarily . . ." Kah interrogation. Air 40/ 2488/107.

61 Kah's knowledge of Scharpwinkel. Kah interrogation. Air 40/2488/ 103-105, 107.

62 "Do you know what happened to him?" Kah interrogation. Air 40/ 2488/107.

62 "No. The capitulation was so much in a hurry . . ." Kah interrogation. Air 40/2488/107.

62 Courtney arrives in Germany with Fritz the German shepherd. Andrews, pg. 112.

63 Lyrics quoted in "German Reactions to Nazi Atrocities." Janowitz, pg. 141.

63 Information at Dachau leads to the arrests of Walde, Grosch, and Hoffman. Investigation progress report: December 5, 1945. Air 40/ 2488/156.

63 Statements of Hoffman, Walde, and Hoffman. Investigation progress report: Dec. 1945–Jan. 1946. Air 40/2489/133-136. (Individual statements are archived as follows: Hoffman—Air 40/2489/049-052; Walde—Air 40/2489/130-132; Grosch—Air 40/2489/137-138.)

64 Information on Fritz Panzinger. Investigation progress report: December 20, 1945. Air 40/2489/106.

64 "The Americans are interested . . ." Investigation progress report: December 20, 1945. Air 40/2489/106.

64 "head of the Reich security office . . ." Gill, pg. 9.

65 Killing of Reinhard Heydrich. MacDonald, pgs. 170–175, 192–196.

65 "seventeen rows of corpses in bloody clothes . . ." *The Massacre at Lidice*

65 German soldiers destroy graveyard, ship women and children off to concentration camp. *The Massacre at Lidice* (Holocaust Education and Research Team).

65 Dr. F. V. van der Bijil allowed to question suspect. Letter to British Ambassador in Prague: December 2, 1945: Air 40/2489/144.

66 "Detailed information has just come into my possession . . ." Letter to British Ambassador in Prague: December 2, 1945: Air 40/2489/144.

66 "The driver of one was Kiowsky . . ." Letter to British Ambassador in Prague: December 2, 1945: Air 40/2489/144.

67 "a harmless person." Letter to British Ambassador in Prague: December 2, 1945: Air 40/2489/144.

67 "Arriving at a spot somewhere between . . ." Letter to British Ambassador in Prague: December 2, 1945: Air 40/2489/144.

67 "It is asserted that these murders . . ." Letter to British Ambassador in Prague: December 2, 1945: Air 40/2489/145.

67 "I, therefore, request [Your] Excellency . . ." Letter to British Ambassador in Prague: December 2, 1945: Air 40/2489/145.

67 "I would add that I am deeply interested . . ." Letter to British Ambassador in Prague: December 2, 1945: Air 40/2489/145.

CHAPTER 4: ZLÍN

68 "overgrown Spaniard." Brickhill, pg. 26.

68 Description of Kirby-Green. Gill, pg. 48

68 Kirby-Green biographical details. Carroll, pgs. 57–58; Gill, pg. 48; *Daily Telegraph.* September 26, 2004.

69 "We were on our way home . . ." *Daily Telegraph.* September 26, 2004.

69 "don't do well . . ." *Daily Telegraph.* September 26, 2004.

70 Kidder biographical details. Vance, pg. 172.

70 "My beloved adored darling . . ." *Daily Telegraph*, September 26, 2004.

71 Kirby-Green in the tunnel. Brickhill, pgs. 184-185; Gill, pgs. 184-185.

71 Kirby-Green and Kidder at the station. Carroll, pg. 209; Gill, pgs. 184–185; Andrews, pg. 68.

71 Kirby-Green and Kidder board 1 A.M. train; captured in Hodinin. Gill, pgs. 186, 210.

72 Bowes background. Andrews, pg. 33.

72 "We can now accept . . ." Special Investigation Branch memo: January 21, 1946. Air 40/2489/142.

73 Lyon's biographical details. Burgess, pg. 239.

73 Details of investigation in Czechoslovakia. Investigation progress report: March 12, 1946. Air 40/2491/041.

74 Questioning Schauschütz. Investigation progress report: March 12, 1946. Air 40/2491/041.

74 Schauschütz dispatched to Zlín as temporary head of police. Schauschütz statement. Air 40/2487/160-161.

74 "As he handed me . . ." Schauschütz statement. Air 40/2487/161.

75 Schauschütz ordered to write report. Schauschütz statement. Air 40/2487/161.

75 Report is approved. Schauschütz statement. Air 40/2487/161.

75 "I had nothing further to do . . ." Schauschütz statement. Air 40/ 2487/165.

75 The naming of other suspects. Schauschütz statement. Air 40/2487/ 166; Nöelle last seen in Prague. Air 40/2493/057.

75 Rumors regarding Nöelle's fate. Air 40/2493/057.

75 "Nöelle would have had to transmit . . ." Schauschütz statement. Air 40/2487/166.

75 "I can only say that . . ." Schauschütz statement. Air 40/2487/166.

76 Names Kiowsky. Schauschütz statement. Air 40/2487/166.

76 "I have been told that driver Fritz . . ." Schauschütz statement. Air 40/2487/166.

76 Relevance of Schauschütz statement. Investigation progress report: March 12, 1946. Air 40/2491/041.

76 Schwarzer's possible whereabouts. Investigation progress report: March 12, 1946. Air 40/2491/041.

76 Vaca and the prison at Pankratz. Burgess, pg. 241.

77 Bowes identifies suspects in bar mural. Brickhill, pg. 253; Burgess, pg. 242.

77 "This is Knuppelberg . . ." Brickhill, pg. 253.

77 Kiowsky questioned in judge's office. Burgess, 243.

78 "You are obliged to say nothing . . ." Kiowsky statement. Air 40/ 2487/157.

78 Kiowsky's biographical details. Kiowsky statement. Air 40/2487/157.

78 "I entered his office . . ." Kiowsky statement. Air 40/2487/157.

78 Kiowsky identifies picture of Knuppelberg. Burgess, pg. 243.

78 Kiowsky retrieves prisoners. Kiowsky statement. Air 40/2487/157.

78 "Both officers were handcuffed . . ." Kiowsky statement. Air 40/ 2487/157.

78 "As I was curious . . ." Kiowsky statement. Air 40/2487/157.

79 "Tell him in English . . ." Kiowsky statement. Air 40/2487/157.

79 "I received the order . . ." Kiowsky statement. Air 40/2487/157.

79 Zacharias gives the thumbs-down. Kiowsky statement. Air 40/ 2487/158.

79 "I knew for the first time . . ." Kiowsky statement. Air 40/2487/158.

79 Cars pull over outside of Zlín. Kiowsky statement. Air 40/2487/158.

79 "I knew that he was carrying a gun . . ." Kiowsky statement. Air 40/ 2487/158.

80 Schwarzer asks for a smoke. Kiowsky statement. Air 40/2487/158.

80 "I gave him a cigarette . . ." Kiowsky statement. Air 40/2487/158.

80 "the dark uniform . . ." Kiowsky statement. Air 40/2487/158.

80 "everything has passed off smoothly . . ." Kiowsky statement. Air 40/ 2487/158.

80 "Ziegler then gave us the strictest instructions . . ." Kiowsky statement. Air 40/2487/159.

81 Kozlowsky constructs cover story. Kiowsky statement. Air 40/ 2487/159.

81 "He showed us a plan . . ." Kiowsky statement. Air 40/2487/159.

81 "If asked, that the two fliers . . ." Kiowsky statement. Air 40/2487/159.

81 "harmless persons and ex–customs officials." Investigation progress report: March 12, 1946. Air 40/2491/042.

81 Frau Zacharias can confirm the information. Investigation progress report: March 12, 1946. Air 40/2491/042.

81 Frau Zacharias confirms information. Andrews, pg. 135; Investigation progress report: March 12, 1946. Air 40/2491/042.

82 Onetime clerk who speaks English. Johann Heger statement. Air 40/2491/065.

82 "I spoke to both the officers in English . . ." Heger statement. Air 40/2491/065.

83 Bowes and Lyon visit crime scene. Investigation progress report: March 12, 1946. Air 40/2491/043.

83 "It's open country . . ." Investigation progress report: March 12, 1946. Air 40/2491/043.

83 "The body of the first man . . ." Statement of Emil Schreier. Air 40/2491/068.

83 "Before I left . . ." Statement of Emil Schreier. Air 40/2491/068.

84 Krupa's account of what transpired at crematorium. Krupa statement. Air 40/2491/069.

84 "The Gestapo men . . ." Krupa statement. Air 40/2491/069.

84 Urn numbers are listed in Krupa's statement. Air 40/2491/069.

84 "I don't know where the urns . . ." Krupa statement. Air 40/2491/069.

84 Ziegler and Kozlowsky spotted at hotel two weeks prior. Investigation progress report: March 12, 1946. Air 40/2491/043.

84 Travel arrangements to meet up with McKenna. Investigation progress report: March 12, 1945. Air 40/2491/044; Andrews, pg. 136.

85 Raid on hotel at 0100 hours. Investigation progress report: March 12, 1945. Air 40/2491/044.

86 "No Gestapo from Brno . . ." Investigation progress report: March 12, 1945. Air 40/2491/044.

86 "They bled me white . . ." Investigation progress report: March 12, 1945. Air 40/2491/044.

86 "With regard to the question . . ." Investigation progress report: March 12, 1945. Air 40/2491/044.

86 McKenna arrives in Bremen and stakes out refrigeration plant. Investigation progress report: April 4, 1946. Air 40/2481/285.

86 McKenna sees Zacharias approaching. Investigation progress report: April 4, 1946. Air 40/2481/285.

87 Zacharias stripped and sent to Karlsburg. Investigation progress report: April 4, 1946. Air 40/2481/285.

87 McKenna seeks permission to take over custody of Zacharias. Investigation progress report: April 4, 1946. Air 40/2481/285.

87 Zacharias escapes. Investigation progress report: April 4, 1946. Air 40/2481/285.

87 Zacharias runs into a bombed-out building. Andrews, pg. 141.

87 McKenna returns to Rinteln to wait. Investigation progress report: April 4, 1946. Air 40/2481/285.

87 "Erich has been ill . . ." Burgess, pg. 247.

87 Return address of house. Investigation progress report: April 4, 1946. Air 40/2481/285.

87 March 31 raid on house. Investigation progress report: April 4, 1946. Air 40/2481/285.

87 McKenna finally takes custody of Zacharias. Investigation progress report: April 4, 1946. Air 40/2481/286.

88 "I bought it in Zlín." Quoted exchange is based on information in investigation progress report: April 4, 1946. Air 40/2481/286.

88 "Why did you escape . . ." Zacharias interrogation. Air 40/2491/287.

88 "I was afraid." Zacharias interrogation. Air 40/2491/287.

88 "Of what?" Zacharias interrogation. Air 40/2491/287.

88 "I know why you arrested me . . ." Zacharias interrogation. Air 40/2491/287.

88 Years serving with the Gestapo. Zacharias interrogation. Air 40/2491/287.

88 "I last saw him in Zlín." Zacharias interrogation. Air 40/2491/287.

88 "I carried out the first task . . ." Zacharias statement. Air 40/2491/292.

88 Kirby-Green protests being shackled. Zacharias statement. Air 40/2491/292.

88 "I reported this to Ziegler . . ." Zacharias statement. Air 40/2491/292.

88 Officers placed in car for supposed transfer. Zacharias statement. Air 40/2491/293.

89 "I had the Canadian officer in my car . . ." Zacharias statement. Air 40/2491/293.

89 Vehicles pull over. Zacharias statement. Air 40/2491/293.

89 "I made the prisoner get out of the car . . ." Zacharias statement. Air 40/2491/293.

89 Zacharias and Knuppelberg fire their guns simultaneously. Zacharias statement. Air 40/2491/293.

89 "I fired a second shot . . ." Zacharias statement. Air 40/2491/293.

89 Zacharias confirms Kidder is dead. Zacharias statement. Air 40/2491/293.

89 "I ran to Knuppelberg and saw his prisoner . . ." Zacharias statement. Air 40/2491/293.

89 Zacharias reports back to Ziegler. Zacharias statement. Air 40/2491/294.

89 "He replied, 'Good, that's all right . . .' " Zacharias statement. Air 40/2491/294.

CHAPTER 5: THE LONDON CAGE

90 Nazi propaganda lies regarding the destruction of London. Andrews, pg. 143.

90 Details about the London Cage, including street address and number of interrogators. "The Secrets of the London Cage," *Guardian,* Saturday, November 12, 2005.

91 "for their height, rather than their brains." *Guardian,* Saturday, November 12, 2005.

91 "groceries and provisions trade." Scotland, pg. 16.

91 Scotland biographical details. Scotland, pgs. 15-29.

91 Guard standing with a foot on the prisoner's back. *Guardian,* Saturday, November 12, 2005.

91 "Abandon all hope ye who enter here." *Guardian,* Saturday, November 12, 2005.

91 Threats of violence and prisoners deprived of sleep. *Guardian,* Saturday, November 12, 2005.

91 Prolonged standing at attention. *Guardian,* Saturday, November 12, 2005.

92 Scotland turns away representative from the Red Cross. *Guardian,* Saturday, November 12, 2005.

92 Scotland writes a letter explaining his actions. *Guardian,* Saturday, November 12, 2005.

92 "must proceed in Germany . . ." *Guardian,* Saturday, November 12, 2005.

92 Allegations of torture made by SS Captain Fritz Knoechlein. *Guardian,* Saturday, November 12, 2005.

93 "a lame allegation." Scotland, pg. 86.

93 "[He] gave us an example of what might have been . . ." Scotland, pg. 86.

93 "a wild young brute." Scotland, pg. 147.

93 "abnormally large, powerful hands [and] remarkably thick neck." Scotland, pg. 148.

93 Escape impossible with Scots Guards watching the premises. Andrews, pg. 143.

93 Girl's rape and murder. Scotland, pg. 148.

94 "He showed neither remorse for the act . . ." Scotland, pg. 148.

94 Zacharias made to strip and kneel for hours. Andrews, pg. 145; Scotland pgs. 148–149.

94 "Take him away . . ." Scotland, pg. 149.

94 Details of Zacharias's escape taken from an *Evening Standard* article filed in Air 40/2492/032; Andrews, pg. 144.

94 "a Nazi police officer." "German Prisoner Recaptured," *Sunday Times,* May 14, 1946.

94 "His escape is one of the boldest . . ." *Evening Standard.* Air 40/2492/032.

94 "a dark blue reefer jacket . . ." *Evening Standard.* Air 40/2492/032.

95 "Italian prisoners of war . . ." *Evening Standard.* Air 40/2492/033.

95 Zacharias found in bush. Andrews, pg. 145.

CHAPTER 6: PRIME SUSPECTS

96 Erich Graes found in Neümunster Civilian Internment Camp. Air 40/ 2722/088.

96 Graes charged with search in Danzig area. Graes statement. Air 40/ 2490/068.

96 Order to police and military personnel quoted by Graes. Air 40/ 2490/071.

97 "in the best room in the police station." Graes statement. Air 40/2490/068.

97 "The next morning I went to the office . . ." Graes statement. Air 40/2490/068.

97 "Top secret." Graes statement. Air 40/2490/068.

97 Graes finds out about the killings. Graes statement. Air 40/2490/ 068.

97 "forty-three or forty-seven." Graes statement. Air 40/2490/069.

98 "Is this true?" based on conversation detailed in Graes statement. Air 40/2490/068.

98 "We do not do that sort of thing." Graes statement. Air 40/2490/068.

98 "It's a rather distant suburb." Graes statement. Air 40/2490/072.

98 "I am at any time ready . . ." Graes statement. Air 40/2490/069.

98 "He's big and elegant looking . . ." Graes statement. Air 40/ 2490/070.

99 "the manners and appearance of a thug." Report on Karl Neitzel interrogation: January 28, 1946. Air 40/2490/42.

99 Identification of Dr. Leopold Spann. Report on Karl Neitzel interrogation: January 28, 1946. Air 40/2490/42.

99 Files in French Zone suffer from poor organization. Investigation progress report: March 16, 1946. Air 40/2491/092-093.

99 French viewing themselves as conquerors. MacDonogh, pgs. 269–270.

99 French atrocities in Stuttgart and Freudenstadt. MacDonogh, pgs. 78, 79.

99 "looting, destruction and rape." Hastings, pg. 477.

99 "It was not that a sex-starved Russian soldier . . ." Hastings, pg. 478.

99 Trying to establish contact with the Russians; believing the Soviet Zone "held the key." Investigation progress report: March 16, 1946. Air 40/2491/091.

100 "The enquiry appears to be opening . . ." Investigation progress report: March 16, 1946. Air 40/2491/091.

100 Escapees shot in Liberec and cremated in Brüx. Air 40/2487/024-025.

100 Affidavit sheds some light on murders. Affidavit by I.P. Tonder: August 24, 1945. Air 40/2491/025.

101 Bull, Kierath, Mondschein, and Williams captured in the mountains. Affidavit by I. P. Tonder: August 24, 1945. Air 40/2491/025.

101 Tonder and Stower's escape and their walk through the woods. Affidavit by I. P. Tonder: August 24, 1945. Air 40/2491/025.

101 Deciding to travel by train and their eventual capture. Affidavit by I. P. Tonder: August 24, 1945. Air 40/2491/025.

102 "During this time . . ." Affidavit by I. P. Tonder: August 24, 1945. Air 40/2491/026.

102 The Gestapo take four men away. Affidavit by I. P. Tonder: August 24, 1945. Air 40/2491/026.

102 "You are a Czech." Affidavit by I. P. Tonder: August 24, 1945. Air 40/2491/026.

102 Tonder eventually ends up in Colditz. Affidavit by I. P. Tonder: August 24, 1945. Air 40/2491/027.

103 Search of records and the discovery of the cremation order. Investigation progress report: April 3, 1946. Air 40/2491/124.

103 "This is conclusive proof . . ." Investigation progress report: April 3, 1946. Air 40/2491/124.

103 Bowes and Lyon visit crematorium, talk with Anton Sawerthal. Investigation progress report: April 3, 1946. Air 40/2491/124.

103 "As the bodies were being unloaded . . ." Sawerthal statement. Air 40/2491/126.

104 The names of the deceased and the corresponding cremation numbers. Sawerthal statement. Air 40/2491/126.

104 "Shot while attempting to escape." Investigation progress report: April 3, 1946. Air 40/2491/124.

104 "The two chief Gestapo officials . . ." Sawerthal statement. Air 40/2491/126.

104 Reviewing the list of Liberec Gestapo. Investigation progress report: April 3, 1946. Air 40/2491/124.

104 "It is possible . . ." Investigation progress report: April 3, 1946. Air 40/2491/124.

105 Bowes and Lyon attempt to pursue Breslau enquiry. Investigation progress report: May 7, 1946. Air 40/2492/155.

105 Bowes and Lyon meet with the attorney for the district. Investigation progress report: May 7, 1946. Air 40/2492/155.

106 Bowes and Lyon denied meeting with Siedwidski or permission to visit other towns. Investigation progress report: May 7, 1946. Air 40/2492/155.

106 Polish police beat and plunder local German populace, "extort[ing] food and money." Bessel, pg. 224.

106 "in a queue of expellees . . ." Bessel, pg. 224.

106 Evacuation of inmates from Stalag Luft III, inmates moved to neighboring farms and eventual liberation. Gill, pg. 238.

106 Bowes and Lyon visit the former site of Stalag Luft III. Andrews, pg. 172.

107 Bowes and Lyon visit memorial to the fifty. Andrews, pg. 172.

CHAPTER 7: MUNICH

108 Biographical information on Johannes Gouws and details of his capture. Vance, pgs. 128–129.

108 Biographical information on Rupert Stevens and details of his capture. Vance, pgs. 56–68.

109 Gouws's and Stevens's travel plans, last seen alive at Breslau station, ashes arrive at Stalag Luft III. Andrews, pg. 67.

110 1936 Winter Olympics; "Jews Not Wanted." *Spiegel Online International,* January 22, 2010.

110 Nuremberg Laws and the concentration camps. *Spiegel Online International,* January 22, 2010.

110 Goring's escape and Hitler's mountain retreat. *Spiegel Online International,* January 22, 2010.

110 Exchange beginning with "Are you a party member?" Gassner interrogation. Air 40/2491/111.

110 Gassner's police service and eventual arrest. Gassner interrogation. Air 40/2491/111.

111 "Do you remember . . ." Gassner interrogation. Air 40/2491/111.

111 "excellent German" and "good impression." Gassner statement. Air 40/2491/197; Neely's name. Andrews, pg. 152, Air 40/2487/029.

111 "The flying officer asked me . . ." Gassner statement. Air 40/2491/197.

111 Gouws and Stevens arrested on separate trains, Neely returned to Stalag Luft III. Gassner statement. Air 40/2491/198.

111 "The two other officers . . ." Gassner statement. Air 40/2491/198.

112 Gassner ordered to deliver parcels. Gassner statement. Air 40/2491/198.

112 "At first, Haselsberger . . ." Gassner statement. Air 40/2491/198.

112 Evidence relating to crime is destroyed. Gassner statement. Air 40/2491/199.

112 "About a fortnight before the arrival . . ." Gassner statement. Air 40/2491/199.

112 "What happened to the two RAF officers?" Greiner interrogation. Air 40/2491/101.

112 "They were handed over to the Gestapo . . ." Greiner interrogation. Air 40/2491/101.

112 "Did you see the urns?" Greiner interrogation. Air 40/2491/101.

112 "No." Greiner interrogation. Air 40/2491/101.

112 "Do you know what happened . . ." Greiner interrogation. Air 40/2491/101.

112 "I don't know . . ." Greiner interrogation. Air 40/2491/101.

113 "As head of the Munich Kripo . . ." Greiner interrogation. Air 40/2491/101.

113 "No, the matter finished for me . . ." Greiner interrogation. Air 40/2491/101.

113 Achter recalls Schneider showing up with a Russian tommy gun. Achter statement. Air 40/2487/185.

113 "I had not seen a model like that before." Achter statement. Air 40/2487/185.

113 Oswald Schäfer summons a meeting. Achter statement. Air 40/2487/185-186.

113 "Weil resumed his seat opposite me . . ." Achter statement. Air 40/2487/186.

113 Achter puts pieces together after his arrest. Achter statement. Air 40/2487/186.

114 "Until then, I did not know this fact." Achter statement. Air 40/2487/186.

114 "I heard Weil worked for the Americans . . ." Achter statement. Air 40/2487/186.

114 "There are various opinions about Schäfer's whereabouts . . ." Achter statement. Air 40/2487/186.

114 Schermer's suicide. Andrews, pg. 154.

114 Details regarding Peter Mohr. Mohr statement. Air 40/2487/089.

115 Gestapo forced to pay cremation expenses. Mohr statement. Air 40/2487/089.

115 Williams find cremation receipts. Andrews, pg. 157.

115 "It was two feet wide . . ." Andrews, pg. 157.

115 Emil Weil's service with the police and Gestapo. Weil statement. Air 40/2487/205.

116 "Orders are orders." Weil statement. Air 40/2487/205.

116 Car ride with prisoners and arrival at scene of execution. Weil statement. Air 40/2487/205-206.

116 "On the right of the prisoners was Geith . . ." Weil statement. Air 40/ 2487/206.

116 "Schermer said he had to drive . . ." Weil statement. Air 40/2487/206.

116 Schermer and Schneider return in a van. Weil statement. Air 40/ 2487/206.

117 "They're dead." Weil statement. Air 40/2487/206.

117 Schermer confers with civilian and officer. Weil statement. Air 40/ 2487/206.

117 "Shortly afterwards, the civilian and the police officer . . ." Weil statement. Air 40/2487/206.

117 Weil removes names from registry; records are destroyed. Weil statement. Air 40/2487/206-207.

118 Schneider's wife leads investigators to Hammelburg. Andrews, pgs. 154, 157.

118 Conditions at Stalag XIII-B grim. RC Nov. 1, 1945.

118 The struggle to keep warm, no washrooms or hot water. RC Nov. 1, 1945.

118 "one-tenth of a loaf of bread . . ." RC Nov. 1, 1945.

119 Men bedridden by malnutrition. RC Nov. 1, 1945.

119 Air raid policies, tensions between prisoners and guards, inmate shootings. RC Nov. 1, 1945.

119 Task Force Baum sets out on rescue operation on March 26. Domes and Heinlein.

119 Ordeal of making it to the camp; Waters shot and carried back to camp. Domes and Heinlein.

120 Negotiations between camp officials and task force go forward; task force moves out at 20:00 hours. Domes and Heinlein.

120 Baum orders his men to fall back to nearby hill. Domes and Heinlein.

121 Baum ordered "every man for himself." Domes and Heinlein.

121 Germans move into position during the night and attack in the morning; Baum is captured. Domes and Heinlein.

121 U.S. 14th Armored Division liberates the camp. Domes and Heinlein.

121 Johann Schneider's background. Schneider statement. Air 40/2487/201.

122 Schneider summoned to headquarters and ordered to prepare a car. Schneider statement. Air 40/2487/201.

122 "We drive to police HQ." Schneider statement. Air 40/2487/201.

122 Prisoners retrieved from police headquarters. Schneider statement. Air 40/2487/201.

122 "Be ready to leave . . ." Schneider statement. Air 40/2487/201.

122 Schermer returns to garage at 4:30 A.M. Schneider statement. Air 40/2487/201.

122 "On Schäfer's orders . . ." Schneider statement. Air 40/2487/201.

122 Car ride to the killing field. Schneider statement. Air 40/2487/201.

122 "Stop. Pull up to the right." Schneider statement. Air 40/2487/201.

122 "Relieve yourselves." Schneider statement. Air 40/2487/201.

122 Prisoners and Gestapo agents exit the vehicle. Schneider statement. Air 40/2487/201-202.

122 "Shoot! Shoot!" Schneider statement. Air 40/2487/202.

122 "I looked at him again briefly . . ." Schneider statement. Air 40/2487/202.

122 Schneider fires machine gun. Schneider statement. Air 40/2487/202.

122 "Take off the chains at once." Schneider statement. Air 40/2487/202.

122 Bodies covered with tarpaulin; shell casings are collected. Schneider statement. Air 40/2487/202.

124 "If there is a commission of enquiry . . ." Schneider statement. Air 40/2487/202.

124 Weil and Geith remain with the bodies. Schneider statement. Air 40/2487/202.

124 "Schermer told me later . . ." Schneider statement. Air 40/2487/202.

124 Geith's biographical details. Geith statement. Air 40/2487/191.

124 Discussing the order of execution and deciding not to use service pistols. Geith statement. Air 40/2487/192-193.

125 "Schneider proposed after long hesitation . . ." Geith statement. Air 40/2487/193.

125 Gestapo agents and captured airmen struggle past language barrier. Geith statement. Air 40/2487/194.

125 "Nothing went quickly enough for him." Geith statement. Air 40/2487/194.

125 The prisoners are loaded into cars for final journey. Geith statement. Air 40/2487/194-195, 196.

125 Cars are stopped and the prisoners are told to relieve themselves. Geith statement. Air 40/2487/195.

125 "In my opinion . . ." Geith statement. Air 40/2487/195.

126 One airman lay twitching on the ground. Geith statement. Air 40/2487/196.

126 "I'll see to that." Geith statement. Air 40/2487/196.

126 The bodies are unshackled and covered with branches. Geith statement. Air 40/2487/196.

126 "After all this had happened . . ." Geith statement. Air 40/2487/196.

126 The coroner arrives on scene. Geith statement. Air 40/2487/197.

126 "Yes, there is certainly no more to be done here." Geith statement. Air 40/2487/197.

126 "inwardly excited." Geith statement. Air 40/2487/196.

126 "smallest detail" Geith statement. Air 40/2487/198.

126 Geith reads newspaper account of Eden's speech. Geith statement. Air 40/2487/199.

127 "I was compelled to agree . . ." Geith statement. Air 40/2487/199.

127 "This is one hell of a business." Geith statement. Air 40/2487/199.

127 Geith told all records pertaining to the murders will be destroyed. Geith statement. Air 40/2487/199.

127 "I did not take part in the happenings of my own free will . . ." Geith statement. Air 40/2487/199.

127 "I can give an assurance . . ." Geith statement. Air 40/2487/199-200.

127 Courtney tracks down Schäfer's onetime secretary. Air 40/2272/065.

CHAPTER 8: A DEATH IN THE MOUNTAINS

129 Death of Cochran's two friends, hatred of Germans, Whitley bomber downed. Gill pg. 148; Vance, pg. 148.

129 Cochran's escape from Dulag Luft. Vance, pg. 148.

130 Cochran's biographical details. Gill, pgs. 147–148, 164; Vance, pg. 148.

130 Escape plan and travel. Gill, pg. 186; Andrews pg. 71.

130 SAS launch sabotage operations behind enemy lines. Scholey, pg. 45.

131	Men and boys rounded up in Moussey. Scholey, pg. 46.

131	Raid on town. *Daily Telegraph,* February 7, 2007.

131	Bodies unearthed and identified as SAS operatives. Charlesworth, pgs. 24–25.

131	French officials release former Nazis from captivity. Charlesworth, pg. 32.

132	Twenty-two thousand inmates die at camp; Eighty-six men and women gassed to provide anatomical specimens. Natzweiler.

132	Law student, sports editor, joins Gestapo in 1934. Herberg statement. Air 40/2487/232.

132	Barkworth forwards Herberg's name to RAF. Investigation progress report: June 7, 1945. Air 40/2492/197.

132	McKenna breaks out of hospital. Andrews, pgs. 174, 175.

132	Herberg learns of escape while on leave. Herberg statement. Air 40/2487/232.

133	"By order of the Reichsführer SS . . ." Reproduced in Herberg statement. Air 40/2487/233.

133	"After I had noted . . ." Herberg statement. Air 40/2487/233.

133	"I'm still on leave." Herberg statement. Air 40/2487/233.

133	"You'll get another day for this." Herberg statement. Air 40/2487/233.

134	Details of the killing are ironed out. Herberg statement. Air 40/2487/233.

134	Gestapo retrieves Cochran from the prison. Herberg statement. Air 40/2487/233-234.

134	"You are to be taken to a camp . . ." Herberg statement. Air 40/2487/234.

134 Cochran becomes defiant when questioned about escape. Herberg statement. Air 40/2487/234.

134 "I can't talk about that . . ." Herberg statement. Air 40/2487/234.

135 Car reaches the gate of the Natzweiler camp. Herberg statement. Air 40/2487/234.

135 "We've lost our way." Herberg statement. Air 40/2487/234.

135 Herberg stays behind as other walk Cochran into the woods; hears two shots. Herberg statement. Air 40/2487/234.

135 Cochran execution and the transporting of the body to the camp. Herberg statement. Air 40/2487/234.

135 "We have been unlucky . . ." Herberg statement. Air 40/2487/234.

135 Ganninger smiles. Herberg statement. Air 40/2487/234.

136 "I am already in the picture." Herberg statement. Air 40/2487/234.

136 "Do you now want a death certificate?" Herberg statement. Air 40/2487/234.

136 "to produce this death certificate in the highest quarters." Herberg statement. Air 40/2487/235.

136 Herberg is denied a death certificate. Herberg statement. Air 40/2487/234-235.

136 "In Karlsruhe, where I reported by telephone . . ." Herberg statement. Air 40/2487/235.

136 Herberg summoned from movie theater and dispatched to Berlin. Herberg statement. Air 40/2487/235.

137 "an unguarded moment." Herberg statement. Air 40/2487/235.

137 Müller dictates report. Herberg statement. Air 40/2487/235.

137 June 4 meeting with Barkworth. Investigation progress report: June 15, 1946. Air 40/2286/007.

138 Wochner's sentence and Ganninger's suicide. Investigation progress report: July 4, 1946. Air 40/2272/074; Investigation progress report: June 15, 1946. Air 40/2286/007.

138 McKenna works his way from camp to camp in the American sector. Andrews, pg. 182.

139 "round, unhealthy face . . ." Air 40/2492/219.

139 Preiss biographical details. Preiss statement. Air 40/2487/236.

139 "The order has been given . . ." Preiss statement. Air 40/2487/237.

139 Preiss shoots Cochran. Preiss statement. Air 40/2487/238.

139 "The pistol did not quite touch his head . . ." Preiss statement. Air 40/2487/238.

140 Preiss takes ashes to *Kripo* in Breslau. Preiss statement. Air 40/2487/239-240.

140 "I declare that I only acted . . ." Preiss statement. Air 40/2487/240.

140 "This was my first and last execution." Preiss statement. Air 40/2487/237.

140 Boschert hospitalized with broken spine; McKenna arrives in Karlsruhe for interrogation. Investigation progress report: July 3, 1946. Air 40/2286/006.

140 Boschert stays with car. Boschert statement. Air 40/2487/225.

140 "After about half a minute to a minute . . ." Boschert statement. Air 40/2487/225.

141 "I never saw the body again." Boschert statement. Air 40/2487/225.

141 Boschert moved to Paderborn for eventual transfer to London. Investigation progress report: July 3, 1946. Air 40/2286/006.

141 Gmeiner in French custody. Investigation progress report: August 6, 1946. Air 40/2493/036.

141 "By order of the Führer . . ." Order reproduced in Gmeiner statement. Air 40/2487/226.

141 "Having received the order . . ." Gmeiner statement. Air 40/ 2487/230.

142 "I became a civil servant . . ." Gmeiner statement. Air 40/2487/ 231.

142 "If in my forty-second year . . ." Gmeiner statement. Air 40/ 2487/231.

142 "This case can now be regarded as completed." Investigation progress report: August 6, 1946. Air 40/2493/036.

CHAPTER 9: SAARBRÜCKEN

143 German hatred toward Allied airmen. Nichol and Rennell, pg. 325.

143 A firsthand account of airgunner Tom Tate's ordeal can be found in Nichol and Rennell, pgs. 338–345.

144 "First of all . . ." Sgt. L. H. Harcus. IWM.

144 Inmates stripped upon arrival at Dulag Luft; measurements of cell. Durand, pgs. 60, 64.

144 Red Cross form and interrogation techniques. Rolf, pgs. 41–43; Durand, pg. 63.

145 "There are too many people . . ." RAF Master Engineer Robert James Goode. IWM.

145 "Go ahead and shoot." RAF Master Engineer Robert James Goode. IWM.

145 Interrogator sends airman back to his cell. RAF Master Engineer Robert James Goode. IWM.

145 "made from various mixtures of hay . . ." Durand, pg. 61.

145 Men denied toiletries and cigarettes; daily rations at Dulag Luft. Durand, pgs. 60, 61.

145 Germans increase heat in cells to stifling levels. Durand, pg. 64; Cell walls heavily insulated and windows sealed. Rolf, pg. 41.

145 "We used to go in these rooms . . ." Flight Lt. H. Burton. IWM.

146 Early escape attempt from Dulag Luft. Gill, pgs. 32–33; Brickhill, pg. 6.

146 Bushell's escape plan. Gill, pgs. 41–42; Brickhill, pgs. 7–8.

146 Bushell runs, is captured, and shipped to Barth. Brichill, pg. 8; Carroll, pg. 33.

146 Bushell loses forty pounds while imprisoned at Barth. Brickhill, pg. 8; Gill, pg. 43.

146 Bushell's escape from the train. Gill, pgs. 41–43; Brickhill, pgs. 8–9.

146 Host family in Prague murdered, Zafouk shipped to Colditz, Bushell held by the Gestapo before arriving at Stalag Luft III. Gill, pg. 10; Brickhill, pg. 9.

148 Scheidhauer's escape by boat. Vance, pg. 203.

148 Scheidhauer's biographical details. Carroll, pgs. 190–191.

148 Bushell and Scheidhauer numbers five and six in tunnel. Gill, pg. 178; Purchase tickets and are approached in Saarbrücken. Carroll, pgs. 223, 240.

149 "Good luck." Carroll, pg. 240.

149 "Thank you." Carroll, pg. 240.

149 Bushell and Scheidhauer are captured and interrogated. Dingermann statement. Air 40/2491/190-191; Brickhill, pg. 258.

149 Dingermann takes call from Spann, makes necessary arrangements; meets with concerned officer. Dingermann statement. Air 40/2491/190.

149 "I heard in confidence . . ." Based on paraphrased conversation in Dingermann statement. Air 40/2491/190.

150 "I seriously do not believe . . ." Dingermann statement. Air 40/2491/190.

150 "What struck me . . ." Dingermann statement. Air 40/2491/189.

150 "When informed a few days later . . ." Dingermann statement. Air 40/2491/190.

150 "About three or four weeks ago . . ." Dingermann statement. Air 40/2491/191.

151 Lampel names Bender as arresting agent. Lampel statement. Air 40/2490/118.

151 "I presume he is still living there." Lampel statement. Air 40/2490/118.

152 Schmoll's statement and Breithaupt's arrest. Andrews, pgs. 203, 204.

152 "to be returned to a camp in the Reich." Breithaupt statement. Air 40/2487/211.

152 Captured airmen retrieved from Lerchesflur prison. Breithaupt statement. Air 40/2487/211.

152 "This is not compatible with the honor of an officer." Breithaupt statement. Air 40/2487/212.

154 Route taken on journey to killing field. Breithaupt statement. Air 40/2487/212.

154 "Don't drive so fast . . ." Breithaupt statement. Air 40/2487/212.

154 Schulz and Spann get out of car. Breithaupt statement. Air 40/2487/212.

154 "I have received an order by teleprint . . ." Breithaupt statement. Air 40/2487/212.

154 Bushell and Scheidhauer are ordered out of the car. Breithaupt statement. Air 40/2487/212.

154 "Shots will be fired immediately . . ." Breithaupt statement. Air 40/ 2487/212.

155 "sounded almost like one." Breithaupt statement. Air 40/2487/ 212.

155 Schulz is ordered to stand watch over the bodies. Breithaupt statement. Air 40/2487/213.

155 "You are not allowed . . ." Based on paraphrased conversation in Breithaupt statement. Air 40/2487/213.

155 Bodies are loaded into a box and driven to Neue Bremm. Breithaupt statement. Air 40/2487/212.

155 "What's going to happen . . ." Based on paraphrased conversation in Breithaupt statement. Air 40/2487/213.

155 "They are to be cremated." Based on paraphrased conversation in Breithaupt statement. Air 40/2487/213.

155 Information on Neue Bremm, including reference to "expanded police prison." Landsman.

155 "He pointed out an empty space . . ." Breithaupt statement. Air 40/ 2487/213.

155 Description of Schulz and his last known address. Breithaupt statement. Air 40/2487/213.

156 Tracking down the Schulz family to Frankenholz. Andrews, pgs. 206–207.

156 McKenna searches the house. Andrews, pg. 207; *Daily Mail*, October 24, 2009.

156 "My dearest, brave darling . . ." *Daily Mail*, October 24, 2009.

156 Frau Schulz denies the letter comes from her husband; McKenna takes letter as evidence. Andrews, pgs. 207–208.

157 "South African born . . ." Andrews, pg. 208.

157 McKenna shows camp commandant letter; guards bring Ernst Schmidt in for interrogation. Andrews, pg. 208.

157 McKenna shows prisoner letter, Schulz confesses to his true identity. Andrews, pg. 209.

157 "*Ich bin Emil Schulz.*" Andrews, pg. 209.

157 Schulz lets prisoner out of vehicle; Spann fires several shots. Schulz statement. Air 40/2487/221.

158 "I also fired one of these shots . . ." Schulz statement. Air 40/2487/221.

158 Schulz shoots Bushell in the temple. Schulz statement. Air 40/2487/221.

158 "Death took place immediately." Schulz statement. Air 40/2487/221.

158 McKenna offers cigarettes to commandant and hurries from French Zone. Andrews, pg. 210.

158 McKenna asks Schulz if he wants to relieve himself. Andrews, pg. 211.

158 "I had never killed a man before . . ." Andrews, pgs. 10-11.

159 "Dear Angela, dear Ingeborg . . ." Letter reproduced in Andrews, pg. 213.

160 "strict rules governing fraternization." Andrews, pg. 213.

160 Schulz joins civil police in 1928, posted to Gestapo ten years later. Schulz statement. Air 40/2487/220.

160 "That's not good . . ." *Daily Mail*, Oct. 24, 2009.

CHAPTER 10: DANZIG

161 Kozlowsky rumored to have been torched to death. Andrews, pg. 148.

161 Knuppelberg freed by the Russians. Andrews, pg. 277; Air 40/2272/023.

162 Monitoring Hans Ziegler's mail. Investigation progress report: March 21, 1947. Air 40/2478/013.

162 "In the death records of the Kriminal Polizei office . . ." Document quoted in Andrews, pg. 215.

163 "Deep powerful voice . . ." Investigation progress report: June 24, 1946. Air 40/2286/009.

163 "It is interesting to point out . . ." Investigation progress report: July 4, 1946. Air 40/2286/005.

163 Graes, in his statement, provided several months earlier. Graes statement. Air 40/2490/070.

164 "One morning in the late summer . . ." Achterberg statement. Air 40/2487/171.

164 "I remember at about that time . . ." Achterberg statement. Air 40/2487/171.

164 "Of course, Bruchardt was subordinated to Venediger directly . . ." Achterberg statement. Air 40/2487/171.

164 "Until then, all I knew . . ." Achterberg statement. Air 40/2487/171.

165 "Never at any time . . ." Achterberg statement. Air 40/2487/171.

165 "Possibly, Berlin got them." Achterberg statement. Air 40/2487/172.

165 "He has not yet been captured." Achterberg statement. Air 40/2487/172-173.

165 Achterberg discovers his wife is having an affair. Achterberg statement. Air 40/2487/173.

165 Bruchardt's bullwhip and his reputation for violence; McKenna told to find Frau Blum. Andrews, pgs. 192, 195.

165 McKenna searches for—and finds—Frau Blum. Andrews, pg. 196.

167 "Please tell Frau Blum . . ." Andrews, pg. 197.

167 Blum reveals Bruchardt's location; leads to a flat above the local police station. Andrews, pg. 197.

168 Arrest and beating of Bruchardt. Andrews, pg. 198.

168 "smoothly." Bruchardt statement. Air 40/2493/115.

168 "formerly employed in the border fights . . ." Bruchardt statement. Air 40/2493/115.

168 "respectively white Russians . . ." Bruchardt statement. Air 40/2493/115.

168 RAF officers shot while trying to escape. Bruchardt statement. Air 40/2493/115.

168 "It appeared to me . . ." Bruchardt statement. Air 40/2493/115.

169 Guard drunk at the time of the shooting. Bruchardt statement. Air 40/2493/115.

169 "When he led me into the woods . . ." Bruchardt statement. Air 40/2493/115.

169 Bruchardt debriefs Venediger. Bruchardt statement. Air 40/2493/115-116.

169 "What purpose would it have served . . ." Bruchardt statement. Air 40/2493/116.

169 Bodies destroyed and shipped to Berlin; destined for England. Bruchardt statement. Air 40/2493/116.

170 "Since the Nuremberg trials . . ." Bruchardt statement. Air 40/2493/116.

CHAPTER 11: FINDING SCHARPWINKEL

171 What the RAF knew about the Breslau murders. War Crimes Report: August 7, 1945. Air 40/2488/032.

171 Threats to captured airmen are quoted in War Crimes Report: August 7, 1945. Air 40/2488/032.

171 "Ten civilians of the Gestapo type"; Six prisoners taken away, their ashes arrive at Stalag Luft III shortly thereafter. War Crimes Report. Air 40/2486/032-033.

172 "battered looking, pugilistic type of face." Ogilvie statement. Air 40/2490/203.

172 Ten prisoners taken from the jail, their ashes returned to Stalag Luft III. War Crimes Report: August 7, 1945. Air 40/2486/032-033.

172 Threats made and Kalanowski's depression. War Crimes Report: August 7, 1945. Air 40/2486/032.

173 "You know darling, I still haven't got over the idea . . ." Letter reproduced in Gill, pg. 255.

173 *Luftwaffe* transports four flight lieutenants back to Stalag Luft III. War Crimes Report: August 7, 1945. Air 40/2486/032.

173 "I remained at Görlitz . . ." Cameron statement. Air 40/2492/008.

173 Threats of decapitation, airmen told they would never see their wives again, bodies burned in Breslau. War Crimes Report: August 7, 1945. Air 40/2486/032.

173 "the work of the Gestapo . . ." Schumacher statement. Air 40/2487/147.

173 "ailing, elderly, and female members of the office." Schumacher statement. Air 40/2487/147.

173 Forty officers for a population of a hundred thousand. Schumacher statement. Air 40/2487/147.

173 Scharpwinkel creates his own unit. Schumacher statement. Air 40/2487/147.

175 Weather and enemy fire kill the majority of men at the front. Schumacher statement. Air 40/2487/147-148.

175 "I cannot imagine Scharpwinkel . . ." Schumacher statement. Air 40/2487/148.

175 "partisan activity, treason . . ." Schumacher statement. Air 40/2487/148.

175 Killing ten to thirty people a week; murder made easy after experiences on Eastern Front. Schumacher statement. Air 40/2487/148.

175 "Frequently, mothers brought . . ." Schumacher statement. Air 40/2487/148.

175 "gas lorries." Schumacher statement. Air 40/2487/148.

175 "Death occurred instantaneously . . ." Schumacher statement. Air 40/2487/148.

176 "I want you to tell me . . ." Hansel interrogation. Air 40/2493/027.

176 "Yes, they escaped from Sagan." Hansel interrogation. Air 40/2493/027.

176 "And how many officers were recaptured?" Hansel interrogation. Air 40/2493/027.

176 "I do not know. I did not hear." Hansel interrogation. Air 40/2493/027.

176 "You do know . . ." Hansel interrogation. Air 40/2493/027.

176 "Six or seven . . ." Hansel interrogation. Air 40/2493/027.

176 "What time of day did they arrive?" Hansel interrogation. Air 40/ 2493/027.

176 "I saw them about 19:30 hours . . ." Hansel interrogation. Air 40/ 2493/027.

176 "What happened then?" Hansel interrogation. Air 40/2493/027.

176 "All the prisoners were taken into my office . . ." Hansel interrogation. Air 40/2493/027.

176 "Who carried out the interrogations . . ." Hansel interrogation. Air 40/2493/028.

176 "Dr. Scharpwinkel . . ." Hansel interrogation. Air 40/2493/028.

176 Questions put to the airmen and their refusal to answer. Hansel statement. Air 40/2493/016-017.

177 "Who are the persons . . ." Hansel statement. Air 40/2493/016.

177 "Take care they don't get away . . ." Hansel statement. Air 40/ 2493/017.

177 "*geheime reichssache*." Hansel statement. Air 40/2493/017.

177 Details of journey taken by six prisoners to the site of execution. Hansel statement. Air 40/2493/017.

177 "Scharpwinkel announced that a short break . . ." Hansel statement. Air 40/2493/017.

178 Hansel eats snack in car, hears gunshots, sees the bodies lying in the woods. Hansel statement. Air 40/2493/017.

178 "Did you believe that?" Hansel interrogation. Air 40/2493/031.

178 "No. They would have been crazy . . ." Hansel interrogation. Air 40/ 2493/031.

178 Hansel makes arrangements with undertaker. Hansel statement. Air 40/2493/017.

178 Bodies taken away to be destroyed and shipped to Breslau. Hansel statement. Air 40/2493/018.

178 "Who paid the cost of the cremations?" Hansel interrogation. Air 40/2493/032.

178 "The Breslau office." Hansel interrogation. Air 40/2493/032.

179 Scharpwinkel coordinates cover stories. Hansel statement. Air 40/2493/018.

179 "I wish only that Scharpwinkel . . ." Hansel statement. Air 40/2493/018.

179 Flying Officer Harrison joins the team. Andrews, pgs. 187–189.

179 "People would recognize . . ." Andrews, pg. 188.

179 Harrison shot at while driving. Andrews, pg. 188.

180 "One was shot at . . ." Andrews, pg. 188.

180 "tended to look on life . . ." Andrews, pg. 188.

180 Rumor the Russians hanged Scharpwinkel. Investigation progress report: March 31, 1946. Air 40/2286/019.

180 Rumor the Russians arrested Scharpwinkel but did not kill him. Investigation progress report: June 13, 1946. Air 40/2286/016.

180 "three Germans accused of war crimes . . ." FO 371/57595/025.

180 "large number of Germans suspected of war crimes . . ." FO 371/57595/025.

180 Arranging food, fuel, and quarters poses significant logistical challenge. Investigation progress report: January 24, 1986. Air 40/2286/047.

181 Nebe background information. Davies, pgs. 154–155; Andrews, pgs. 113–114.

181 Nebe commands *Einsatzgruppen* B. Davies, pg. 154.

182 Daniel interviews Babette Helmut's brothers, tracks down Frau Mül-
     ler, learns of Anny Schmid. Andrew, pgs. 162–163; Investigation
     progress report: September 24, 1946. Air 40/2272/065.

182 Information provided by Reinhardt Müller. Andrews, pg. 165.

183 Daniel questions Müller's father, reads embarrassing letter. Andrews,
     pgs. 163–164.

183 "My relations have told me . . ." from letter reproduced in Andrews,
     pg. 163.

184 "We were together . . ." Andrews, pg. 165.

184 Daniel orders surveillance, doubts Schmid would confess to ruse.
     Andrews, pg. 165.

184 "an expert." Foreign Office memo: June 17, 1946. FO 371/57595/040.

184 "Should Captain C. wear mufti or uniform?" Foreign Office telegram:
     July 2, 1946. FO 371/57595/044. (Official records do not record the
     response.)

184 Interview witnessed by four Russian soldiers, Cornish warned intimi-
     dation of Scharpwinkel will not be tolerated. Andrews, pg. 217.

185 Scharpwinkel implicates Wielen, says Breslau *Kripo* chief wanted to
     oversee executions. FO 371/57595/056.

185 "come across with some admission . . ." Scotland, pg. 137.

185 "It's a damn swindle . . ." Scotland, pg. 137.

185 "Look at the signature . . ." Scotland, pg. 137.

185 "I don't believe you . . ." Scotland, pg. 137.

185 "If you were not the old man that you are . . ." Scotland, pg. 137.

185 "I believe that in my district . . ." Scharpwinkel statement. Air 40/
     2487/143.

185 "in order to carry out his mission." Scharpwinkel statement. Air 40/2487/143.

185 "The first six were shot . . ." Scharpwinkel statement. Air 40/2487/143.

186 "My driver was Schröder." Andrews, pg. 239.

186 Names of the first six men shot. Air 40/2487/022.

186 "As regards my activities . . ." Scharpwinkel statement. Air 40/2487/144.

187 "account for the murder . . ." Foreign Office letter: November 22, 1946. FO 371/57595/091.

187 "held positions of importance on the camp staff." Judge Advocate General letter: October 17, 1946. FO 371/57595/069.

187 "intended to set a standard for other concentration camps . . ." JVL.

187 Thirty thousand Russians die in camp. New York Times, December 17, 2001.

187 Thirty-three thousand inmates vacated on forced march. JVL.

187 Camps becomes a prison run by NKVD. New York Times, December 17, 2001.

187 "the former Counselor of the German Embassy in Moscow . . ." Foreign Office memo: December 2, 1946. FO 371/57595/094.

187 Scharpwinkel hospitalized with pneumonia and pleurisy. FO 371/57595/069.

188 Scharpwinkel orders driver to stage a breakdown. Andrews, pg. 240; Twitching lip. Air 40/2493/049.

188 Sound of screaming and machine gun fire, a scene of pandemonium. Andrews, pg. 241.

188 "The officials were running around excitedly . . ." Wieczorek statement reproduced in Andrews, pg. 241.

188 Death of gunmen. Investigation progress report: June 29, 1946. Air 40/2493/047.

189 Names of the ten executed airmen. Air 40/2487/022.

189 "The lorry stood forty meters behind me . . ." Schröder statement reproduced in Andrews, pg. 241.

190 "not only investigated the escape . . ." Andrews, pg. 240.

CHAPTER 12: ALONE

191 Hayter's name on list of deceased. Andrews, pg. 246.

191 Hayter's passion for and interest in flying. Vance, pg. 81.

191 Hayter's biographical information and the details of his capture. Vance, pgs. 81–82.

192 Herberg interviewed a second time at the London Cage, names Hilker. Investigation progress report: November 14, 1946. Air 40/2272/60-61.

193 "should be treated with reserve." Investigation progress report: November 14, 1946. Air 40/2272/61.

193 Details of Anthony Hayter's arrest. Arrest report: March 31, 1944. Air 40/2278/016.

194 "It would be very useful . . ." Arrest report: March 31, 1944. Air 40/2278/016.

195 "executioner for the Strasbourg Gestapo." Investigation progress report: December 16, 1946. Air 40/2272/053.

195 Gehrum would have been triggerman. Air 40/2278/019.

195 Gehrum questions Harrison's involvement in Dresden. Andrews, pgs. 188–189.

195 Committing murder versus the following of a legitimate order. Andrews, pg. 189.

195 Interrogating members of Strasbourg Gestapo. Investigation progress report: December 16, 1946. Air 40/2272/053.

195 Schimmel denies knowledge of murder. Investigation progress report: March 21, 1947. Air 40/2278/011.

196 Fear of being charged in the murder of paratroopers. Investigation progress report: March 21, 1947. Air 40/2278/011.

196 "Shortly after the end of the war . . ." Investigation progress report: March 21, 1947. Air 40/2278/011.

196 "special mission." Investigation progress report: March 21, 1947. Air 40/2278/011.

196 "a man caught on the frontier during the *Fahndung.*" Investigation progress report: March 21, 1947. Air 40/2278/011.

196 "been shot by Hilker whilst trying to escape." Investigation progress report: March 21, 1947. Air 40/2278/012.

196 Hilker's activities following Hayter affair; false papers. Investigation progress report: March 21, 1947. Air 40/2278/012.

196 "In the beginning of 1945 . . ." Investigation progress report: March 21, 1947. Air 40/2278/012.

197 Description of Hilker. Investigation progress report: March 21, 1947. Air 40/2278/012.

197 Cremation records examined at Strasbourg. Investigation progress report: December 14, 1946. Air 40/2272/053.

197 "All the entries are in name form . . ." Investigation progress report: December 12, 1946. Air 40/2278/019.

197 Information provided by Rudolf Peters. Peters statement. Air 40/2278/03.

197 "That's an English Air Force officer." Peters statement. Air 40/2278/03.

197 "In my presence . . ." Peters statement. Air 40/2278/03.

197 Hayter is questioned in Peters's room. Peters statement. Air 40/2278/03.

198 Hayter is placed in a cell. Peters statement. Air 40/2278/03.

198 Peters sees Hayter bundled into a waiting car. Peters statement. Air 40/2278/03.

198 Peters told to mind his own business. Peters statement. Air 40/2278/03.

198 "Stop asking questions . . ." Peters statement. Air 40/2278/03.

198 No paperwork filed regarding Hayter's capture. Peters statement. Air 40/2278/003.

198 Schimmel accused of being soft. Andrews, pg. 250.

199 Shooting of Hayter is based on Schimmel's statement quoted in Andrews, pgs. 249–250.

199 Hayters's shooting and cremation. Andrews, pgs. 249, 250.

199 Hilker's wife and inquiries in Karlsruhe. Investigation progress report: December 14, 1946. Air 40/2272/053; Air 40/2278/020.

199 The fates of Dissner and Hilker. Andrews, pgs. 250, 260.

CHAPTER 13: THE ORDER OF THE BLOOD

201 Catanach's love of adventure and his joining the air force. Vance, pg. 92.

202 "Take care of it . . ." Vance, pg. 92.

202 Catanach and crew fly against Cologne. Vance, pg. 93.

203 "Boys, I think we'd better be getting home now." Vance, pg. 93.

203 Catanach awarded DFC, becomes squadron leader, assigned to protect arctic convoys. Vance, pg. 93.

203 Catanach and crew shot down and taken prisoner. Vance, pg. 93.

203 Details of Christensen's wartime experiences leading up to capture. Vance, pgs. 74–75.

204 Christensen's Danish lineage, responsible for intelligence on Denmark. Gill, pgs. 91, 147.

204 Espelid responsible for intelligence on Norway. Gill, pg. 147.

204 Espelid's wartime service and capture; meets Fuglesang in Stalag Luft III. Vance, pgs. 175, 176.

205 Fuglesang shot down over Flushing and captured. Vance, pg. 176.

205 Lyon commences investigation with "battle order" of Kiel Gestapo. Investigation progress report: September 24, 1946. Air 40/2493/113.

205 Schafer produces cremation records. Schafer statement. Air 40/2493/156.

206 Town clerk is told Gestapo does not require permission to conduct its business. Fahl statement. Air 40/2493/154.

206 "The corpses were cremated . . ." Schafer statement. Air 40/2493/156.

206 "No, I didn't know their names . . ." Schafer statement. Air 40/2493/156.

206 Russian laborer suspects bodies are British or Australian officers. Schafer statement. Air 40/2493/156.

206 Tischendorf recalls the night of the murders. Tischendorf statement. Air 40/2493/138.

207 "I cannot remember the date and times very clearly . . ." Tischendorf statement. Air 40/2493/138.

207 Four airmen recaptured as they make their way through town, confess to being British officers. Linke statement. Air 40/2493/141.

207 "Concerning the escape proper . . ." Linke statement. Air 40/2493/141.

208 List of police record numbers for the recaptured men. Linke statement. Air 40/2493/141.

208 "In the built-up area of the town . . ." Linke statement. Air 40/2493/141.

208 Berlin notified of capture; Post shows up to take men away. Linke statement. Air 40/2493/141.

208 Typists confirm Post's presence during interrogations. Christiansen statement. Air 40/2493/140; Rodenberg statement. Air 40/2493/153.

208 Clausen provides Oskar Schmidt's name. Clausen statement. Air 40/2493/146.

209 "Officially, I had nothing to do with the case . . ." Mueller statement. Air 40/2493/152.

209 Kaehler, Jacobs, Franz and Oskar Schmidt are arrested. Andrews, pg. 222.

209 "This looks bad." Andrews, pg. 222.

209 "sworn under penalty of death and degradation . . ." Investigation progress report: November 18, 1946. Air 40/2493/174.

209 Summary of Kiel murders. Investigation progress report: November 18, 1946. Air 40/2493/174-175.

210 Franz Schmidt hangs himself. Andrews, pg. 224; Investigation progress report: November 18, 1946. Air 40/2493/176.

210 *Schlechter mann, schlechter mann . . .* Andrews, pg. 224.

210 Oskar Schmidt details shootings and is summoned to chief's office. Schmidt statement. Air 40/2493/170.

211 "He told me that he would merely believe . . ." Schmidt statement. Air 40/2493/170.

211 Jacobs details Post's brutality, turns back on scene. Jacobs statement. Air 40/2493/164.

211 "I wish to emphasize . . ." Jacobs statement. Air 40/2493/164.

211 Kaehler says both Schmidts and Jacobs took part in shooting. Kaehler statement. Air 40/2493/159.

211 "All of the prisoners fell forward . . ." Kaehler statement. Air 40/2493/159.

212 "I can just as well recall . . ." Kaehler statement. Air 40/2493/160.

212 "I wish to finish this statement . . ." Kaehler statement. Air 40/2493/160.

212 Oskar Schmidt concedes he may have fired one shot. Schmidt statement. Air 40/2493/151.

212 "If Kaehler says that I shot . . ." Schmidt statement. Air 40/2493/151.

212 Arrest of Struve and Denkmann. Struve statement. Air 40/2493/166; Investigation progress report: November 18, 1946. Air 40/2493/173; Andrews, pg. 222.

212 Types of the cars used in the killing. Struve statement. Air 40/2493/166.

212 Struve drops off prisoners, hears shots fired. Struve statement. Air 40/2493/167.

212 "one loud detonation." Struve statement. Air 40/2493/167.

212 "They are lying there." Struve statement. Air 40/2493/167.

212 Struve peers over the bush and sees the bodies. Struve statement. Air 40/2493/167.

213 "On the return journey . . ." Struve statement. Air 40/2493/167.

213 "Sturmbannführer Schmidt and Kriminalkommissar Post . . ." Investigation progress report: November 18, 1946. Air 40/2493/175, 176-177.

213 "I believe this was the most-bitter winter . . ." Andrews, pg. 232.

213 "appalling." Andrews, pg. 232.

213 Winter conditions kill twelve thousand Germans. MacDonogh, pg. 497.

213 "Whenever I recall the winter of 1946 to 1947 . . ." Carl Zuckmayer quoted in MacDonogh, pg. 496.

213 "I shall never forget that drive . . ." Andrews, pg. 233.

213 "After the rigors of the winter . . ." Andrews, pg. 233.

213 Post and Schmidt's postwar travels. Baumann statement. Air 40/2493/148.

215 Details regarding Schmidt's clothing and family. Baumann statement. Air 40/2493/148.

215 Details regarding Post's family and mistress. Baumann statement. Air 40/2493/148.

216 Raid on Heidt household; McKenna gets hands on photograph. Andrews, pg. 225; Investigation progress report: January 26, 1947. Air 40/2279/010.

216 Searching houses in Kiel, information provided by Heidt's cousin, Post's P.O. Box. Investigation progress report: January 26, 1947. Air 40/2279/010.

217 "From all police offices . . ." quoted in Bessel, pg. 55.

217 German military not immune to Nazi brutality; Berlin residents shot or hanged from trees. Bessel, pg. 63; Ryan, pg. 480.

217 List of war crimes against Allied soldiers and airmen. Cab 66/56/4.

219 "very old and an imbecile." Investigation progress report: August 7, 1947. Air 40/2272/010.

219 Visiting Schmidt's mother; two decades to find Schmidt. Investigation progress report: August 7, 1947. Air 40/2272/010; Andrews, pg. 231.

219 "spasmodic . . . of information given to various officials . . ." Investigation progress report: May 23, 1947. Air 40/2272/028.

219 Number and status of wanted men tracked down by the RAF. Loose minute: May 23, 1947. Air 40/2272/026-027.

219 Daniel hunts for Ziegler, interrogates the man's mother, sister, and nephew. Andrews, pgs., 165–166; Investigation progress report: September 24, 1946. Air 40/2272/064.

220 McKenna notified of Pohlmann's arrest. Investigation progress report: May 21, 1947. Air 40/2272/033.

220 "a haulage contractor." Andrews, pg. 225.

220 "in connection with the murders of 300 people . . ." Investigation progress report: May 21, 1947. Air 40/2272/033.

220 McKenna travels to Minden to interview the prisoner. Investigation progress report: May 21, 1947. Air 40/2272/033.

220 McKenna studies prisoner through spy hole in cell door and examines picture of Post and Heidt. Andrews, pg. 226.

221 "That's me. I am Post." Andrews, pg. 226.

221 Catanach asks, "Why?" Andrews, pg. 231.

221 "How could you do such a thing as this?" Andrews, pg. 12.

221 "Inhuman! I was dealing with sub-humans . . ." Andrews, pg. 12.

222 McKenna and Bowes consider the Kiel case closed. Investigation progress report: June 30, 1947. Air 40/2492/020.

222 "It has now been established . . ." Investigation progress report: June 30, 1947. Air 40/2492/020.

222 "This can be considered . . ." Investigation progress report: June 30, 1947. Air 40/2492/021.

CHAPTER 14: REMEMBRANCE

223 McKenna distributes photo sheets. Air 40/2272/007-010; information provided by Schäfer's wife. Air 40/2272/010.

223 Mug shots of wanted men are published in *Rogue's Gallery*. Air 40/2272/007.

223 Ziegler is captured and commits suicide. Andrews, pg. 258.

223 Eighteen defendants go on trial in Hamburg. UNWCC, pg. 31.

224 Charges quoted in UNWCC, pg. 31.

224 Individual charges leveled against defendants. UNWCC, pgs. 31–32.

225 Specific charges against Wielen; all defendants plead not guilty. UNWCC, pg. 32.

225 "Owing to the *Grossfahndung* (the nation-wide search) . . ." UNWCC, pg. 35.

225 "I could not have been a National Socialist . . ." Carroll, pg. 297.

225 "the plea of superior orders." UNWCC, pg. 46.

225 "International law must not place the subject . . ." UNWCC, pg. 50.

225 "My attitude is quite clear . . ." Andrews, pg. 256.

226 "statute or decree . . ." UNWCC, pg. 50.

226 "a British hospital ship which was sunk by a submarine." UNWCC, pg. 48.

226 "Patzig's order does not free the accused of guilt." UNWCC, pg. 48.

226 "infringement of civil or military law." UNWCC, pg. 48.

226 "liable to punishment." UNWCC, pg. 48.

226 "The term 'war crime' is a technical expression . . ." UNWCC, pg. 51.

226 "on the uncorroborated evidence . . ." UNWCC, pg. 51.

226 "that the evidence given was true." UNWCC, pg. 51.

227 Zacharias claims he was penetrated by an electric probe. Andrews, pg. 145.

227 "information on Gestapo hot-iron methods . . ." Andrews, pg. 145.

227 Zacharias made to strip and kneel for hours. Andrews, pg. 145.

227 "I can only die once . . ." Andrews, pg. 145.

227 Testimony: "I did not want . . . I could not get a confession of torture." Reproduced in Andrews, pg. 145.

227 Testimony: "Surely as a British soldier . . . singular punishments were given in the London Cage?" Reproduced in Scotland, pgs. 155–156.

228 "Yes." Scotland, pg. 156.

228 "If that were true . . ." Scotland, pg. 156.

228 "would become common property." Scotland, pgs. 156–157.

228 "manufactured tales." Scotland, pg. 158.

228 "the brutal fate of those fifty RAF officers." Scotland, pg. 158.

228 "I did not make this statement upon oath . . ." Andrews, pg. 147.

229 "It was to be expected that the world . . ." Scotland, pgs. 158, 159.

229 "It is only when you lose the war . . ." Andrews, pg. 255.

229 Details of the defendants on the stand come from Scotland, pg. 154.

230 Exchange between Judge Advocate and Schimmel: "Why did you not carry . . . passing on the order to another official." Andrews, pgs. 254, 255.

230 Court considerations when determining verdicts. UNWCC, pg. 52.

230 Verdicts rendered by the court. UNWCC, pgs. 52, 57-58.

230 Russians inform the British that Scharpwinkel is dead. Andrews, pg. 258.

231 Second trial, verdicts, and sentences. Davies, pgs. 143–144; *New York Times,* November 7, 1948.

231 Death of Absalon, OBE honors for McKenna and Bowes. Andrews, pg. 258.

232 British Foreign Secretary announces an end to war crimes prosecutions. Andrews, pg. 258.

232 Schäfer never charged in Munich murders. Andrews, pg. 259.

232 Venediger and Schmidt eventually come out of hiding and each receives two years for their involvement in the Sagan murders. Andrews, pg. 260.

233 "by British authorities as an act of clemency." *New York Times,* October 25, 1952.

233 "duty to avoid capture" and "duty to escape." Davies, pg. 173.

233 "didn't see escaping as a sport . . ." Davies, pg. 173.

233 The seventy-two men identified by the RAF and their fates. Andrews, pg. 261.

INDEX

Page numbers in italic indicate photographs; those followed by "n" indicate notes.

ABOUT THE AUTHOR

Simon Read is the author of five previous works of nonfiction, including *War of Words*, *On the House*, and *In the Dark*. He lives in Northern California with his wife and son. You can reach him through his website at www.simon-read.com.